WHITE DEATH

ROBBIE MORRISON
CHARLIE ADLARD

WHITE DEATH
First printing
September 2014

Printed in South Korea

For international rights, contact:
foreignlicensing@imagecomics.com

ISBN: 978-1-63215-142-1

ROBBIE MORRISON
writer

CHARLIE ADLARD
artist

On a sunlit day in September 2013, 500 people attended a double funeral in the small alpine ski resort village of Peio, northern Italy. The bodies were those of two Austrian males, aged 17 and 18 years old. They weren't, however, holiday-makers who had fallen victim to a tragic ski accident. Both had bullet-holes in their skulls and had been frozen in the snow and ice of the Presana glacier for almost 100 years. They were First World War soldiers who had fought in a relatively obscure part of that conflict, now known as the White War.

The Italian Front stretched across the borders separating Italy and the Austro-Hungarian Empire. The main battles were waged in mountain regions claimed by Italy, part of the Allied Powers, from Austria, allied to the Kaiser. They confronted each other in a conflict strategically similar to trench warfare, but played out in the frozen heights of the Trentino, Dolomite and Caporetto mountains. In this, the centenary year of World War 1, the discovery of their bodies is a sad, haunting reminder that the past never truly dies.

I first became aware of the White War after watching a documentary, which quoted a chilling statistic: on the Italian Front in WWI, an estimated 60 - 100,000 troops were killed in avalanches deliberately caused by the enemy. To me this seemed to take the ruthlessness and inhumanity of warfare to new heights — turning nature itself into a weapon of war.

'White Death' is a slang term used to describe avalanches in French and Italian Alpine regions, and in my head, the avalanche became a metaphor for war — a terrifying, irresistible force that remorselessly consumes and destroys everything on its path. Around the same time, Charlie Adlard, who had just finished a long, acclaimed run on *The X-Files* comic, got in touch. He had been experimenting with an illustration technique more associated with fine art than comic books — a combination of charcoal and chalk on grey paper. He felt that this moody, highly atmospheric style of rendering would be perfect for a historical piece and asked if I had any ideas for a First World War story. *White Death*, based upon historical fact, grew from the initial idea into a fully-fledged graphic novel through research. I wrote a detailed outline of the story, coincidentally while I was in Italy, taking character names from a First World War memorial in the town of Frascati, where I was staying. At the same time, Charlie produced preliminary sketches and visuals, including an incredibly powerful opening sequence that I only wish I could claim credit for. *White Death* came about not only through a passion for the material, but also for the comics medium and what we thought it was capable of. I'm obviously biased, but I feel the book is one of the best things Charlie's done. It's a departure from the style he's become known for – an example of an artist pushing himself creatively - but still retains the superlative storytelling skills that make *The Walking Dead* such a huge success.

Charlie not only captures the grand spectacle of the high-altitude locations, the numbing reality of life in the trenches, the desperation and brutality of hand-to-hand combat, and the thundering power of the avalanches, he also portrays the subtler emotional interplay of the characters in moving and poignant detail.

Of all the projects I've worked on, *White Death* is quite possibly the one that remains closest to my heart. To this day, I'm immensely proud of the book and hope we managed to say something about the horror and futility of war, and the cruelty, compassion and camaraderie of those trapped within it.

Robbie Morrison

It all started with *White Death*.

I could divide my career into two halves - pre *White Death* and post *White Death*. Before I drew this book, I was floundering, not really knowing what I wanted to do with my career. I'd worked for 2000AD and the Judge Dredd Megazine, Marvel, Defiant — had a prosperous run on *The X-Files* for Topps — but nothing to give me real direction.

I'd made quite a bit of money with *The X-Files* and I wanted to put it to good use. I was experimenting too with other drawing techniques and needed an outlet for my newer creative urges. It was no secret that I'd finished my run on *The X-Files* in not the best circumstances and was feeling somewhat disillusioned with the industry. Time for a change.

All these elements finally came together in the book you now hold in your hand. I could do my OWN thing. This, to me at the time, was a revelation. I hadn't been aware very much of the concept of creator-owned comics and, yet, here I was, doing just that. *White Death* eventually formulated my world view and opinions on where I wanted my career to go after this. And it wasn't going to be anything to do with other peoples' characters, that's for sure. OK, I had a family to feed, so the road was going to be rocky, and I wasn't going to turn down paying work-for-hire just to keep my morals intact.... But eventually, a few years after *White Death*'s inspiration, I started *The Walking Dead* and haven't looked back since.

White Death started all that and I cannot emphasise how important to me that is.

White Death would not have existed though without another important element - Robbie's script. His story is probably one of the best and most moving comic scripts I have ever read, let alone worked on.

Once I had the technique together to actually realise the book and the script to work from, we were off.

The gestation of the original book was tough. I'm not a self-publisher, so — with the help of some like-minded friends — we formed a co-operative called Les Cartoonistes Dangereux. We all had a mutual love affair with the European comics industry — hence the French name — and *White Death* was initially going to be our first foray into that world. After finishing the book in a cloud of charcoal and chalk dust and getting high on fixative, we then had to letter the thing — in French AND English. This was pretty much pre-digital lettering, so our little group spent many sleepless nights hand sticking the lettering on acetate over the art to meet the impending deadline... happy days... So thank you, Brad and Liz, Faz, Paul, Tim, Roger and Sylvie, and anyone else involved with the creation of our inaugural book. I could not have done it without you!

White Death will always be one of the most important books of my career, a book I'm justifiably proud of, and it's wonderful to see it continue into this new millennia.

Charlie Adlard

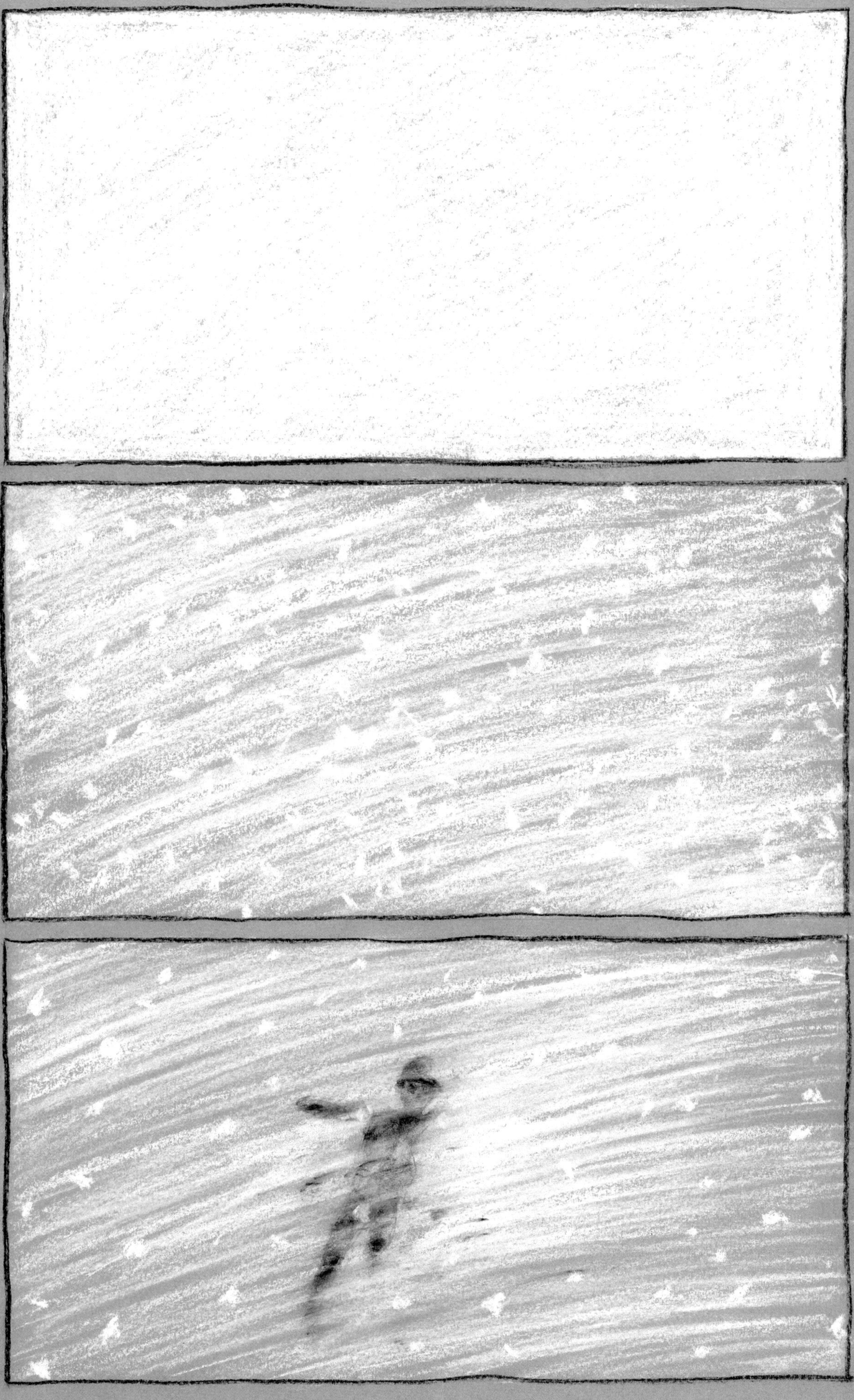

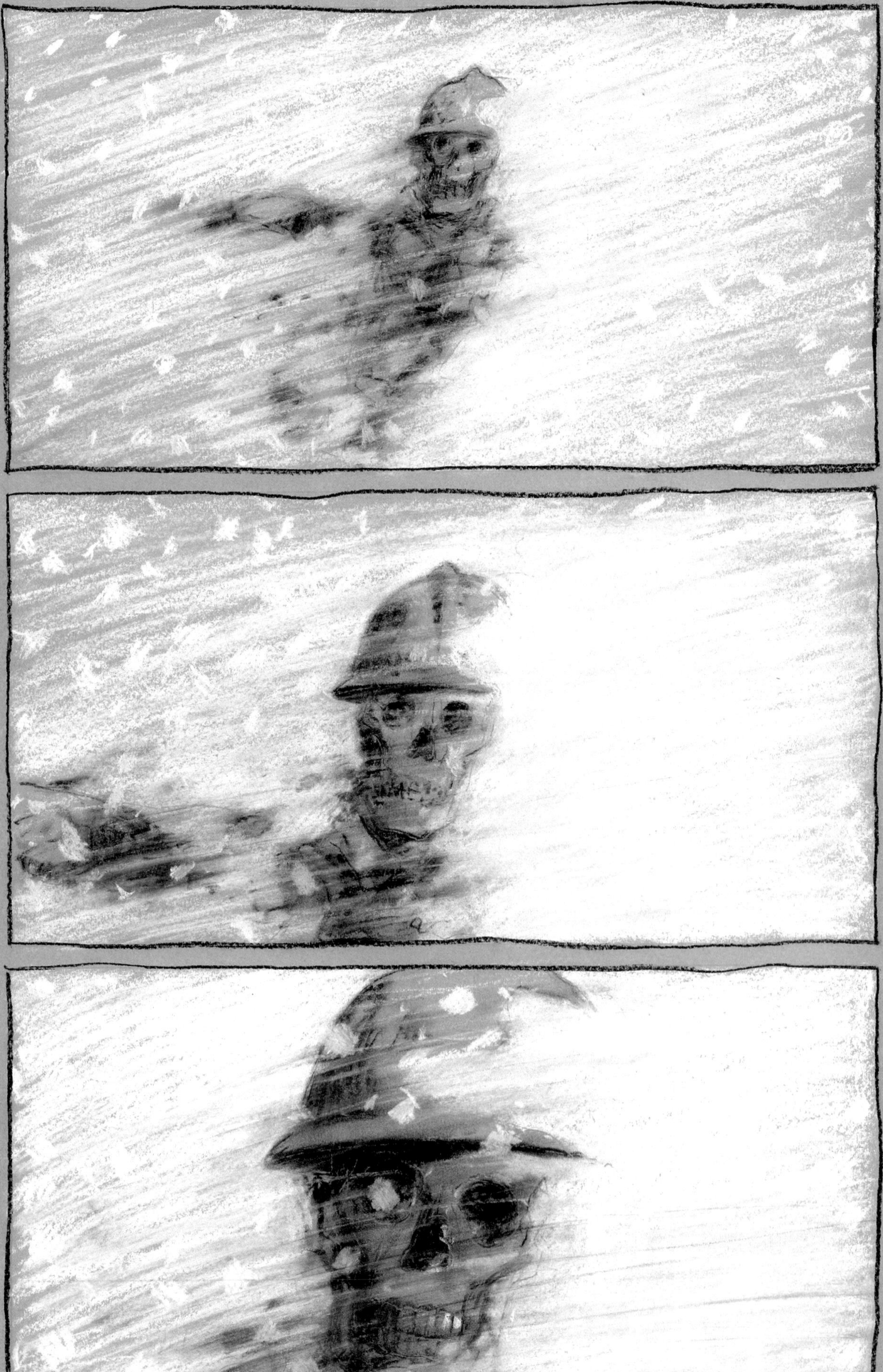

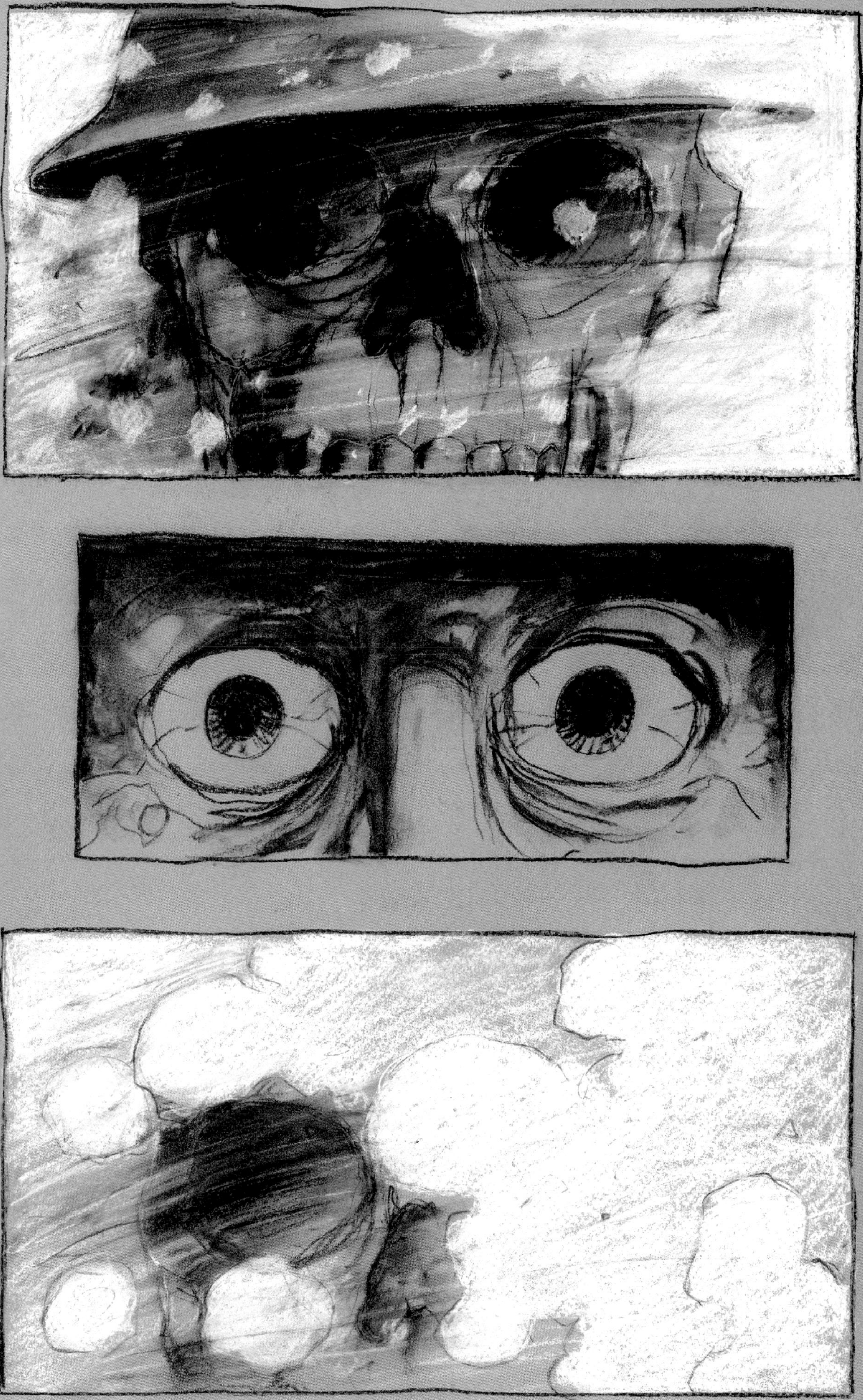

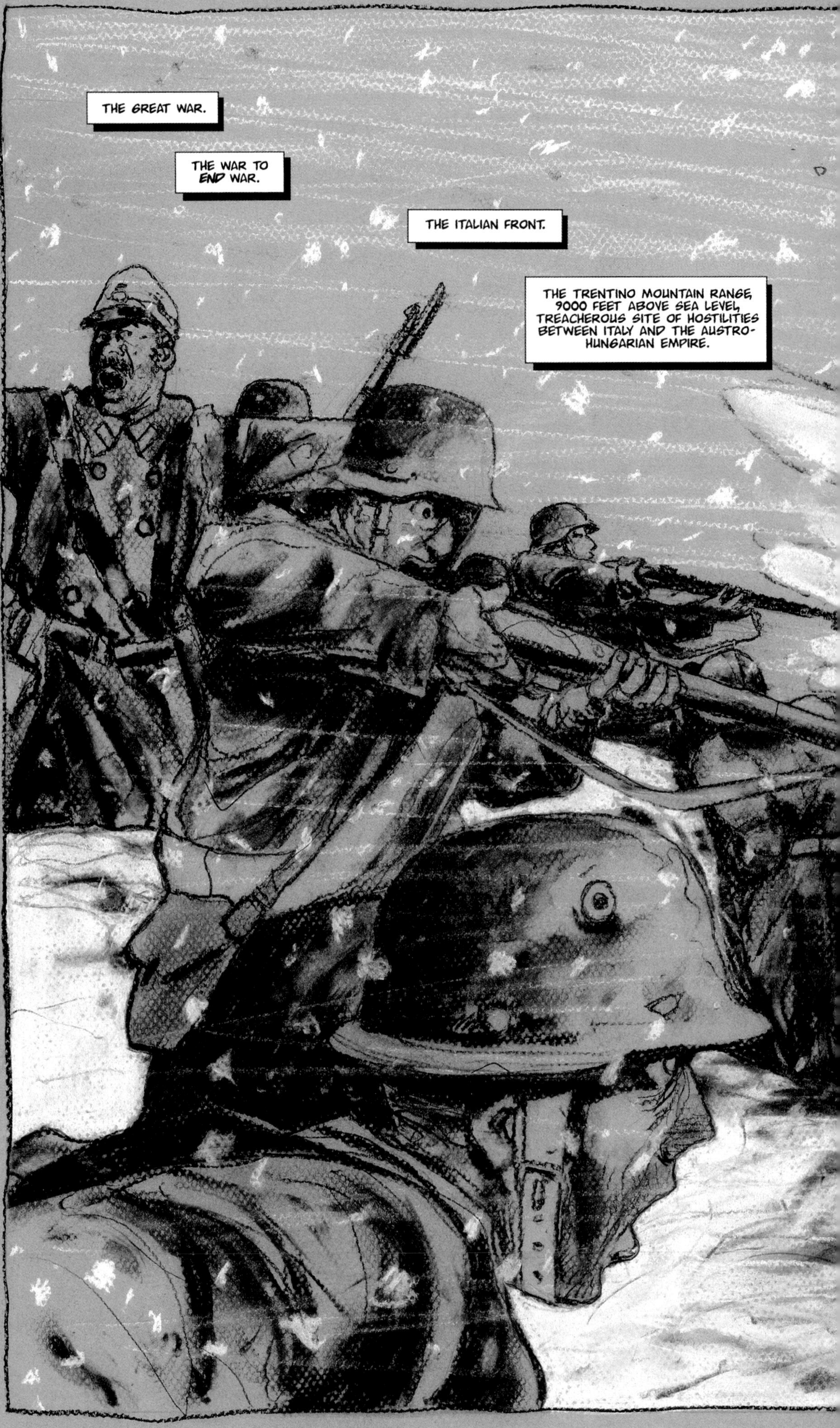
THE GREAT WAR.
THE WAR TO END WAR.
THE ITALIAN FRONT.
THE TRENTINO MOUNTAIN RANGE, 9000 FEET ABOVE SEA LEVEL, TREACHEROUS SITE OF HOSTILITIES BETWEEN ITALY AND THE AUSTRO-HUNGARIAN EMPIRE.

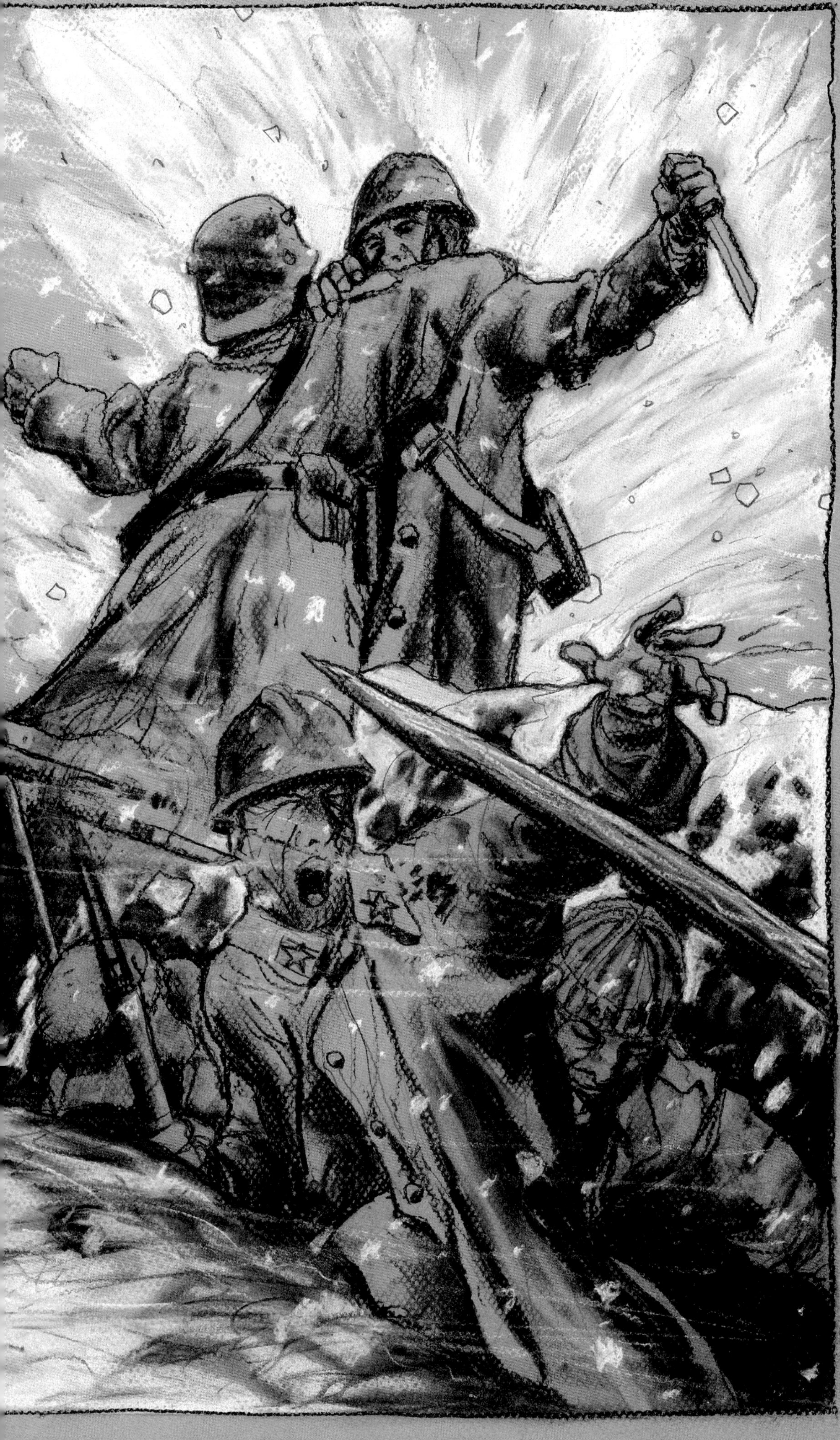

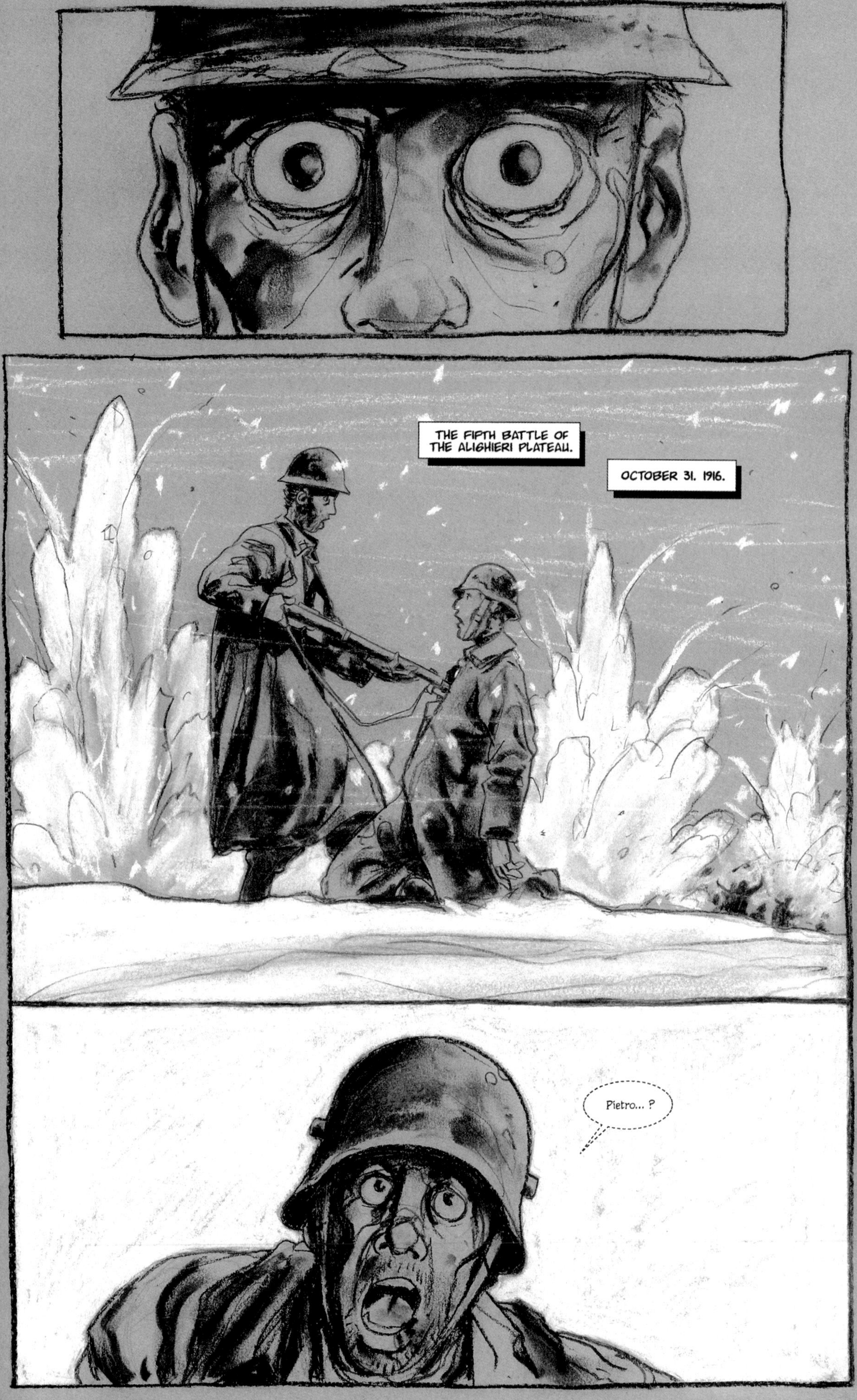
THE FIFTH BATTLE OF
THE ALIGHIERI PLATEAU.
OCTOBER 31. 1916.
Pietro... ?

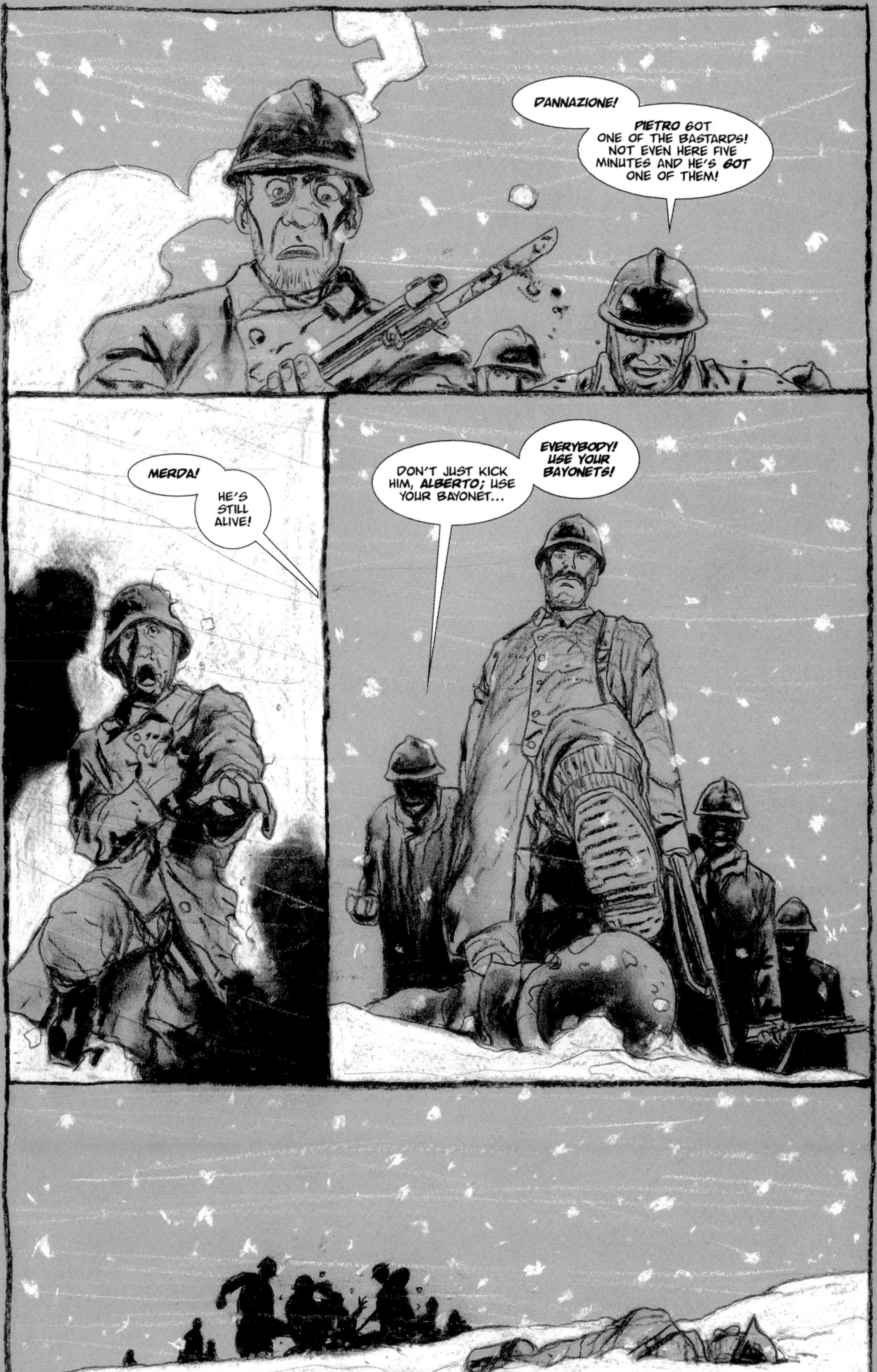
DANNAZIONE!
PIETRO GOT ONE OF THE BASTARDS! NOT EVEN HERE FIVE MINUTES AND HE'S GOT ONE OF THEM!
MERDA!
HE'S STILL ALIVE!
DON'T JUST KICK HIM, ALBERTO; USE YOUR BAYONET...
EVERYBODY! USE YOUR BAYONETS!

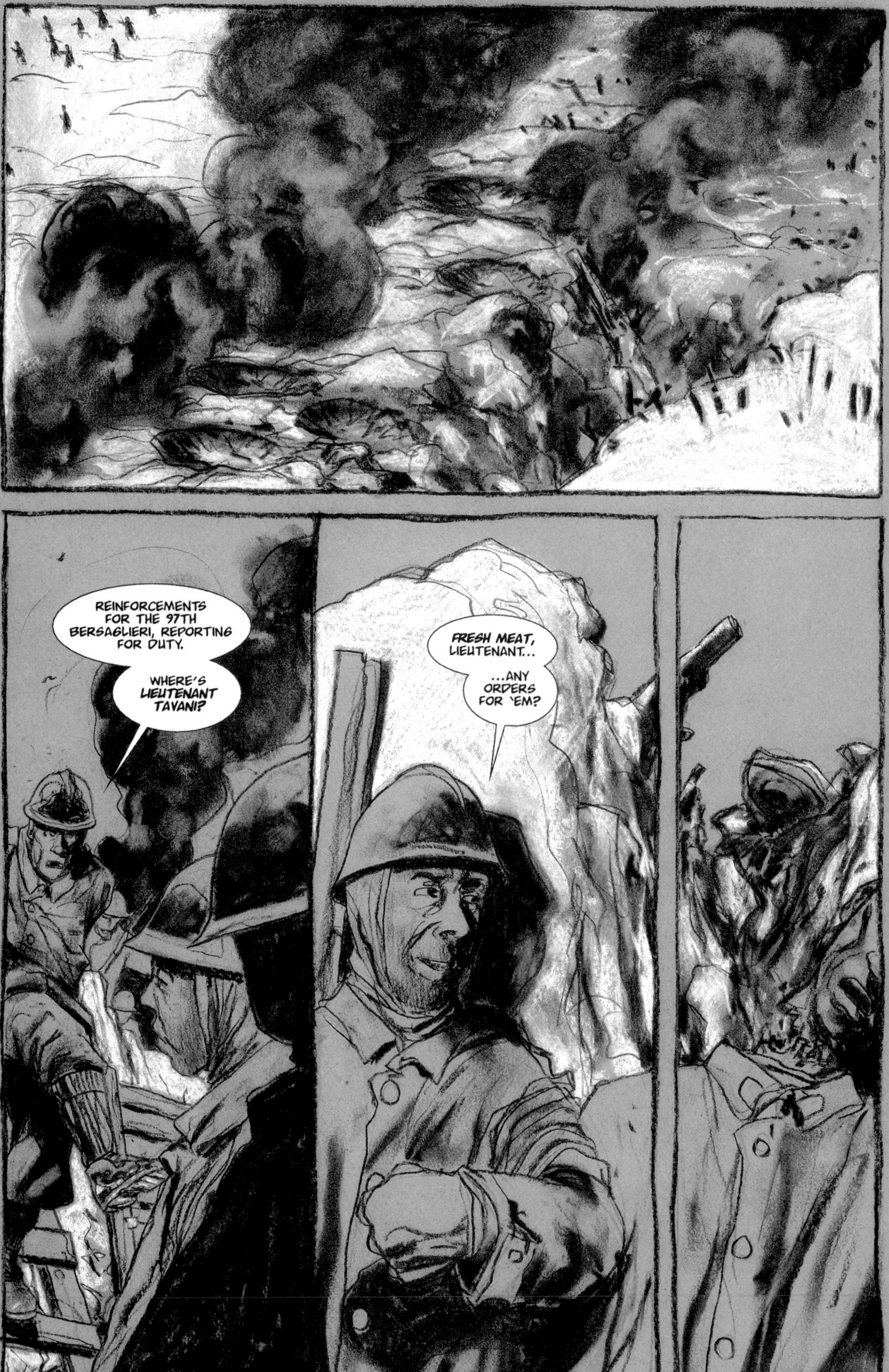
REINFORCEMENTS FOR THE 97TH BERSAGLIERI, REPORTING FOR DUTY.
WHERE'S LIEUTENANT TAVANI?
FRESH MEAT, LIEUTENANT...
...ANY ORDERS FOR 'EM?

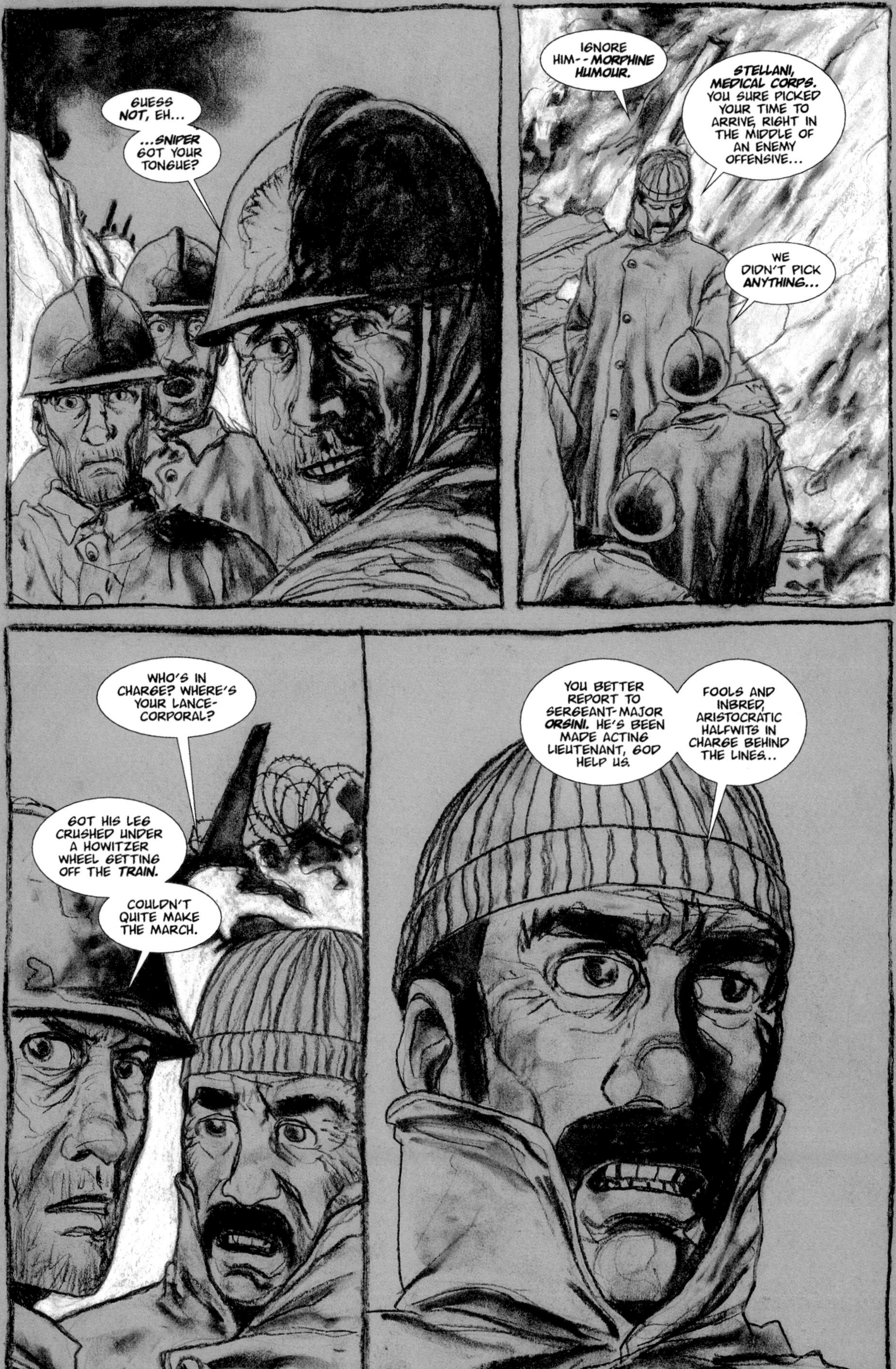
GUESS NOT, EH...
...SNIPER GOT YOUR TONGUE?
IGNORE HIM--MORPHINE HUMOUR.
STELLANI, MEDICAL CORPS. YOU SURE PICKED YOUR TIME TO ARRIVE, RIGHT IN THE MIDDLE OF AN ENEMY OFFENSIVE...
WE DIDN'T PICK ANYTHING...
WHO'S IN CHARGE? WHERE'S YOUR LANCE-CORPORAL?
GOT HIS LEG CRUSHED UNDER A HOWITZER WHEEL GETTING OFF THE TRAIN.
COULDN'T QUITE MAKE THE MARCH.
YOU BETTER REPORT TO SERGEANT-MAJOR ORSINI. HE'S BEEN MADE ACTING LIEUTENANT, GOD HELP US.
FOOLS AND INBRED, ARISTOCRATIC HALFWITS IN CHARGE BEHIND THE LINES...

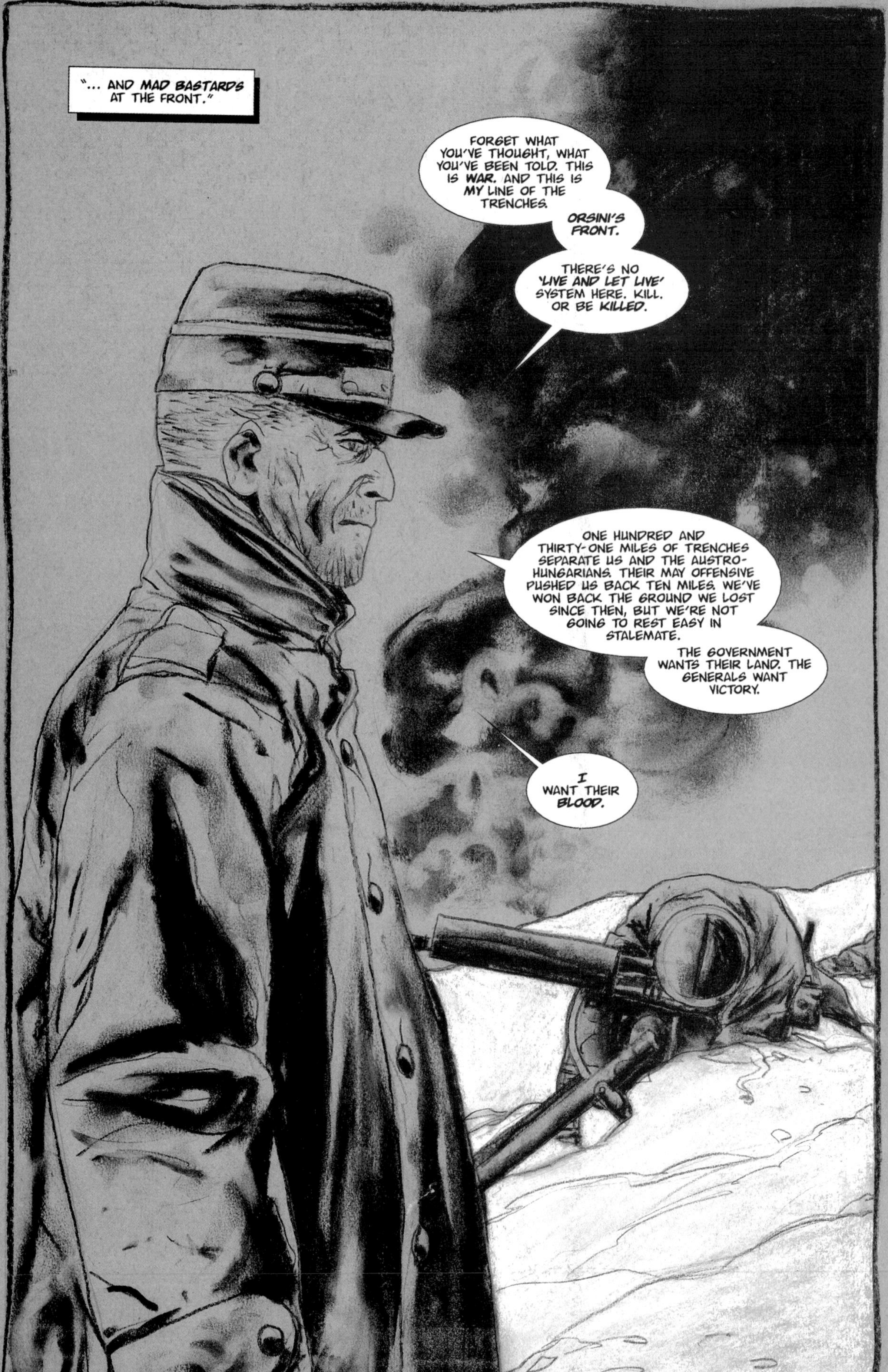
"... AND MAD BASTARDS AT THE FRONT."
FORGET WHAT YOU'VE THOUGHT, WHAT YOU'VE BEEN TOLD. THIS IS WAR. AND THIS IS MY LINE OF THE TRENCHES.
ORSINI'S FRONT.
THERE'S NO 'LIVE AND LET LIVE' SYSTEM HERE. KILL. OR BE KILLED.
ONE HUNDRED AND THIRTY-ONE MILES OF TRENCHES SEPARATE US AND THE AUSTRO-HUNGARIANS. THEIR MAY OFFENSIVE PUSHED US BACK TEN MILES. WE'VE WON BACK THE GROUND WE LOST SINCE THEN, BUT WE'RE NOT GOING TO REST EASY IN STALEMATE.
THE GOVERNMENT WANTS THEIR LAND. THE GENERALS WANT VICTORY.
I WANT THEIR BLOOD.

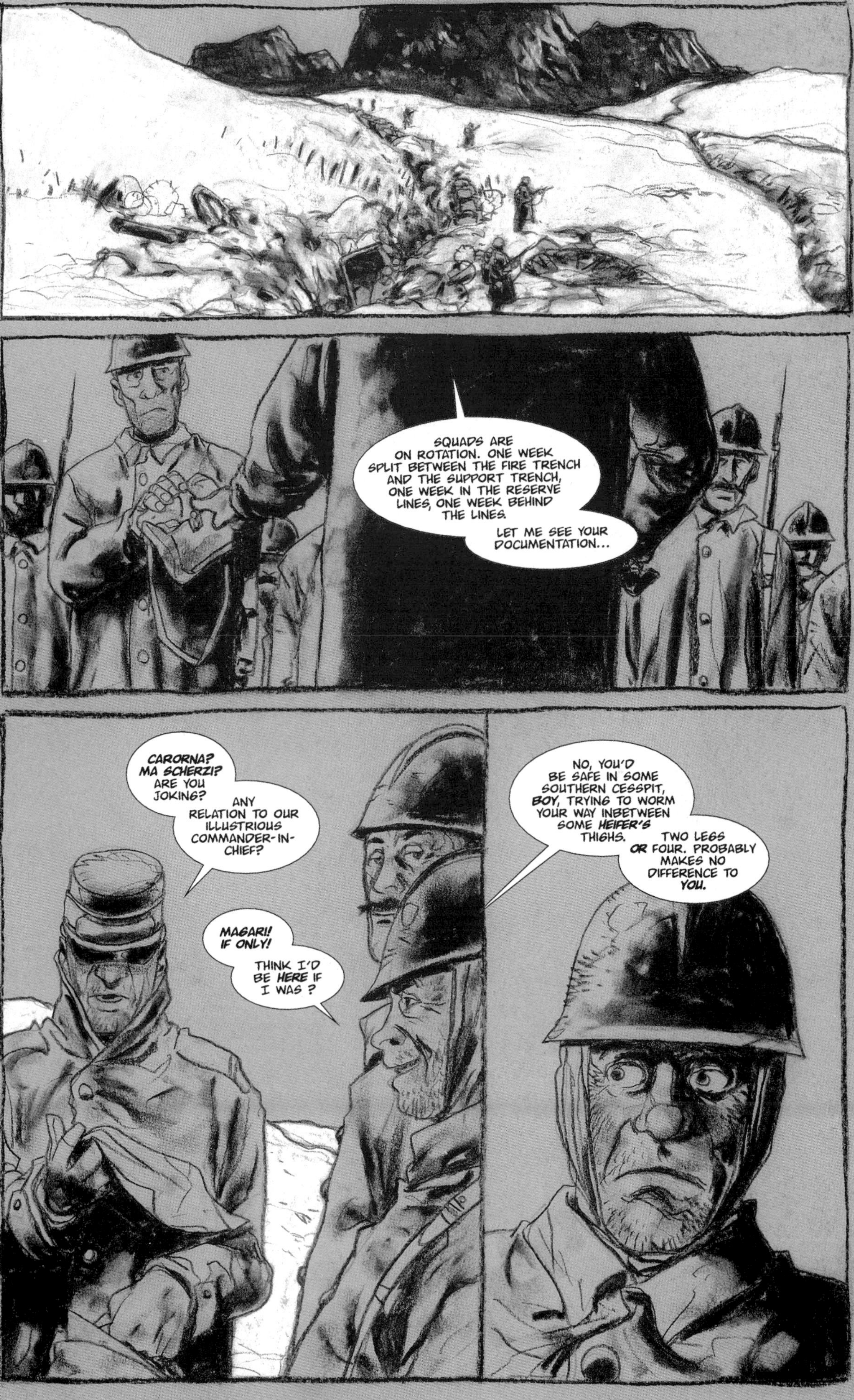
SQUADS ARE ON ROTATION. ONE WEEK SPLIT BETWEEN THE FIRE TRENCH AND THE SUPPORT TRENCH, ONE WEEK IN THE RESERVE LINES, ONE WEEK BEHIND THE LINES.
LET ME SEE YOUR DOCUMENTATION...
CARORNA? MA SCHERZI? ARE YOU JOKING?
ANY RELATION TO OUR ILLUSTRIOUS COMMANDER-IN-CHIEF?
MAGARI! IF ONLY!
THINK I'D BE HERE IF I WAS ?
NO, YOU'D BE SAFE IN SOME SOUTHERN CESSPIT, BOY, TRYING TO WORM YOUR WAY INBETWEEN SOME HEIFER'S THIGHS.
TWO LEGS OR FOUR. PROBABLY MAKES NO DIFFERENCE TO YOU.

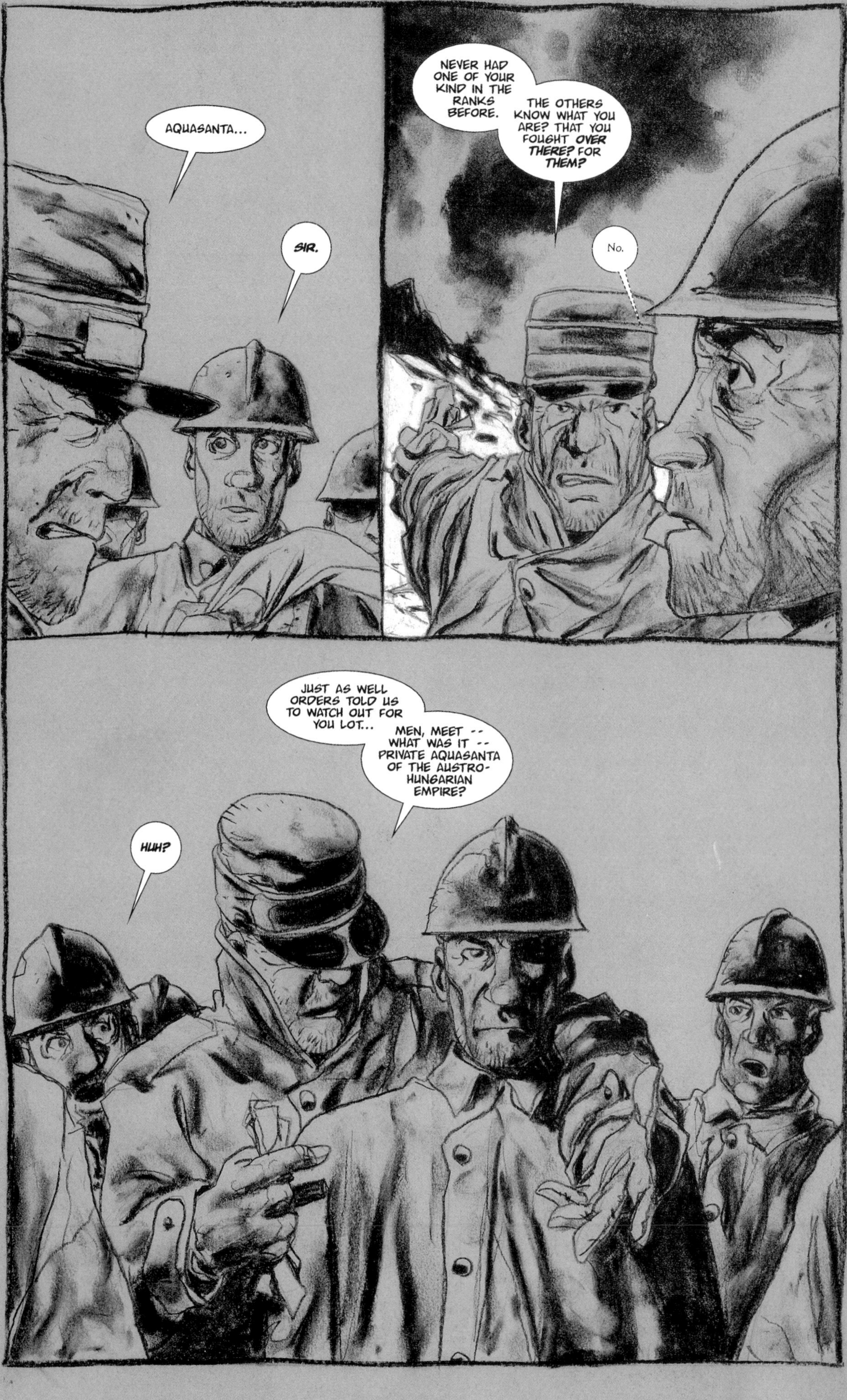
AQUASANTA...
SIR.
NEVER HAD ONE OF YOUR KIND IN THE RANKS BEFORE.
THE OTHERS KNOW WHAT YOU ARE? THAT YOU FOUGHT OVER THERE? FOR THEM?
No.
JUST AS WELL ORDERS TOLD US TO WATCH OUT FOR YOU LOT...
MEN, MEET -- WHAT WAS IT -- PRIVATE AQUASANTA OF THE AUSTRO-HUNGARIAN EMPIRE?
HUH?

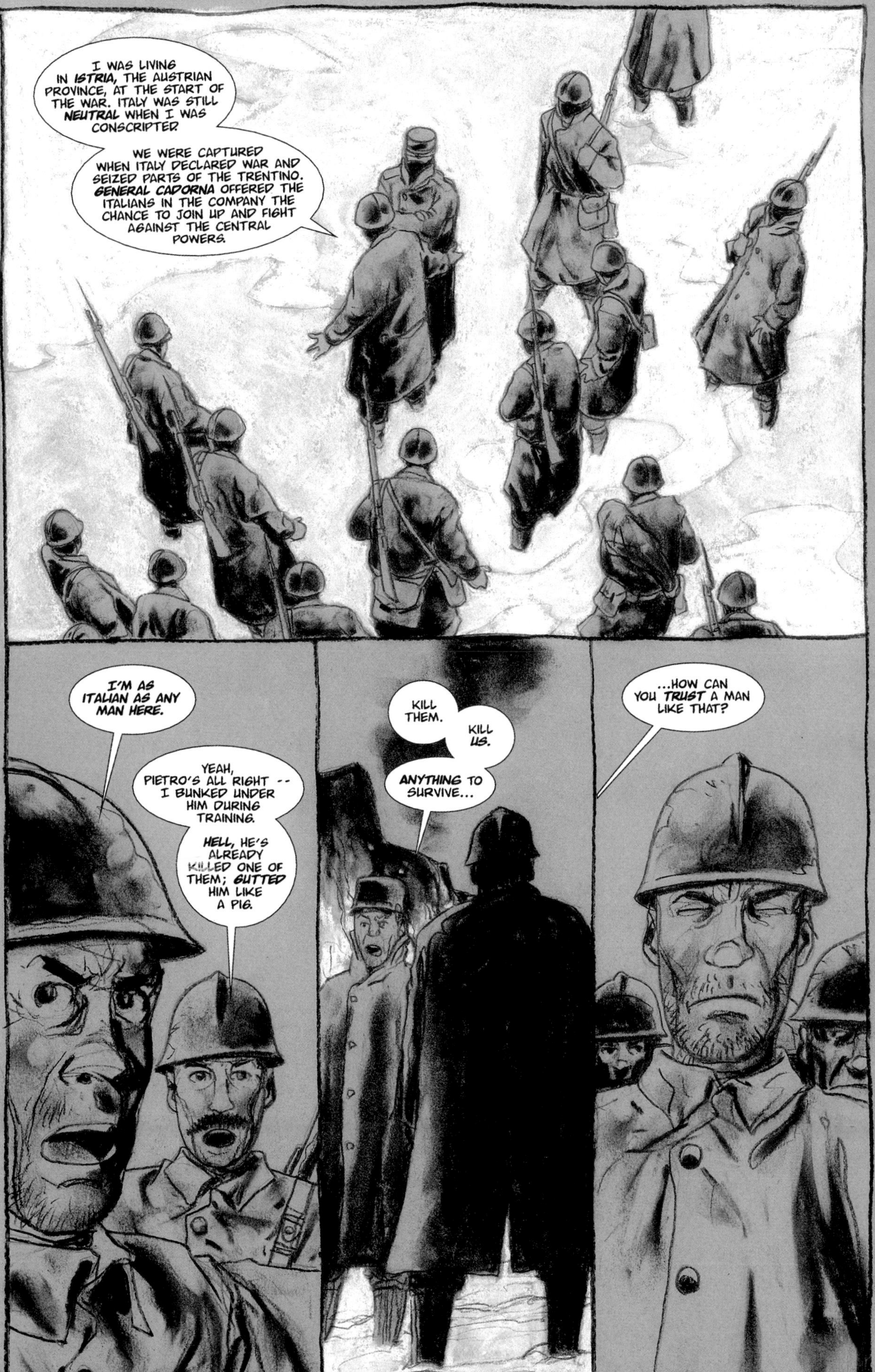
I WAS LIVING IN ISTRIA, THE AUSTRIAN PROVINCE, AT THE START OF THE WAR. ITALY WAS STILL NEUTRAL WHEN I WAS CONSCRIPTED.
WE WERE CAPTURED WHEN ITALY DECLARED WAR AND SEIZED PARTS OF THE TRENTINO. GENERAL CADORNA OFFERED THE ITALIANS IN THE COMPANY THE CHANCE TO JOIN UP AND FIGHT AGAINST THE CENTRAL POWERS.
I'M AS ITALIAN AS ANY MAN HERE.
YEAH, PIETRO'S ALL RIGHT -- I BUNKED UNDER HIM DURING TRAINING.
HELL, HE'S ALREADY KILLED ONE OF THEM; GUTTED HIM LIKE A PIG.
KILL THEM.
KILL US.
ANYTHING TO SURVIVE...
...HOW CAN YOU TRUST A MAN LIKE THAT?

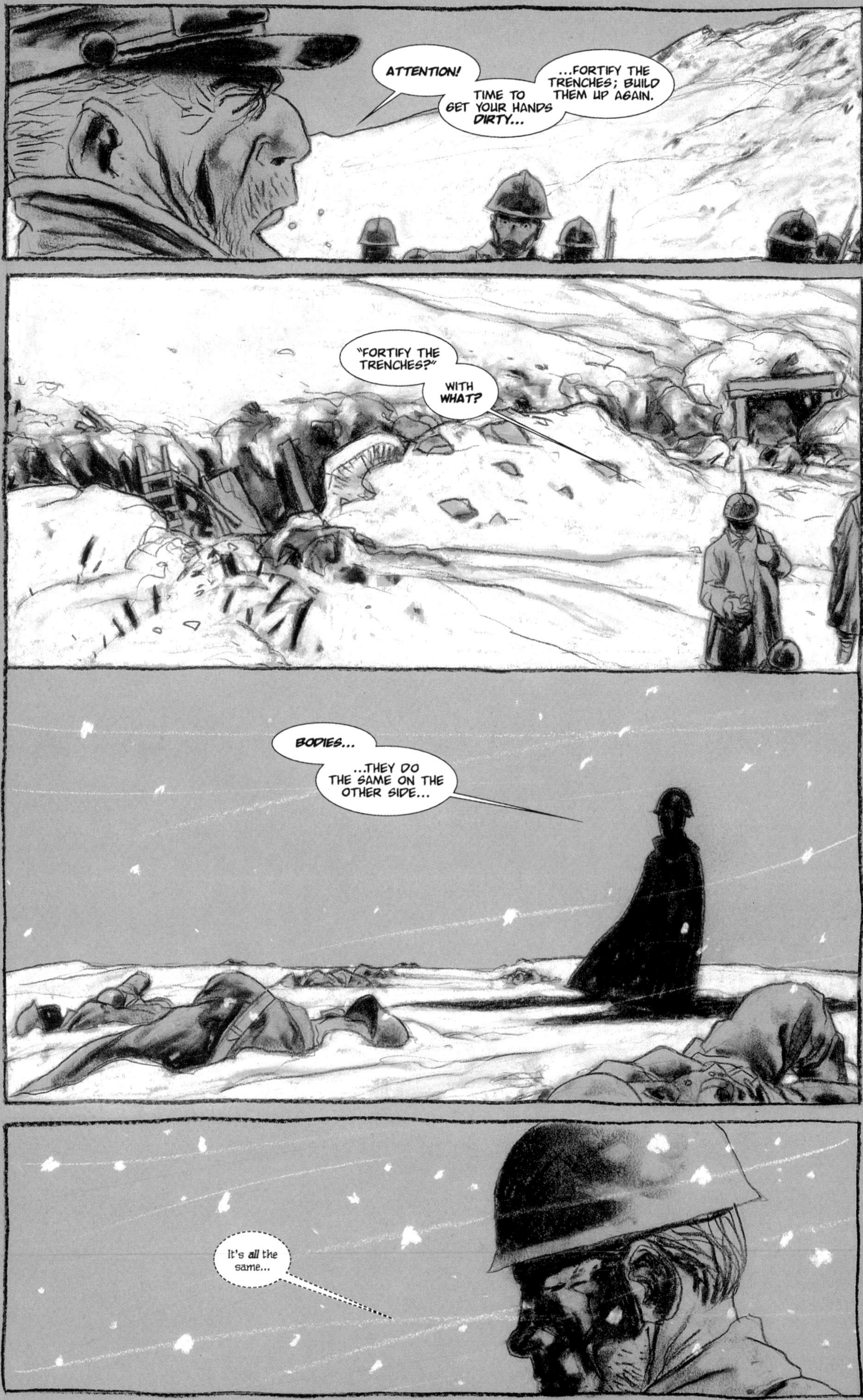
ATTENTION!
TIME TO GET YOUR HANDS DIRTY...
...FORTIFY THE TRENCHES; BUILD THEM UP AGAIN.
"FORTIFY THE TRENCHES?"
WITH WHAT?
BODIES...
...THEY DO THE SAME ON THE OTHER SIDE...
It's all the same...

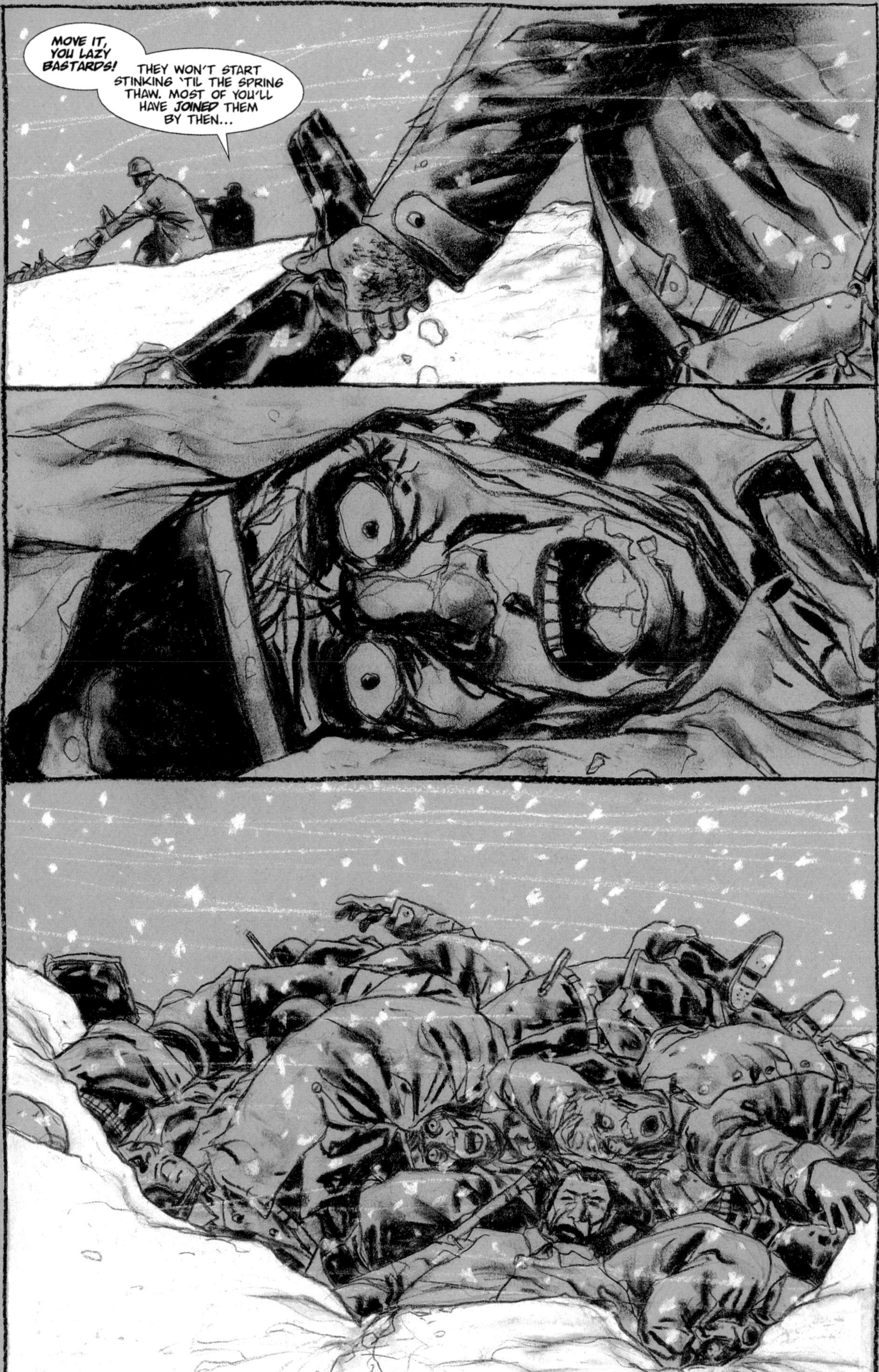
MOVE IT, YOU LAZY BASTARDS!
THEY WON'T START STINKING 'TIL THE SPRING THAW. MOST OF YOU'LL HAVE JOINED THEM BY THEN...

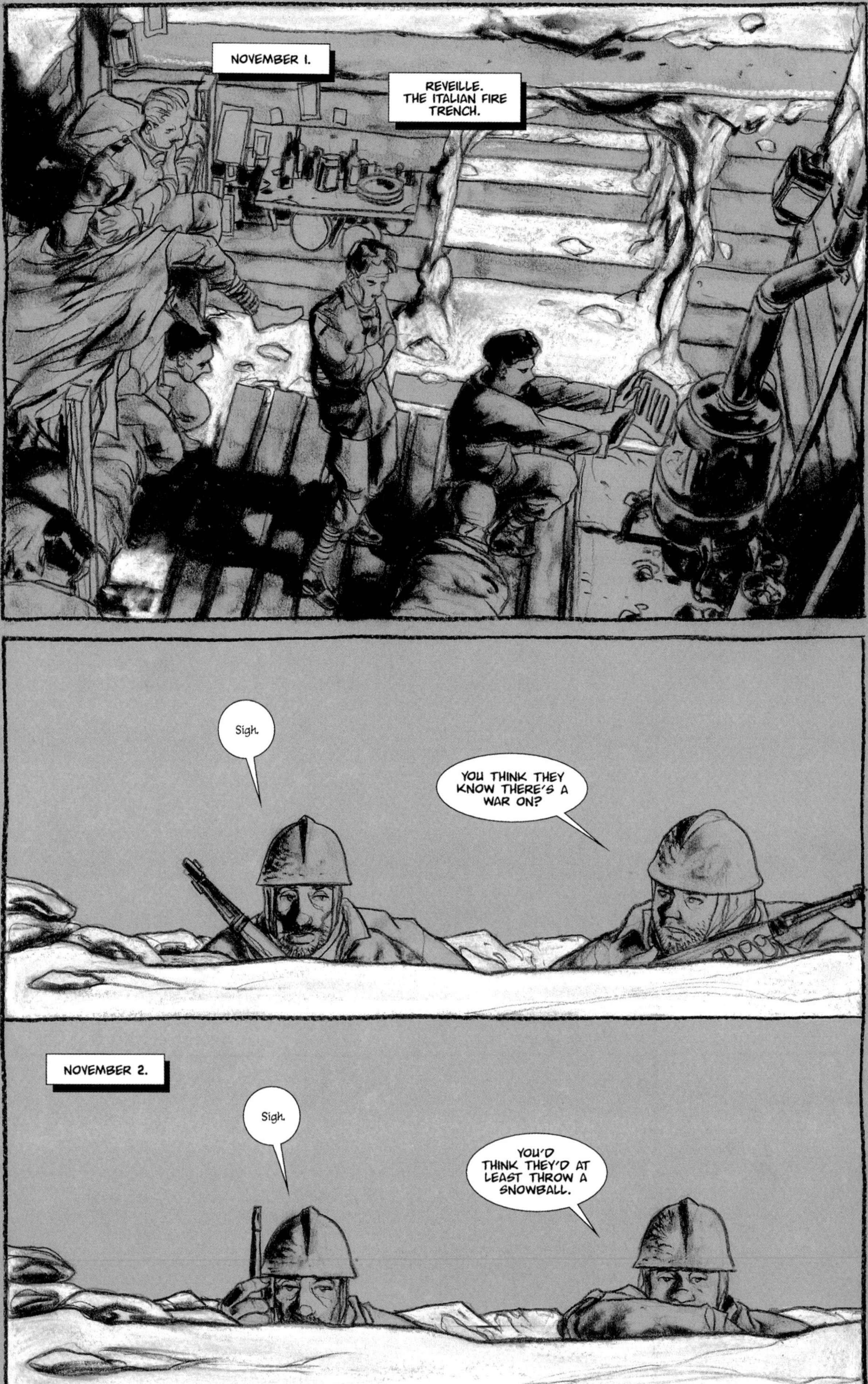

NOVEMBER 1.
REVEILLE. THE ITALIAN FIRE TRENCH.
Sigh.
YOU THINK THEY KNOW THERE'S A WAR ON?
NOVEMBER 2.
Sigh.
YOU'D THINK THEY'D AT LEAST THROW A SNOWBALL.

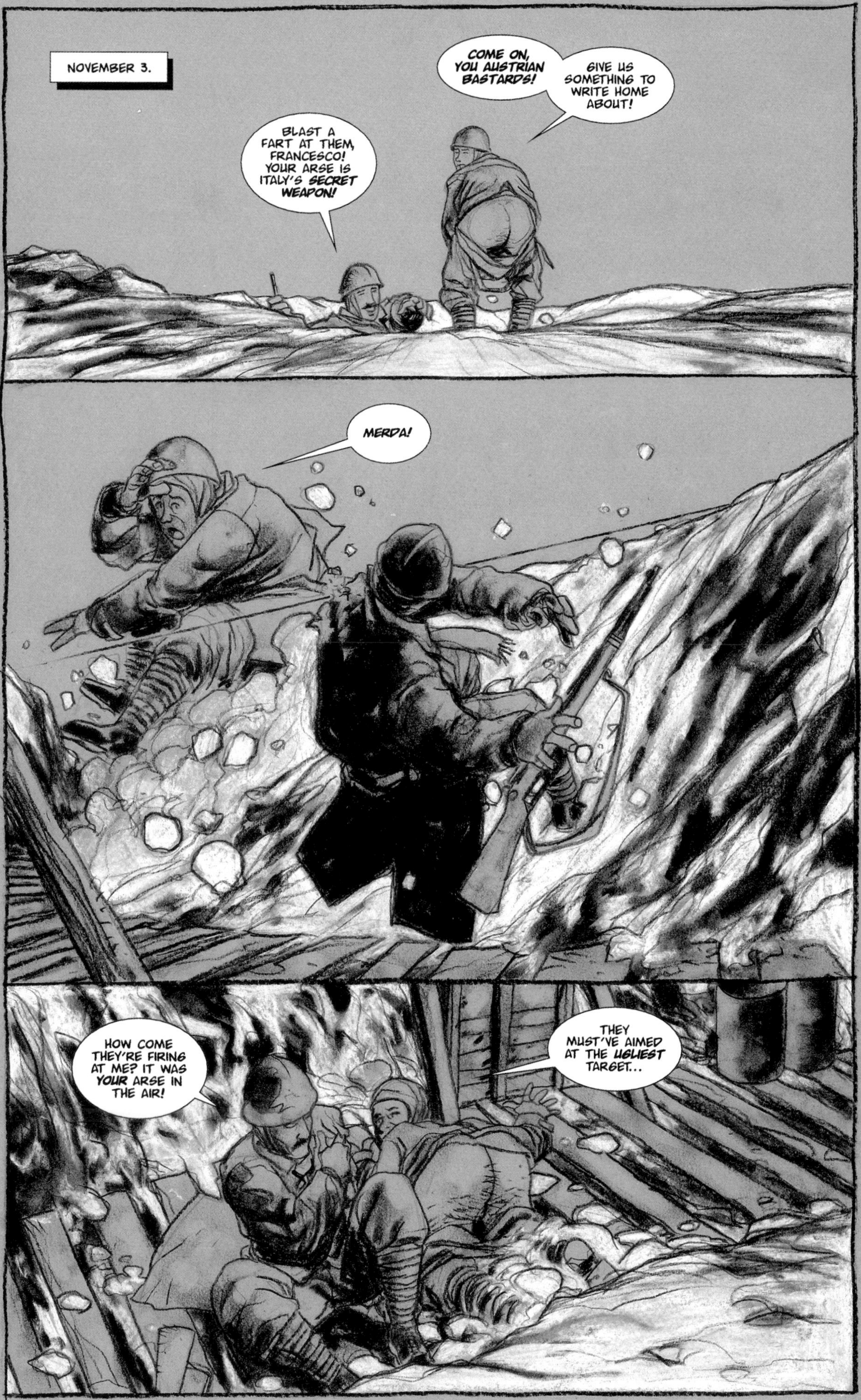
NOVEMBER 3.
COME ON, YOU AUSTRIAN BASTARDS!
GIVE US SOMETHING TO WRITE HOME ABOUT!
BLAST A FART AT THEM, FRANCESCO! YOUR ARSE IS ITALY'S SECRET WEAPON!
MERDA!
HOW COME THEY'RE FIRING AT ME? IT WAS YOUR ARSE IN THE AIR!
THEY MUST'VE AIMED AT THE UGLIEST TARGET...

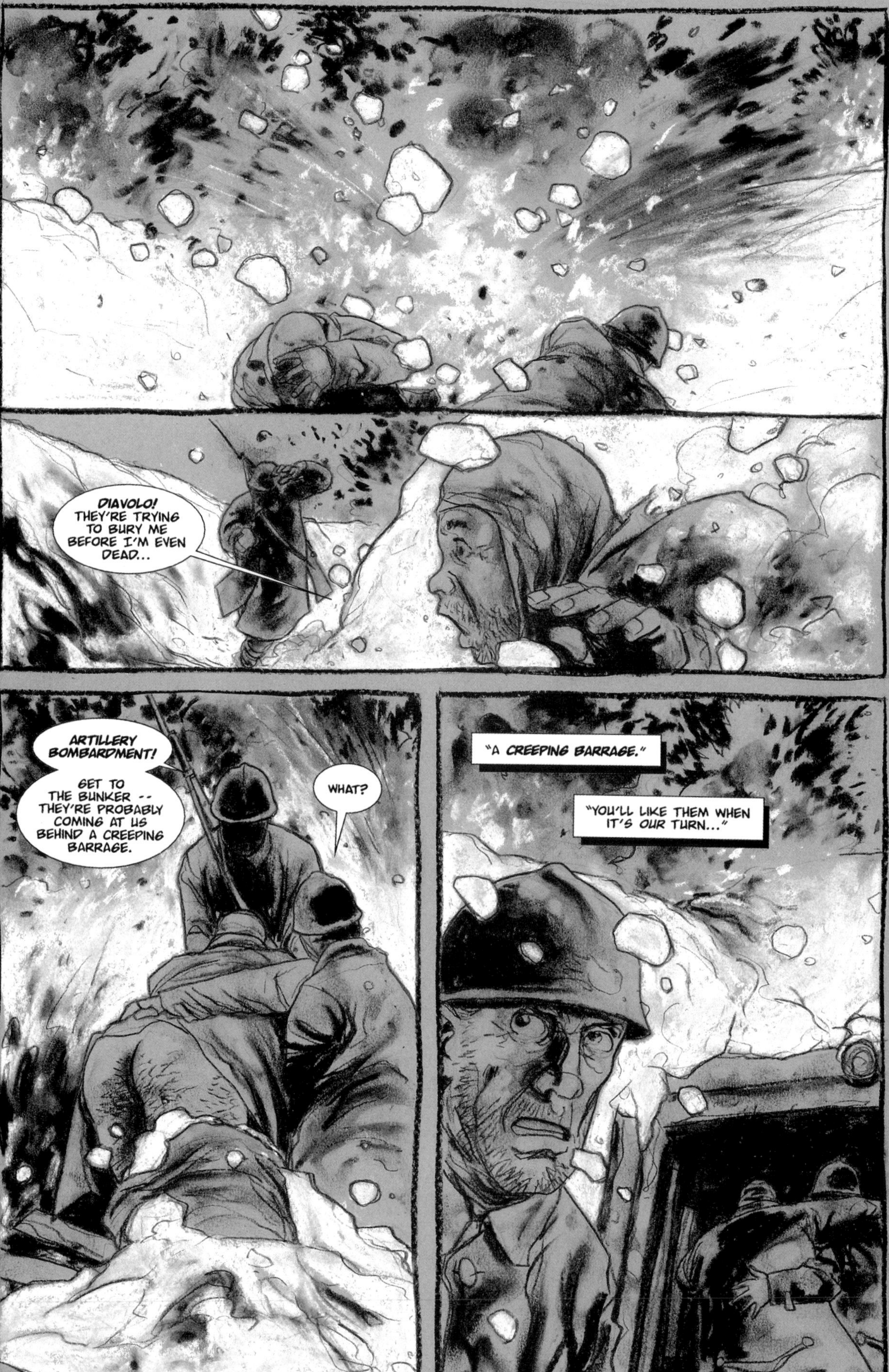
DIAVOLO! THEY'RE TRYING TO BURY ME BEFORE I'M EVEN DEAD...
ARTILLERY BOMBARDMENT!
GET TO THE BUNKER -- THEY'RE PROBABLY COMING AT US BEHIND A CREEPING BARRAGE.
WHAT?
"A CREEPING BARRAGE."
"YOU'LL LIKE THEM WHEN IT'S OUR TURN..."

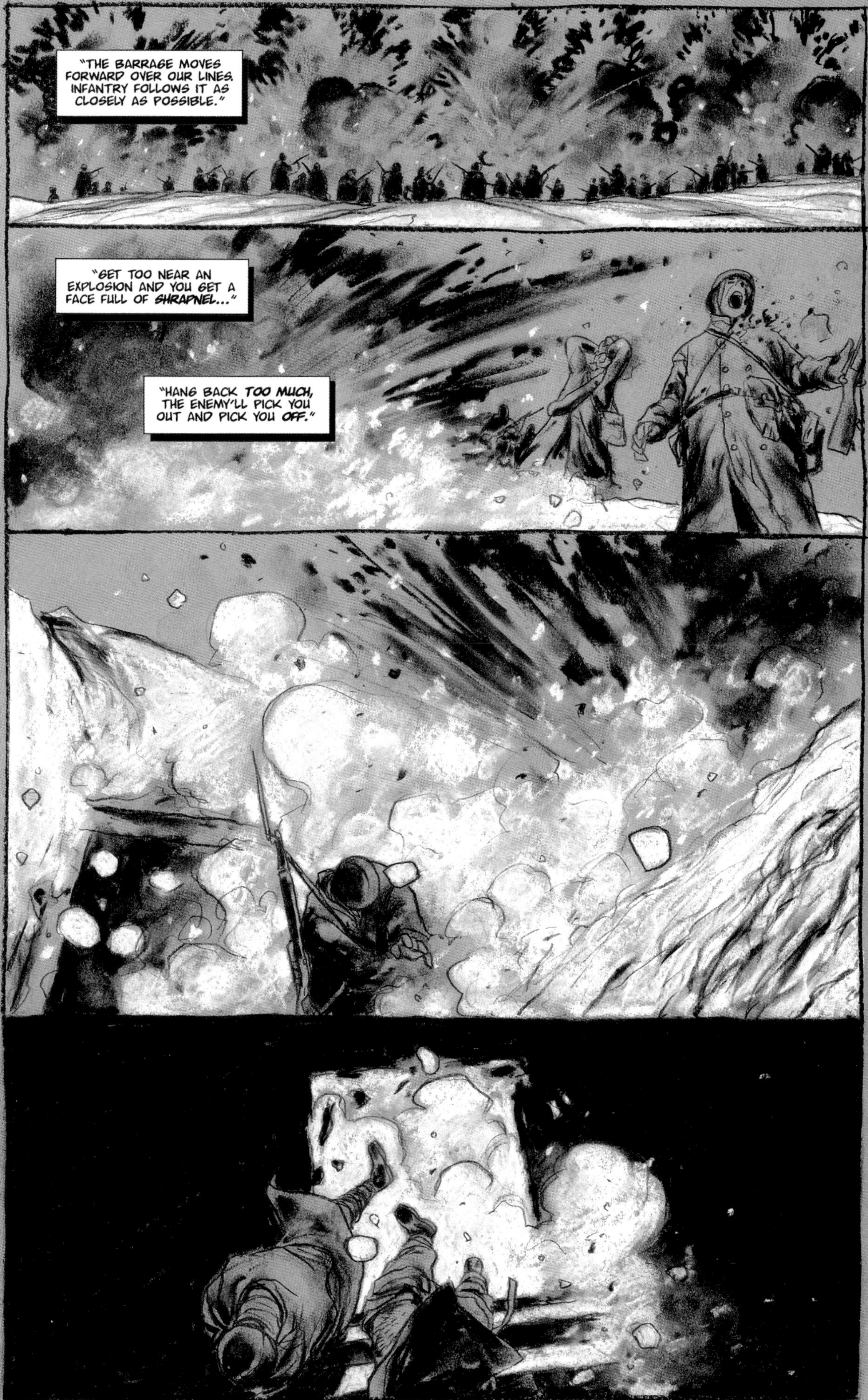
"THE BARRAGE MOVES FORWARD OVER OUR LINES. INFANTRY FOLLOWS IT AS CLOSELY AS POSSIBLE."
"GET TOO NEAR AN EXPLOSION AND YOU GET A FACE FULL OF SHRAPNEL..."
"HANG BACK TOO MUCH, THE ENEMY'LL PICK YOU OUT AND PICK YOU OFF."

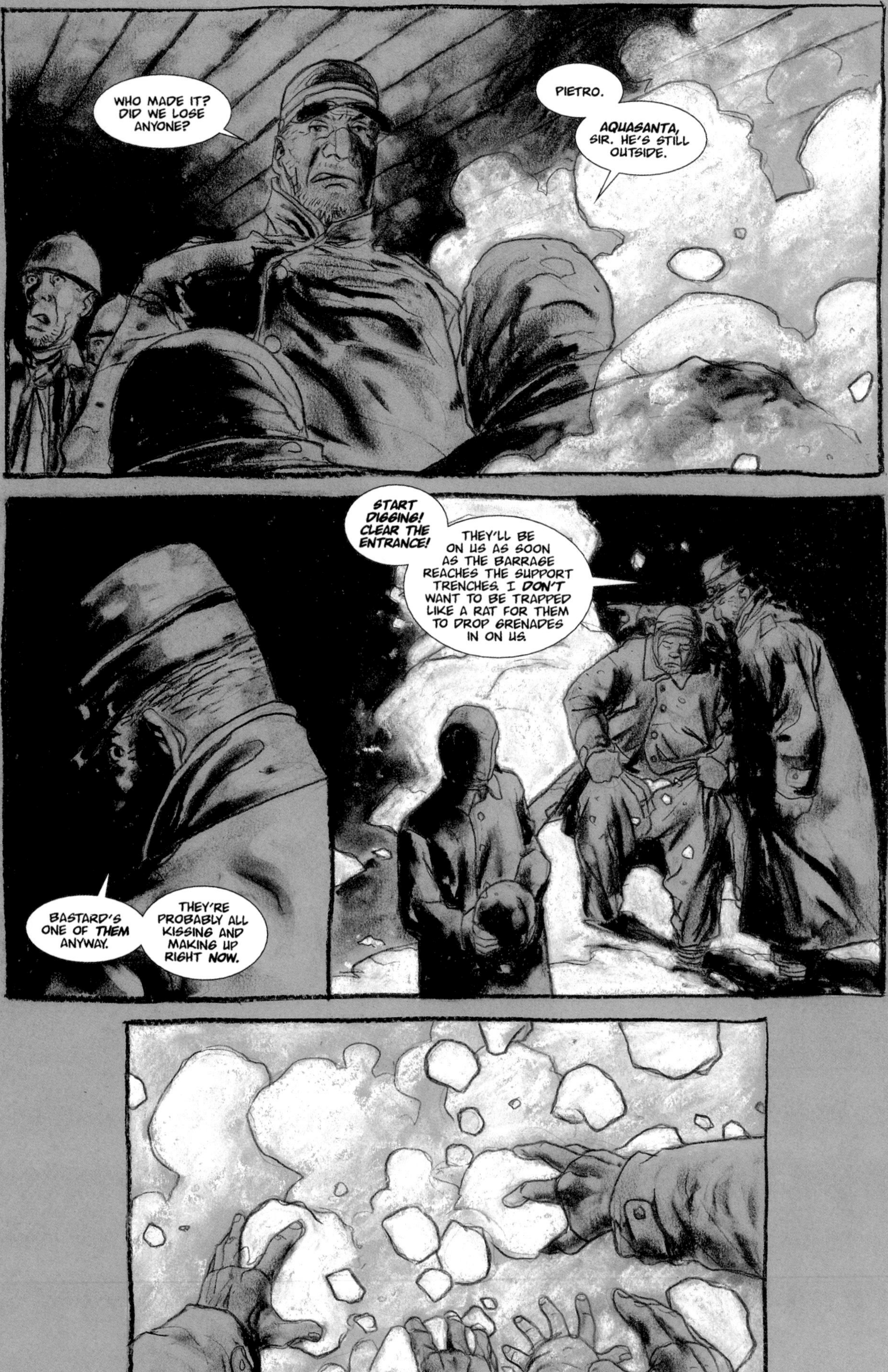
WHO MADE IT? DID WE LOSE ANYONE?
PIETRO.
AQUASANTA, SIR. HE'S STILL OUTSIDE.
START DIGGING! CLEAR THE ENTRANCE!
THEY'LL BE ON US AS SOON AS THE BARRAGE REACHES THE SUPPORT TRENCHES. I DON'T WANT TO BE TRAPPED LIKE A RAT FOR THEM TO DROP GRENADES IN ON US.
BASTARD'S ONE OF THEM ANYWAY.
THEY'RE PROBABLY ALL KISSING AND MAKING UP RIGHT NOW.

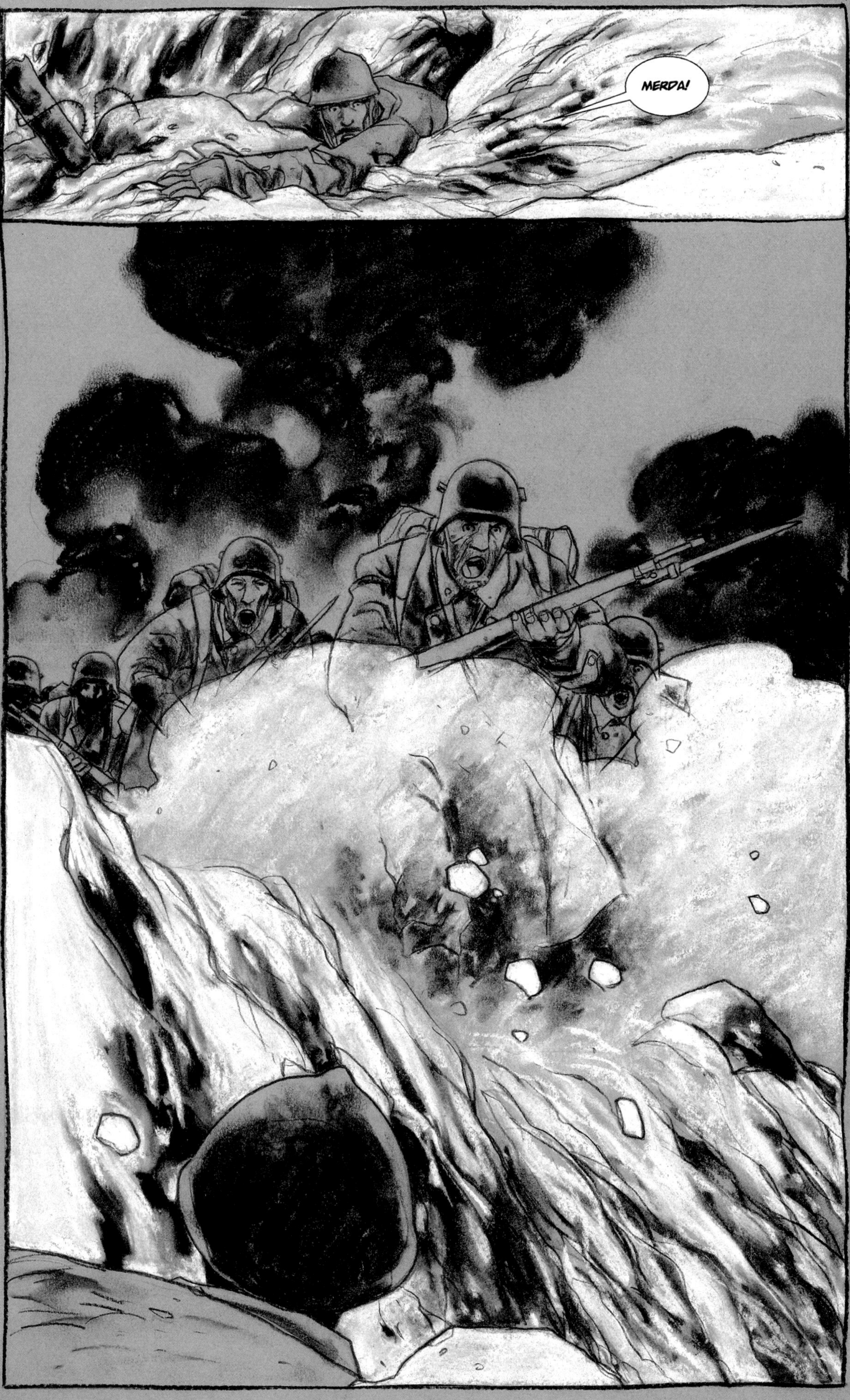
MERDA!

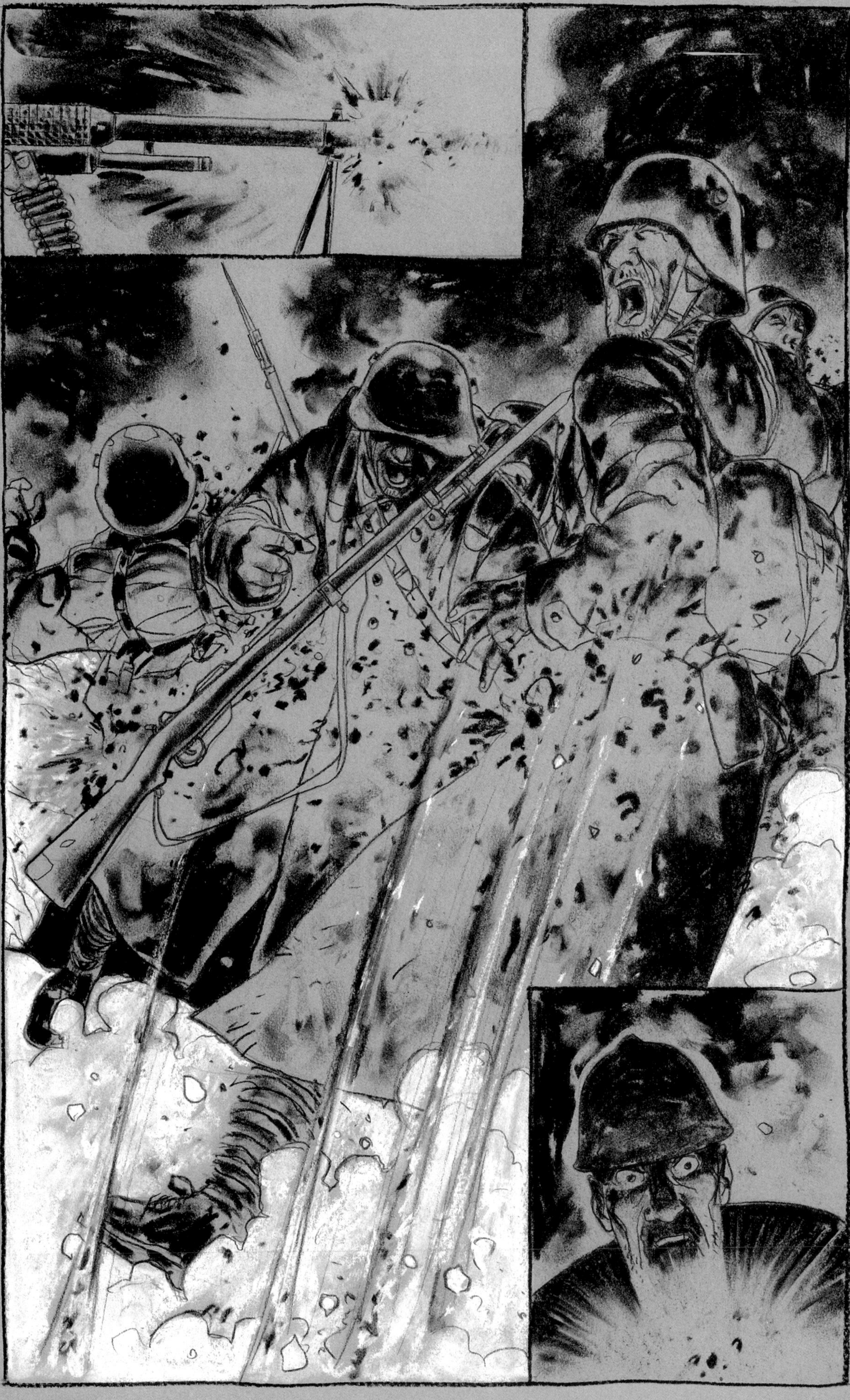

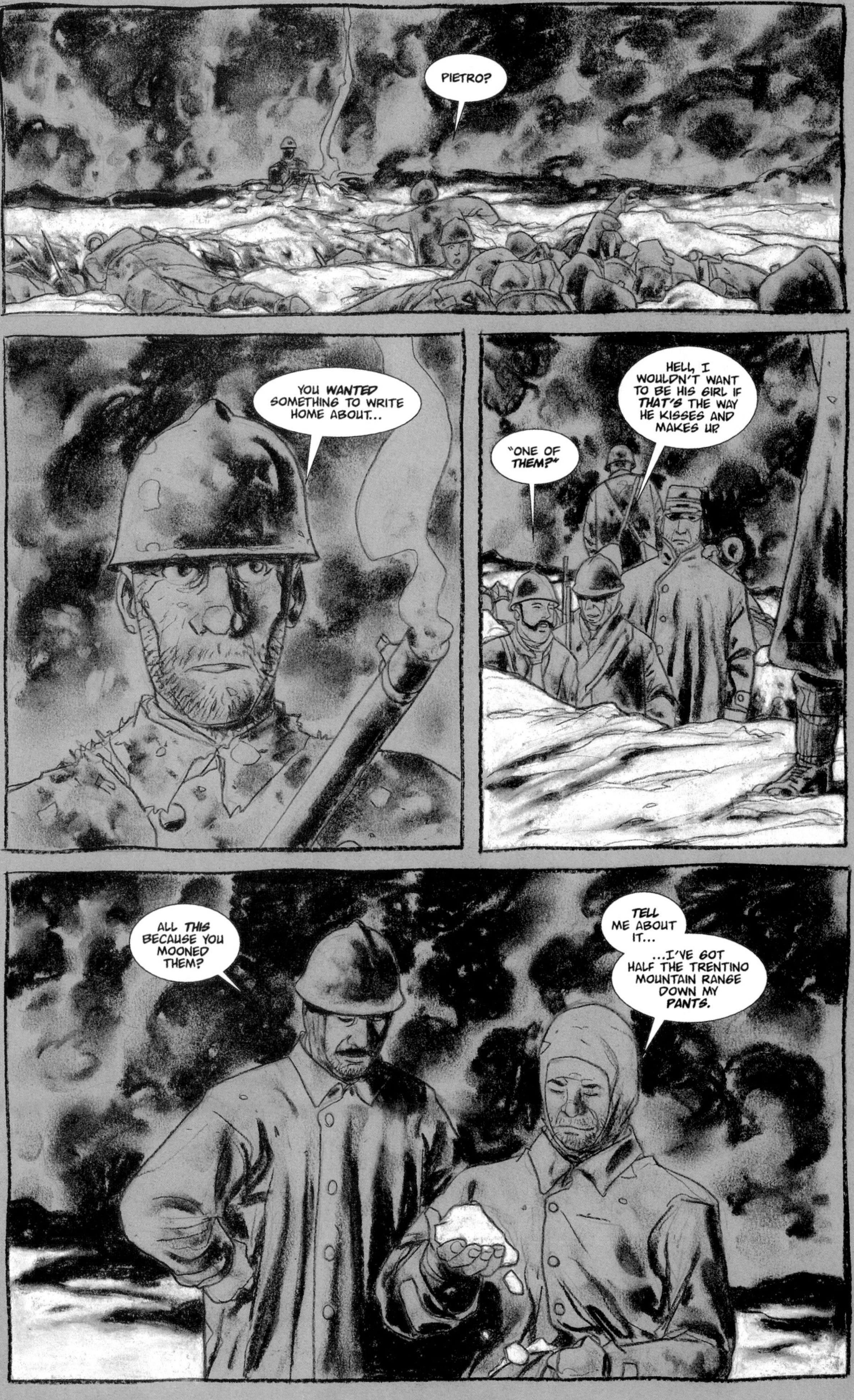
PIETRO?
YOU WANTED SOMETHING TO WRITE HOME ABOUT...
HELL, I WOULDN'T WANT TO BE HIS GIRL IF THAT'S THE WAY HE KISSES AND MAKES UP.
"ONE OF THEM?"
ALL THIS BECAUSE YOU MOONED THEM?
TELL ME ABOUT IT...
...I'VE GOT HALF THE TRENTINO MOUNTAIN RANGE DOWN MY PANTS.

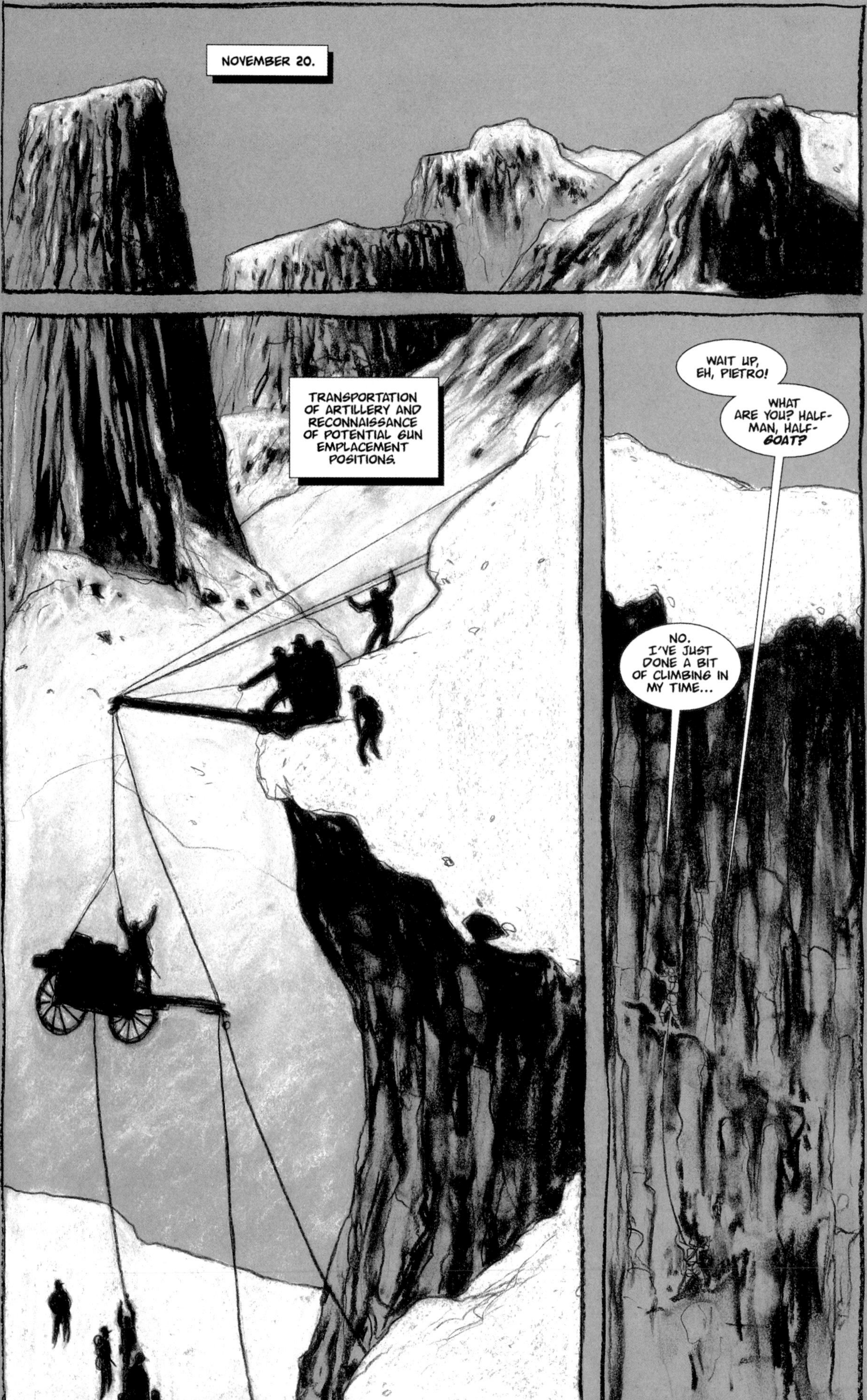
NOVEMBER 20.
TRANSPORTATION OF ARTILLERY AND RECONNAISSANCE OF POTENTIAL GUN EMPLACEMENT POSITIONS.
WAIT UP, EH, PIETRO!
WHAT ARE YOU? HALF-MAN, HALF-GOAT?
NO. I'VE JUST DONE A BIT OF CLIMBING IN MY TIME...

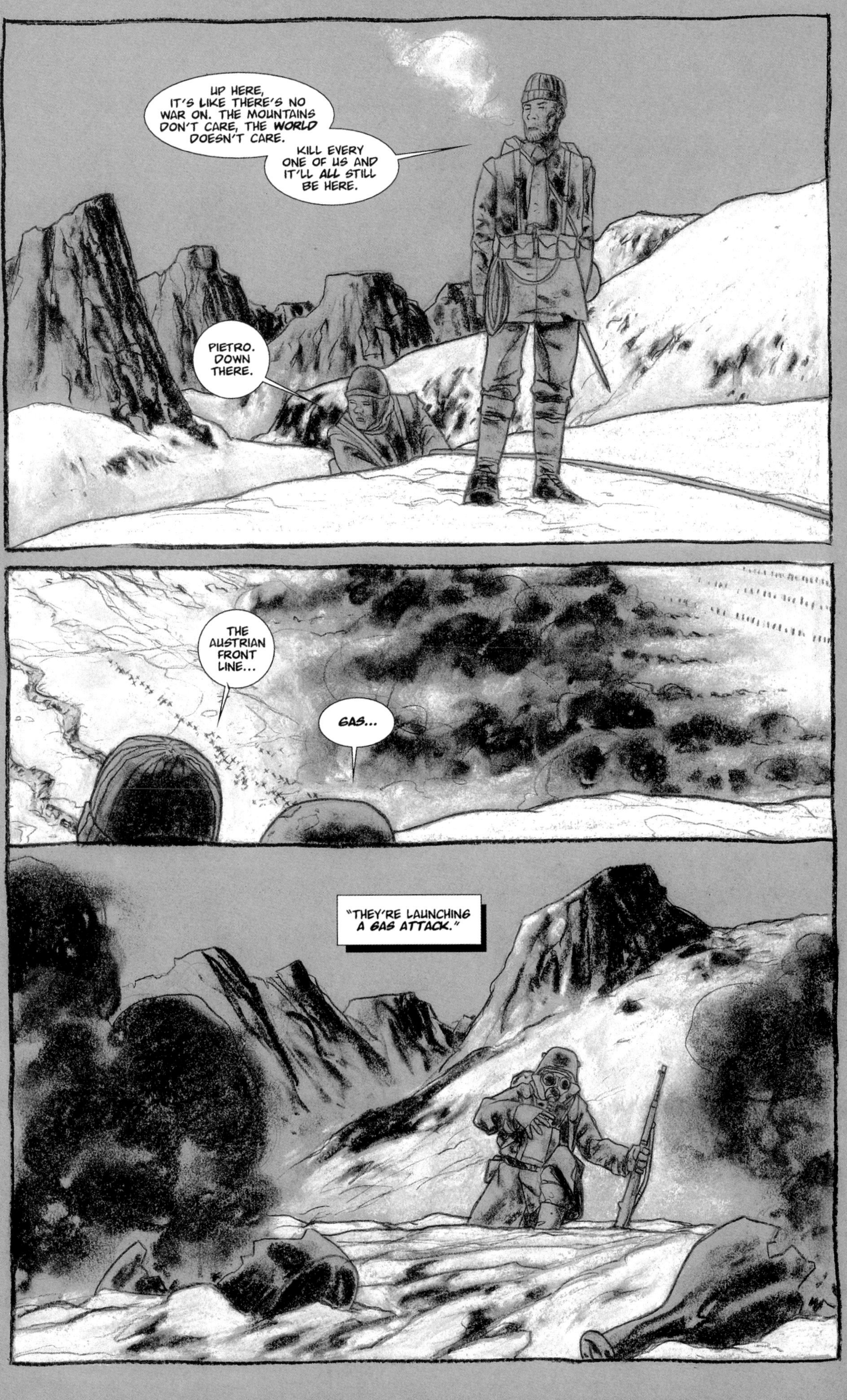
UP HERE, IT'S LIKE THERE'S NO WAR ON. THE MOUNTAINS DON'T CARE, THE WORLD DOESN'T CARE.
KILL EVERY ONE OF US AND IT'LL ALL STILL BE HERE.
PIETRO. DOWN THERE.
THE AUSTRIAN FRONT LINE...
GAS...
"THEY'RE LAUNCHING A GAS ATTACK."

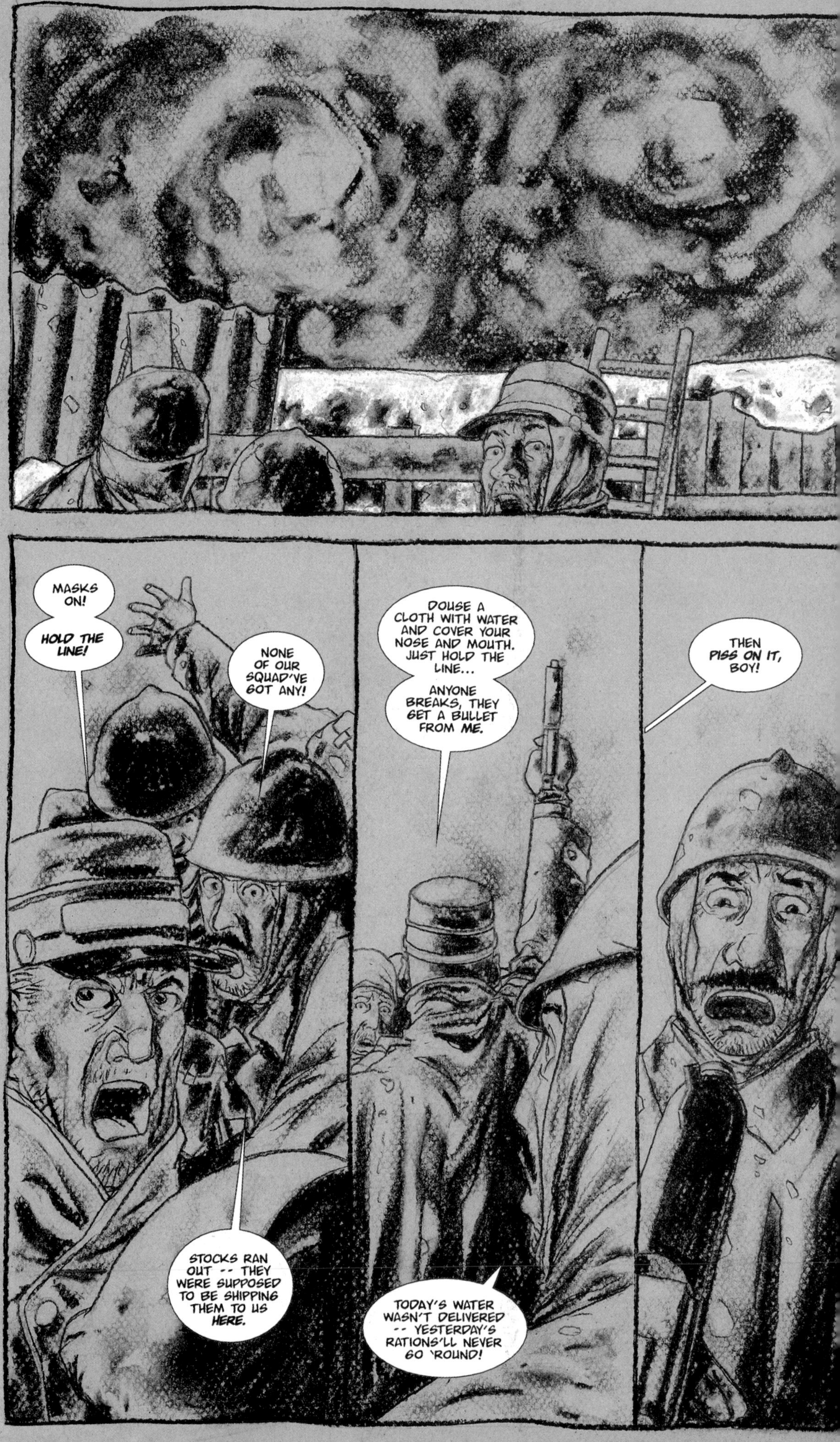
MASKS ON!
HOLD THE LINE!
NONE OF OUR SQUAD'VE GOT ANY!
STOCKS RAN OUT -- THEY WERE SUPPOSED TO BE SHIPPING THEM TO US HERE.
DOUSE A CLOTH WITH WATER AND COVER YOUR NOSE AND MOUTH. JUST HOLD THE LINE...
ANYONE BREAKS, THEY GET A BULLET FROM ME.
TODAY'S WATER WASN'T DELIVERED -- YESTERDAY'S RATIONS'LL NEVER GO 'ROUND!
THEN PISS ON IT, BOY!

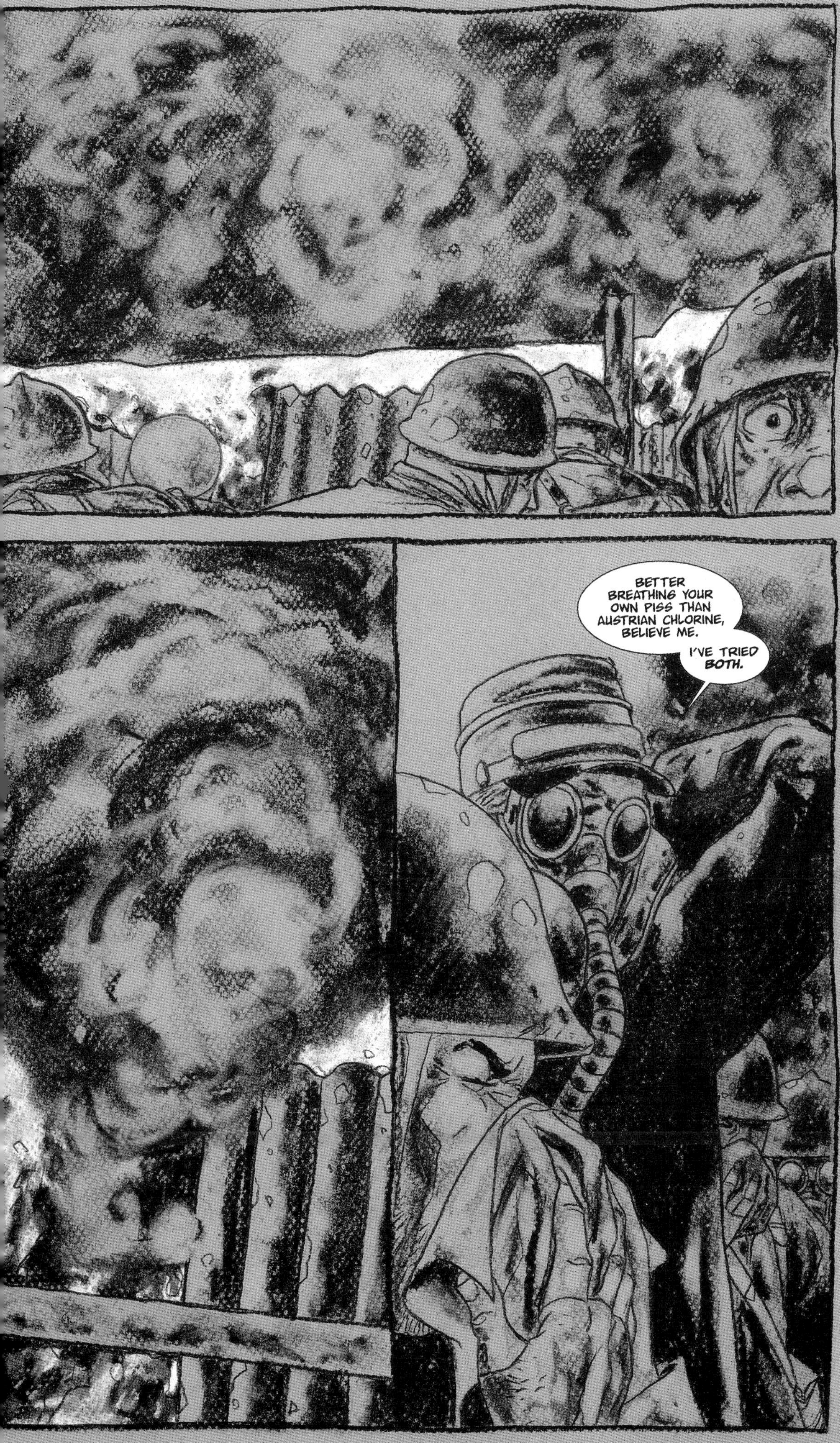
BETTER BREATHING YOUR OWN PISS THAN AUSTRIAN CHLORINE, BELIEVE ME.
I'VE TRIED BOTH.

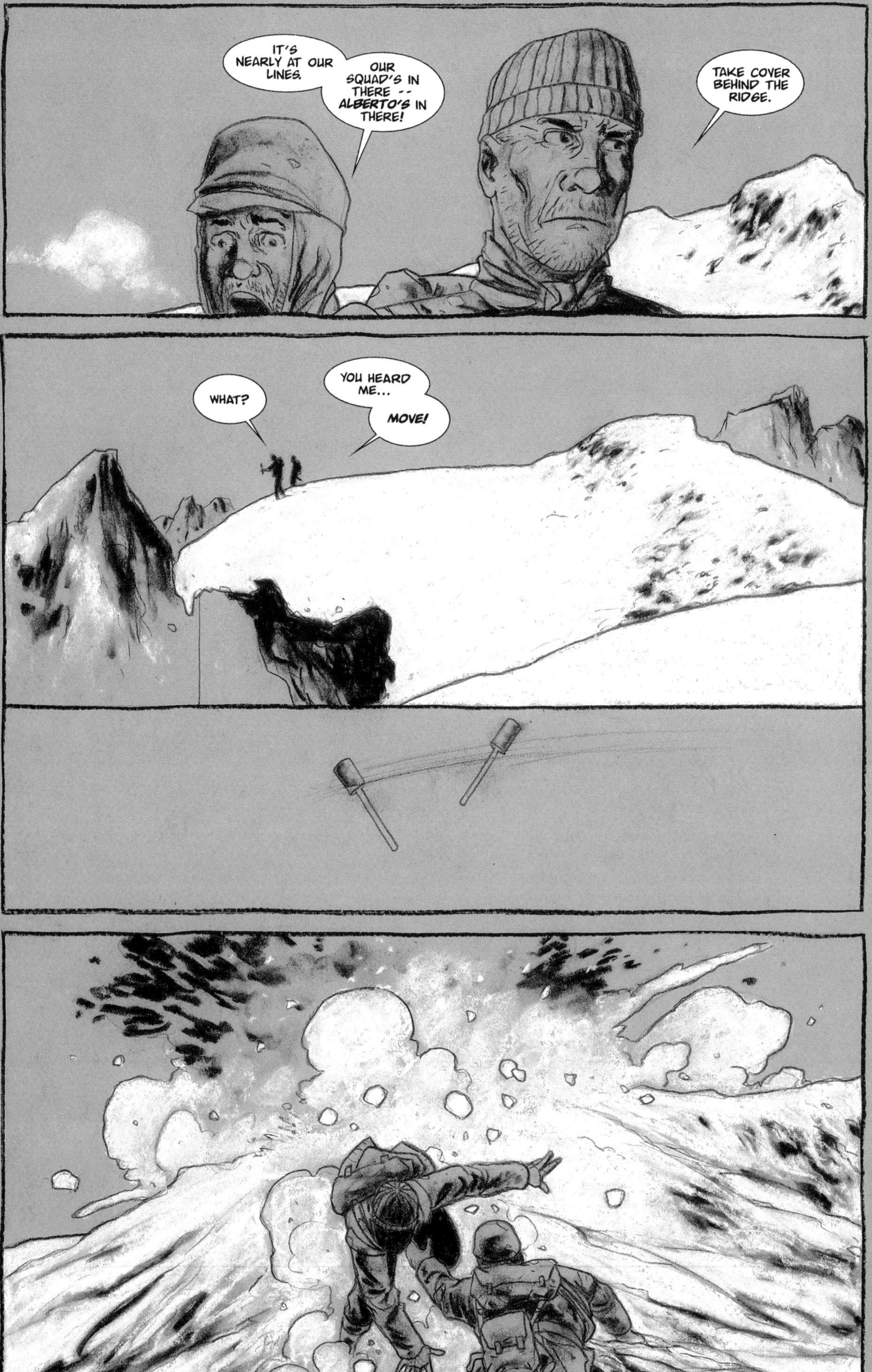
IT'S NEARLY AT OUR LINES.
OUR SQUAD'S IN THERE -- ALBERTO'S IN THERE!
TAKE COVER BEHIND THE RIDGE.
WHAT?
YOU HEARD ME...
MOVE!

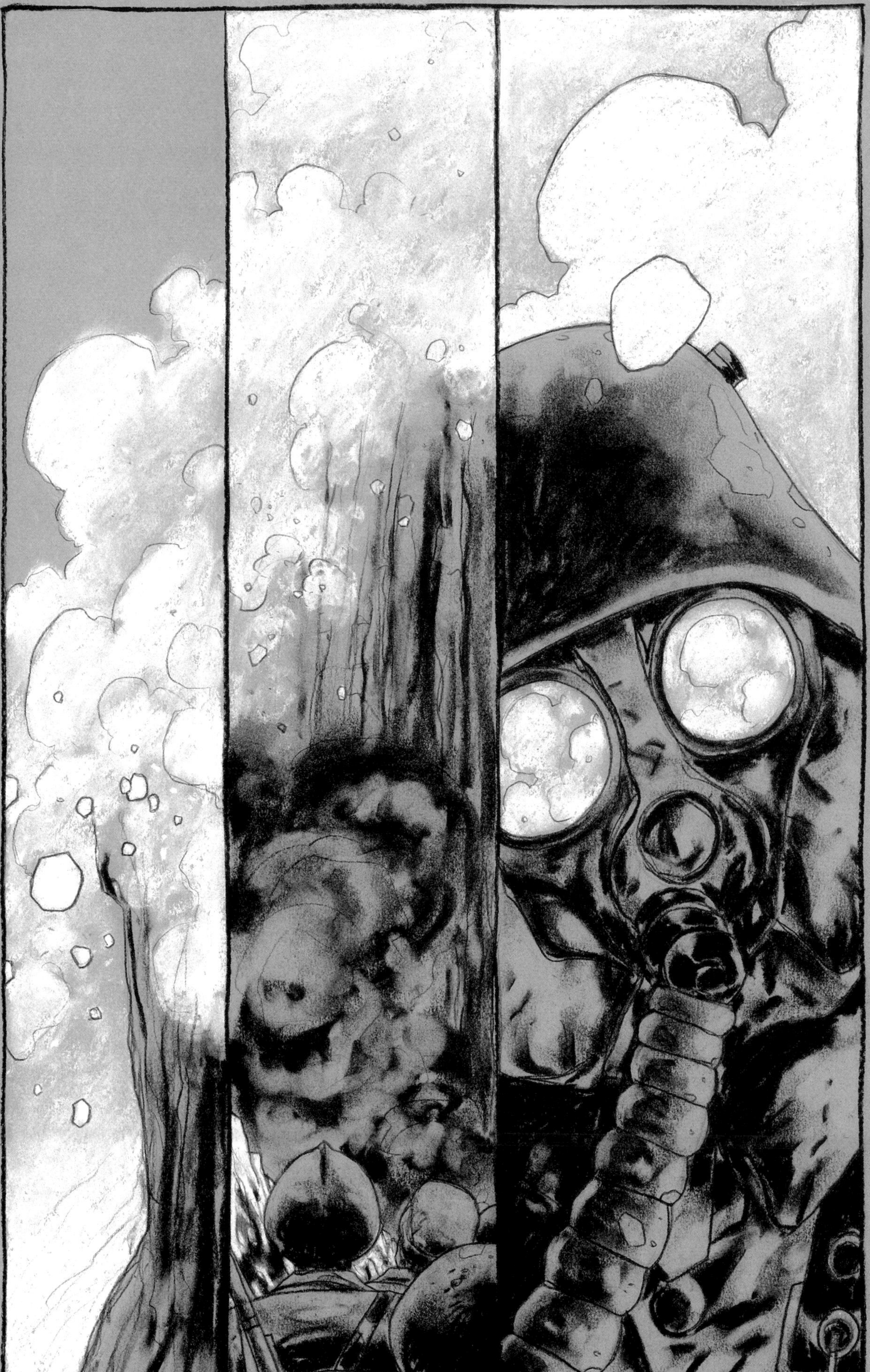

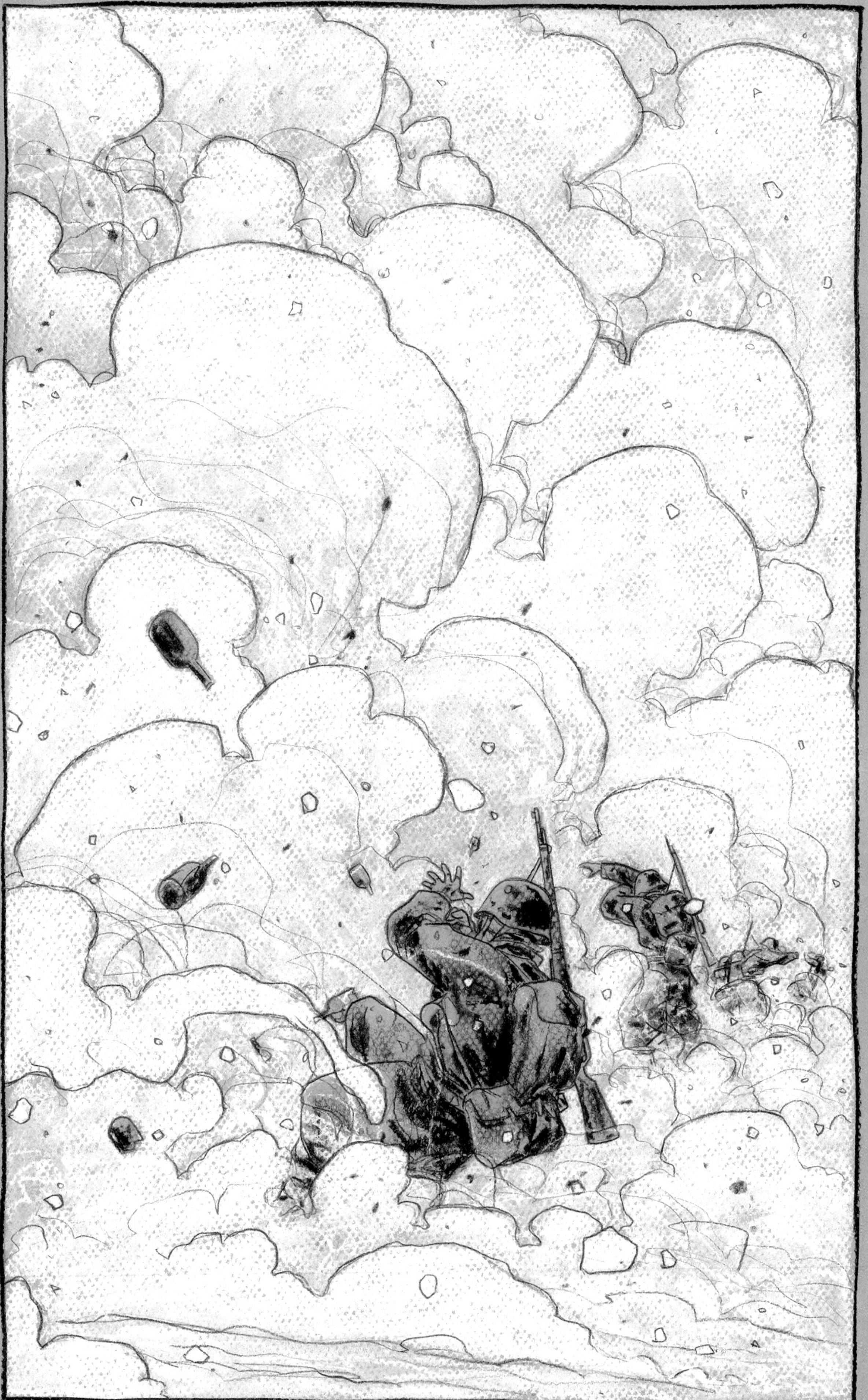

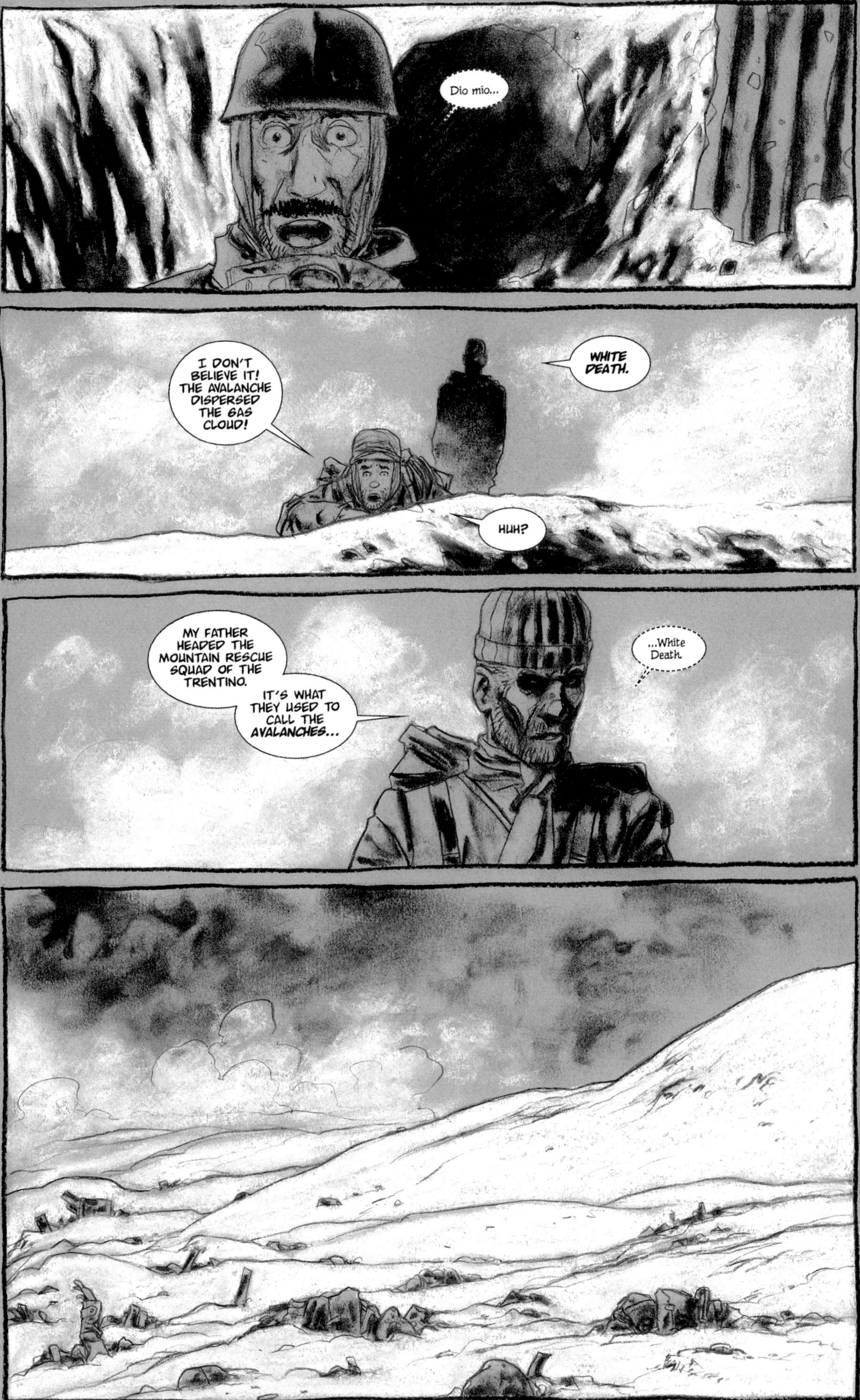
Dio mio...
I DON'T BELIEVE IT! THE AVALANCHE DISPERSED THE GAS CLOUD!
WHITE DEATH.
HUH?
MY FATHER HEADED THE MOUNTAIN RESCUE SQUAD OF THE TRENTINO.
IT'S WHAT THEY USED TO CALL THE AVALANCHES...
...White Death.

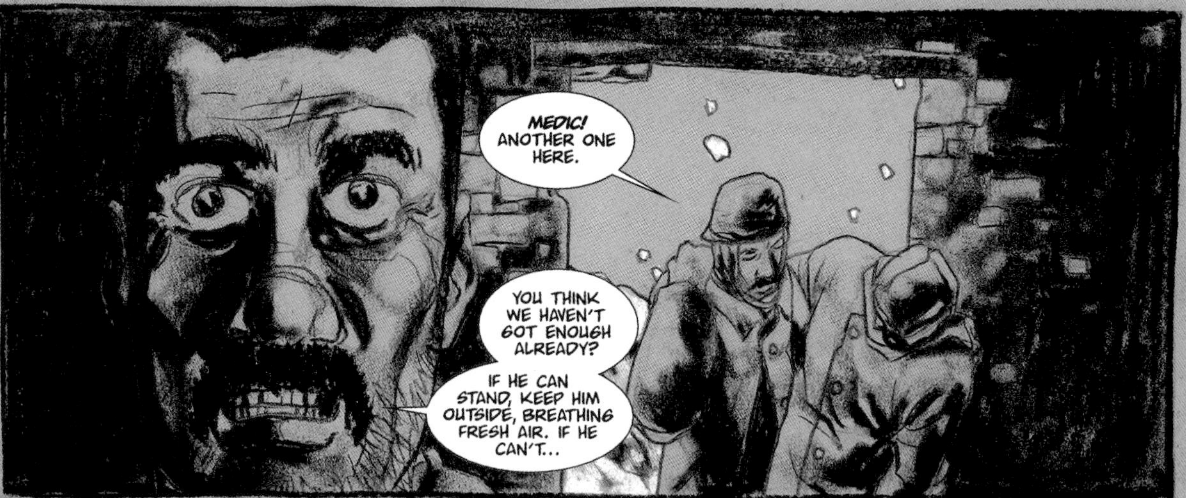
MEDIC! ANOTHER ONE HERE.
YOU THINK WE HAVEN'T GOT ENOUGH ALREADY?
IF HE CAN STAND, KEEP HIM OUTSIDE, BREATHING FRESH AIR. IF HE CAN'T...

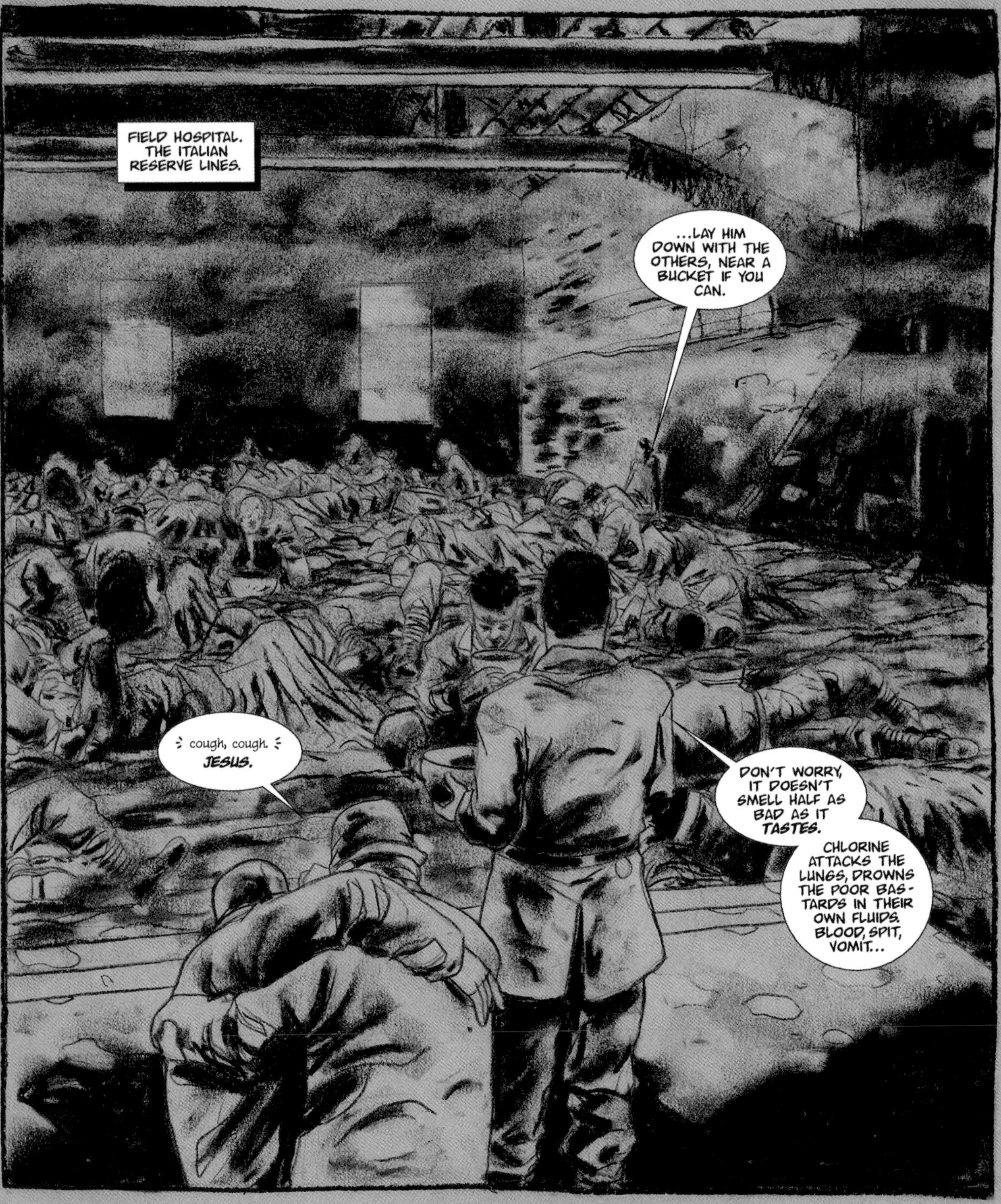
FIELD HOSPITAL. THE ITALIAN RESERVE LINES.
...LAY HIM DOWN WITH THE OTHERS, NEAR A BUCKET IF YOU CAN.
cough, cough. JESUS.
DON'T WORRY, IT DOESN'T SMELL HALF AS BAD AS IT TASTES.
CHLORINE ATTACKS THE LUNGS, DROWNS THE POOR BAS-TARDS IN THEIR OWN FLUIDS. BLOOD, SPIT, VOMIT...

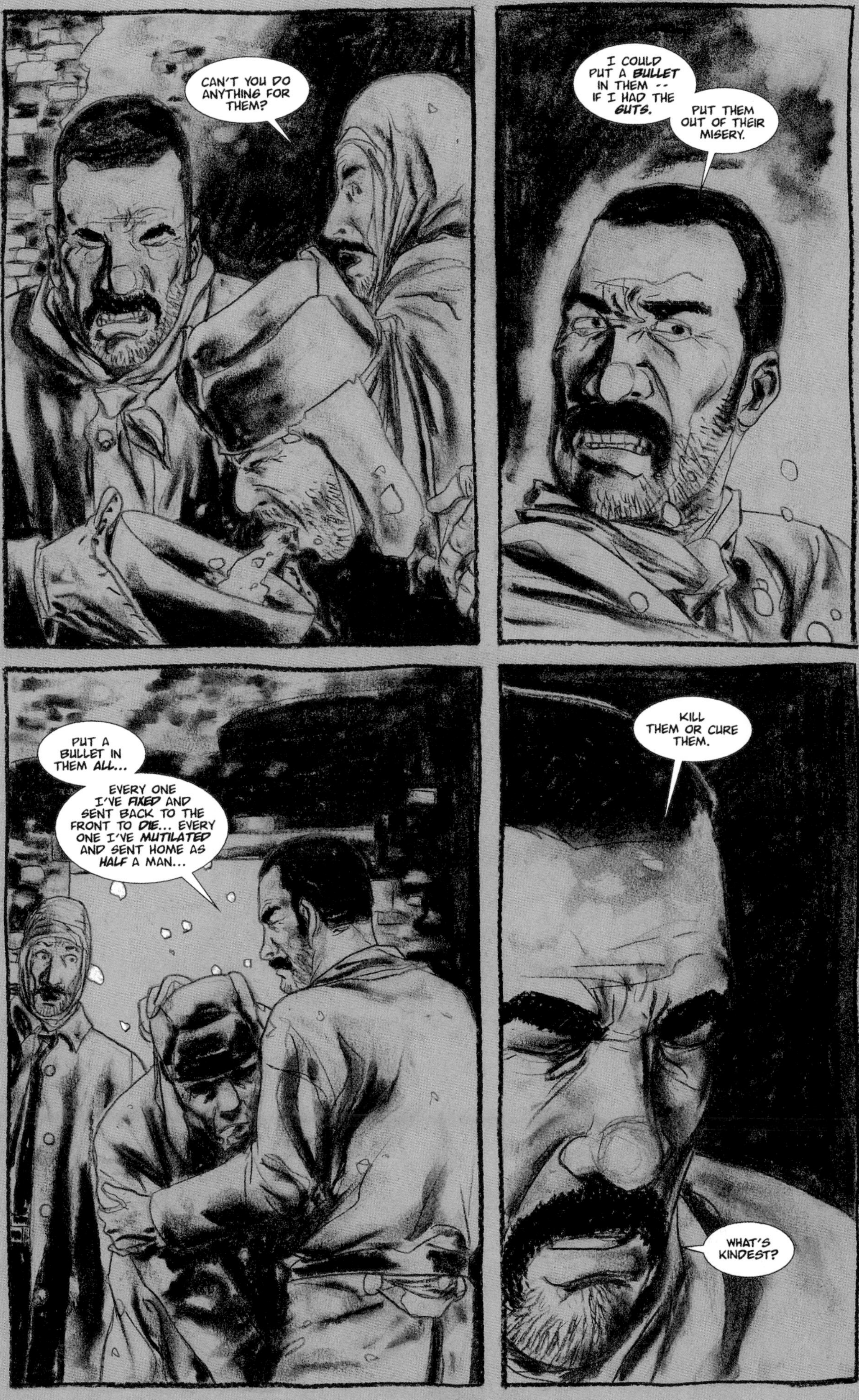
CAN'T YOU DO ANYTHING FOR THEM?
I COULD PUT A BULLET IN THEM -- IF I HAD THE GUTS.
PUT THEM OUT OF THEIR MISERY.
PUT A BULLET IN THEM ALL...
EVERY ONE I'VE FIXED AND SENT BACK TO THE FRONT TO DIE... EVERY ONE I'VE MUTILATED AND SENT HOME AS HALF A MAN...
KILL THEM OR CURE THEM.
WHAT'S KINDEST?

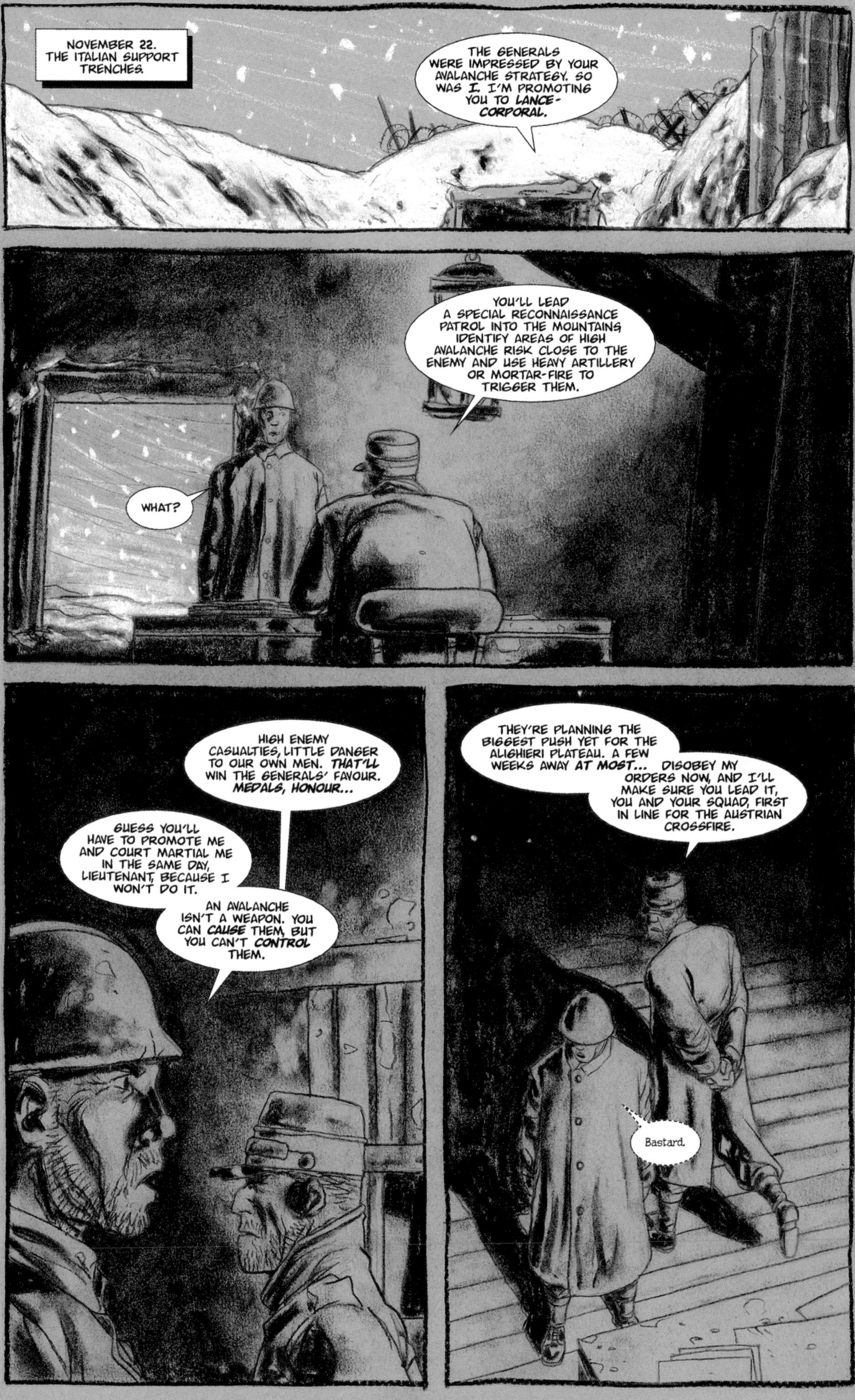
NOVEMBER 22. THE ITALIAN SUPPORT TRENCHES.
THE GENERALS WERE IMPRESSED BY YOUR AVALANCHE STRATEGY. SO WAS I. I'M PROMOTING YOU TO LANCE-CORPORAL.
YOU'LL LEAD A SPECIAL RECONNAISSANCE PATROL INTO THE MOUNTAINS IDENTIFY AREAS OF HIGH AVALANCHE RISK CLOSE TO THE ENEMY AND USE HEAVY ARTILLERY OR MORTAR-FIRE TO TRIGGER THEM.
WHAT?
HIGH ENEMY CASUALTIES, LITTLE DANGER TO OUR OWN MEN. THAT'LL WIN THE GENERALS' FAVOUR. MEDALS, HONOUR...
GUESS YOU'LL HAVE TO PROMOTE ME AND COURT MARTIAL ME IN THE SAME DAY, LIEUTENANT, BECAUSE I WON'T DO IT.
AN AVALANCHE ISN'T A WEAPON. YOU CAN CAUSE THEM, BUT YOU CAN'T CONTROL THEM.
THEY'RE PLANNING THE BIGGEST PUSH YET FOR THE ALIGHIERI PLATEAU. A FEW WEEKS AWAY AT MOST... DISOBEY MY ORDERS NOW, AND I'LL MAKE SURE YOU LEAD IT, YOU AND YOUR SQUAD, FIRST IN LINE FOR THE AUSTRIAN CROSSFIRE.
Bastard.

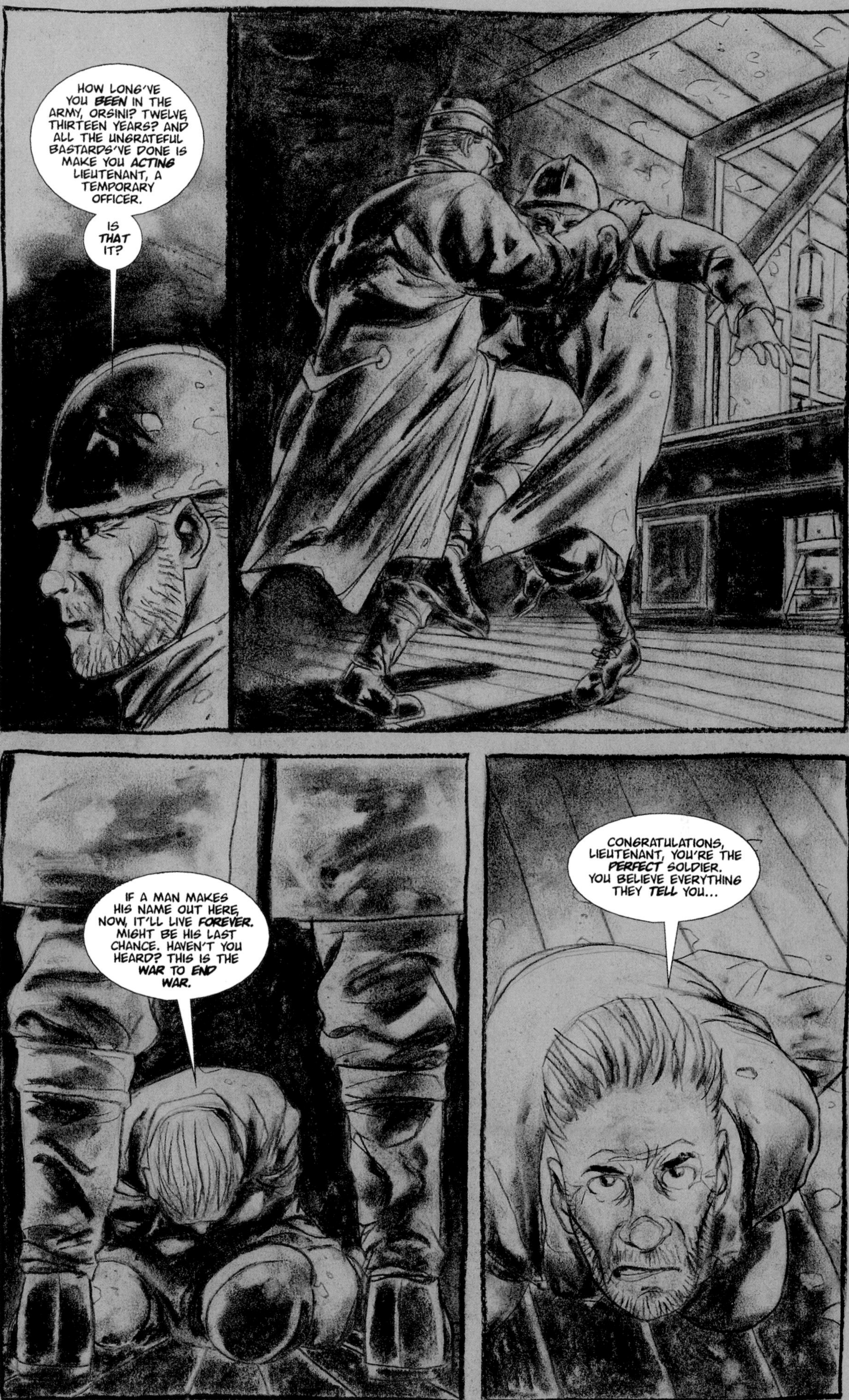

HOW LONG'VE YOU BEEN IN THE ARMY, ORSINI? TWELVE, THIRTEEN YEARS? AND ALL THE UNGRATEFUL BASTARDS'VE DONE IS MAKE YOU ACTING LIEUTENANT, A TEMPORARY OFFICER.
IS THAT IT?
IF A MAN MAKES HIS NAME OUT HERE, NOW, IT'LL LIVE FOREVER. MIGHT BE HIS LAST CHANCE. HAVEN'T YOU HEARD? THIS IS THE WAR TO END WAR.
CONGRATULATIONS, LIEUTENANT, YOU'RE THE PERFECT SOLDIER. YOU BELIEVE EVERYTHING THEY TELL YOU...

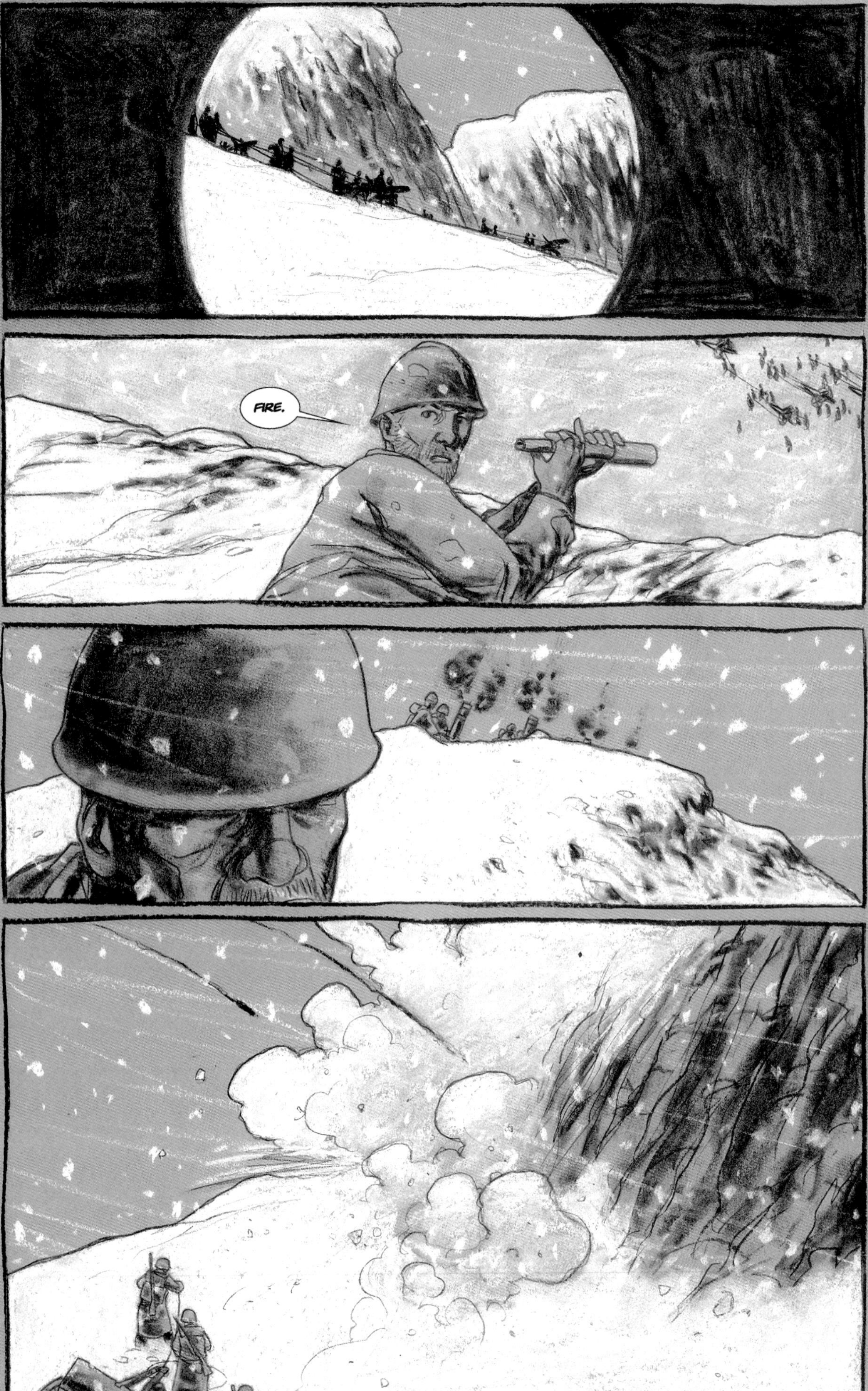
FIRE.

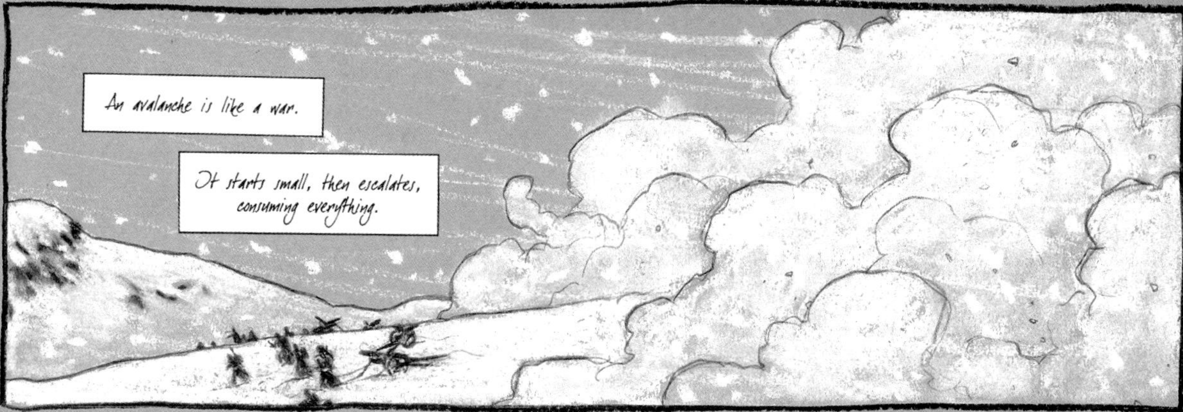
An avalanche is like a war.
It starts small, then escalates, consuming everything.

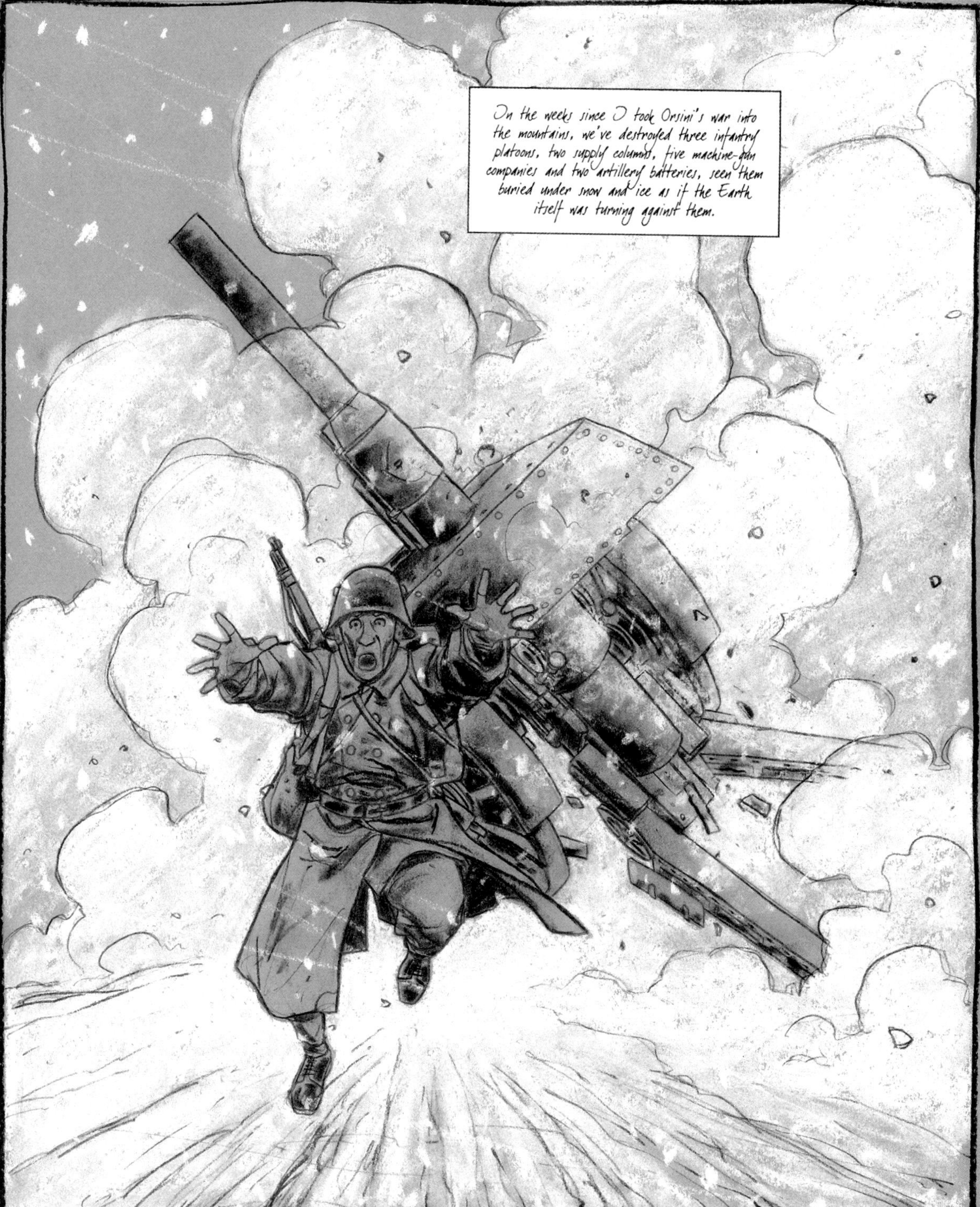
In the weeks since I took Orsini's war into the mountains, we've destroyed three infantry platoons, two supply columns, five machine-gun companies and two artillery batteries, seen them buried under snow and ice as if the Earth itself was turning against them.

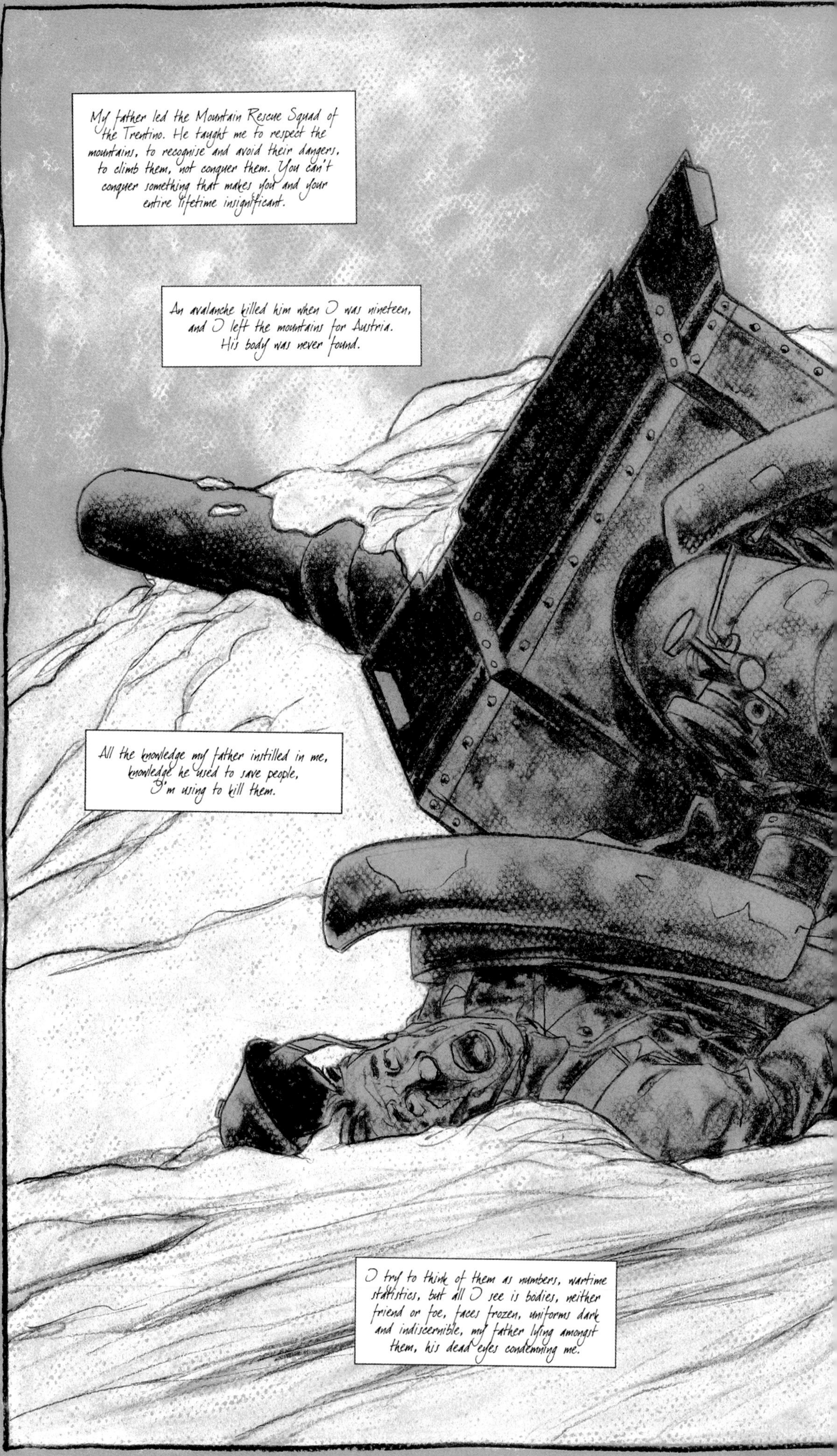
My father led the Mountain Rescue Squad of the Trentino. He taught me to respect the mountains, to recognise and avoid their dangers, to climb them, not conquer them. You can't conquer something that makes you and your entire lifetime insignificant.
An avalanche killed him when I was nineteen, and I left the mountains for Austria. His body was never found.
All the knowledge my father instilled in me, knowledge he used to save people, I'm using to kill them.
I try to think of them as numbers, wartime statistics, but all I see is bodies, neither friend or foe, faces frozen, uniforms dark and indiscernible, my father lying amongst them, his dead eyes condemning me.

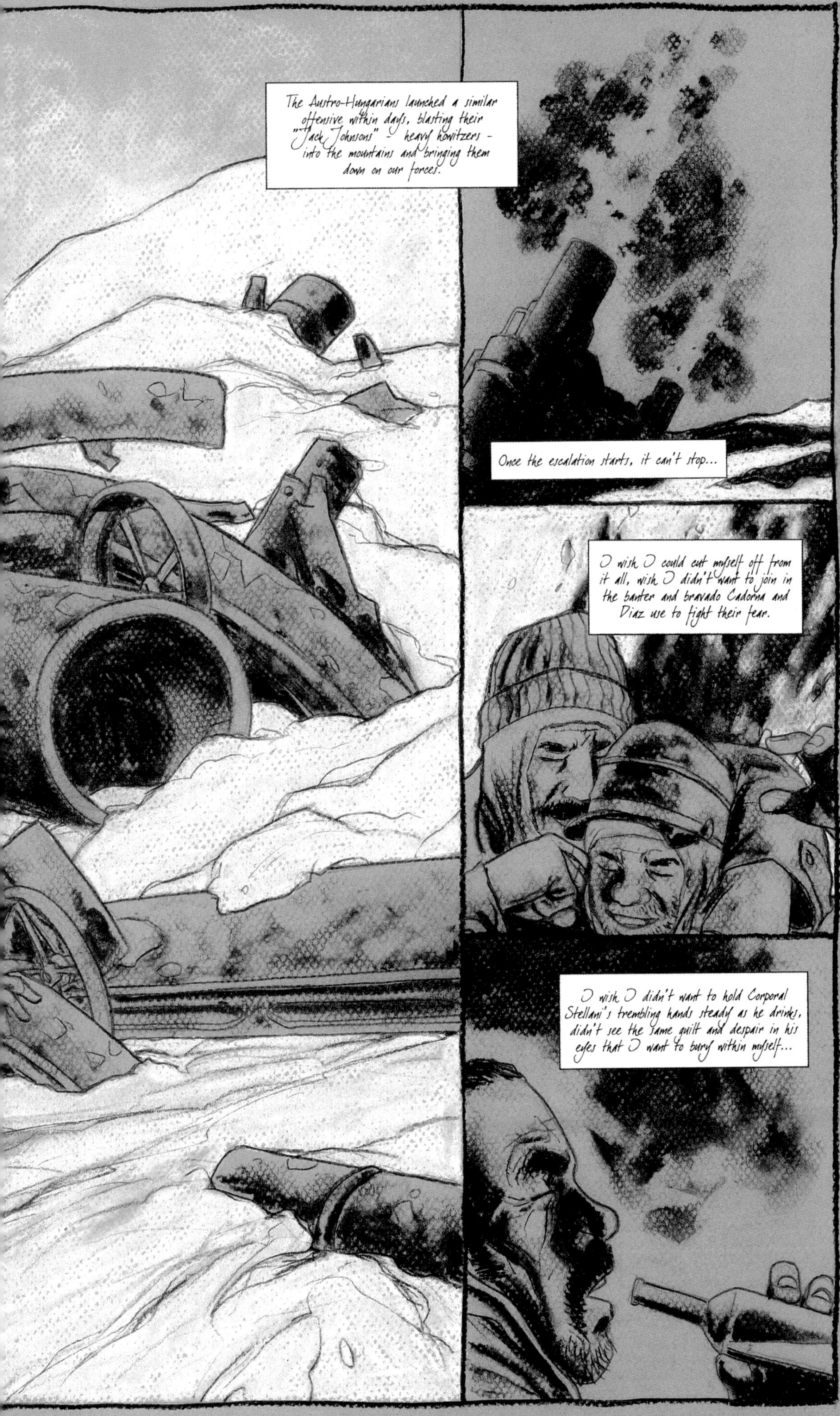
The Austro-Hungarians launched a similar offensive within days, blasting their "Jack Johnsons" - heavy howitzers - into the mountains and bringing them down on our forces.
Once the escalation starts, it can't stop...
I wish I could cut myself off from it all, wish I didn't want to join in the banter and bravado Cadorna and Diaz use to fight their fear.
I wish I didn't want to hold Corporal Stellani's trembling hands steady as he drinks, didn't see the same guilt and despair in his eyes that I want to bury within myself...

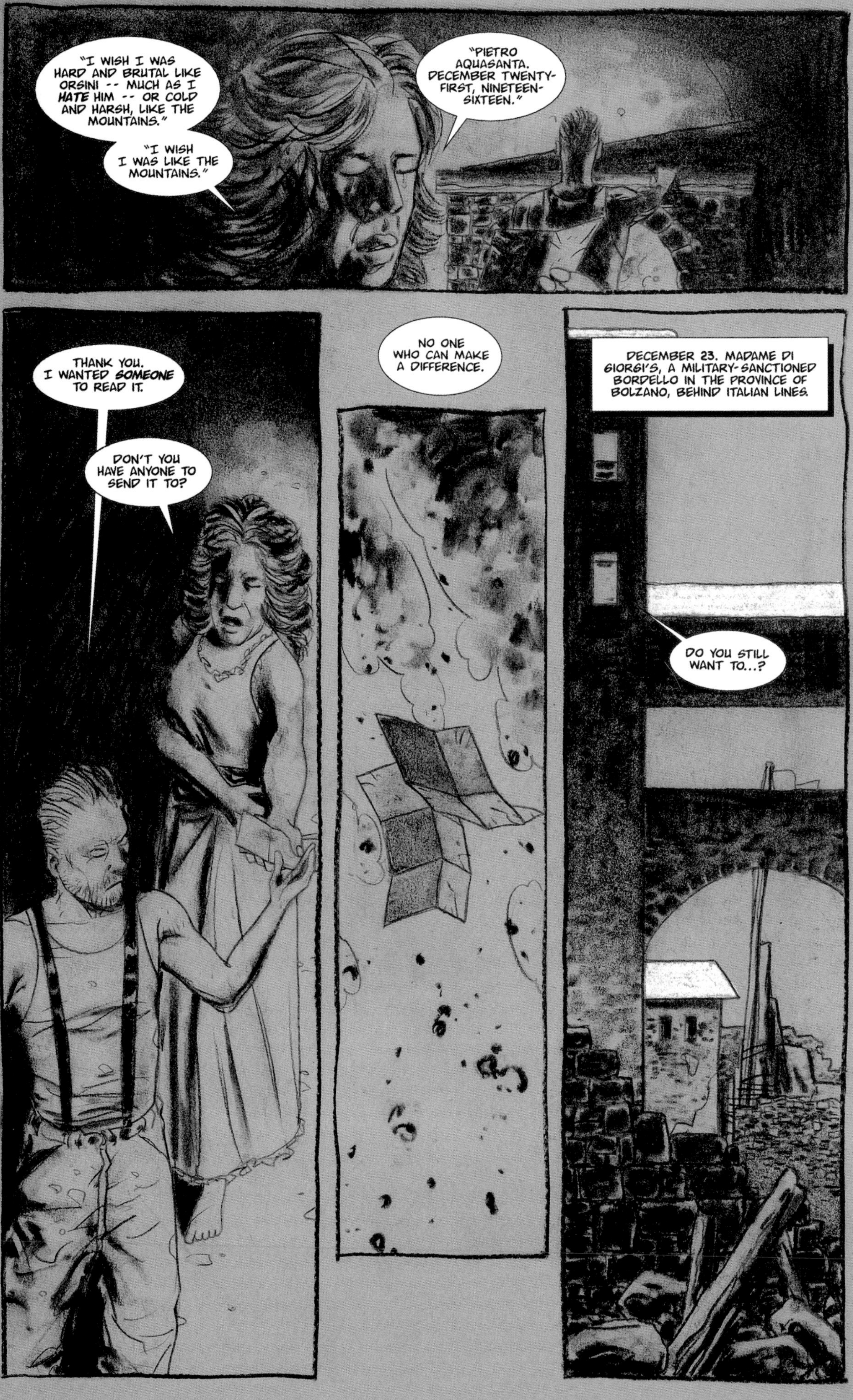
"I WISH I WAS HARD AND BRUTAL LIKE ORSINI -- MUCH AS I HATE HIM -- OR COLD AND HARSH, LIKE THE MOUNTAINS."
"I WISH I WAS LIKE THE MOUNTAINS."
"PIETRO AQUASANTA. DECEMBER TWENTY-FIRST, NINETEEN-SIXTEEN."
THANK YOU. I WANTED SOMEONE TO READ IT.
DON'T YOU HAVE ANYONE TO SEND IT TO?
NO ONE WHO CAN MAKE A DIFFERENCE.
DECEMBER 23. MADAME DI GIORGI'S, A MILITARY-SANCTIONED BORDELLO IN THE PROVINCE OF BOLZANO, BEHIND ITALIAN LINES.
DO YOU STILL WANT TO...?

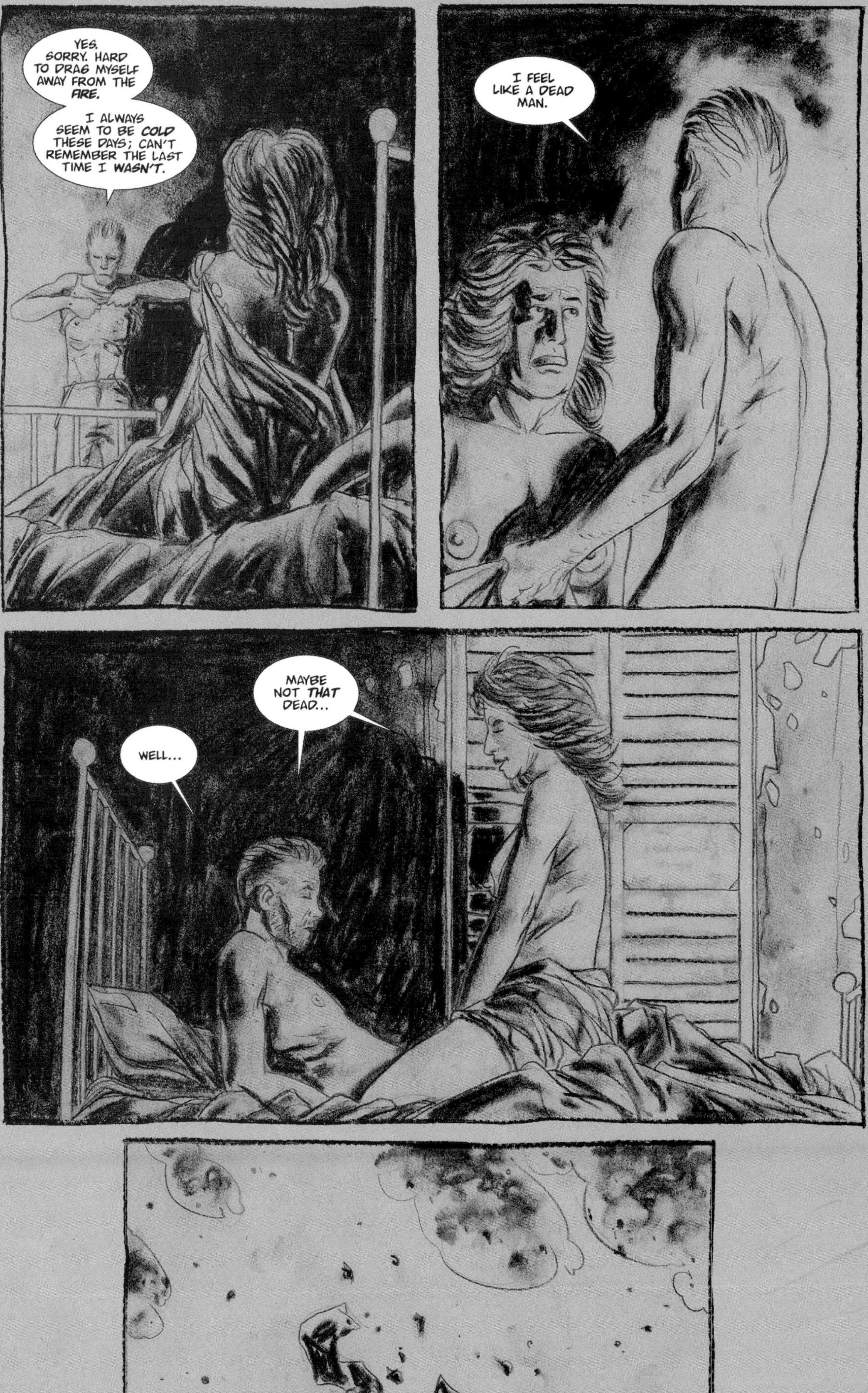
YES. SORRY. HARD TO DRAG MYSELF AWAY FROM THE FIRE.
I ALWAYS SEEM TO BE COLD THESE DAYS; CAN'T REMEMBER THE LAST TIME I WASN'T.
I FEEL LIKE A DEAD MAN.
WELL...
MAYBE NOT THAT DEAD...

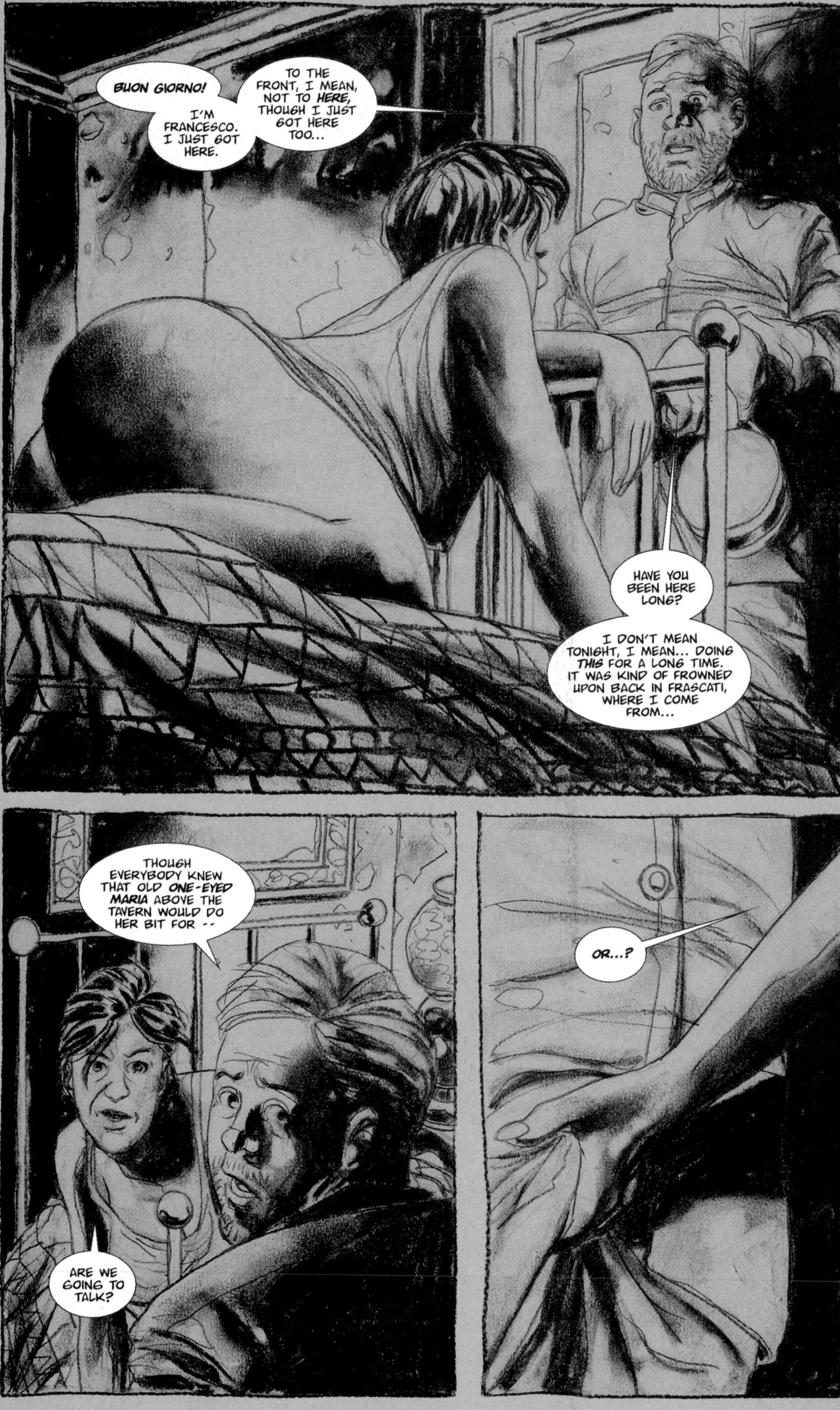
BUON GIORNO!
I'M FRANCESCO. I JUST GOT HERE.
TO THE FRONT, I MEAN, NOT TO HERE, THOUGH I JUST GOT HERE TOO...
HAVE YOU BEEN HERE LONG?
I DON'T MEAN TONIGHT, I MEAN... DOING THIS FOR A LONG TIME. IT WAS KIND OF FROWNED UPON BACK IN FRASCATI, WHERE I COME FROM...
THOUGH EVERYBODY KNEW THAT OLD ONE-EYED MARIA ABOVE THE TAVERN WOULD DO HER BIT FOR --
ARE WE GOING TO TALK?
OR...?

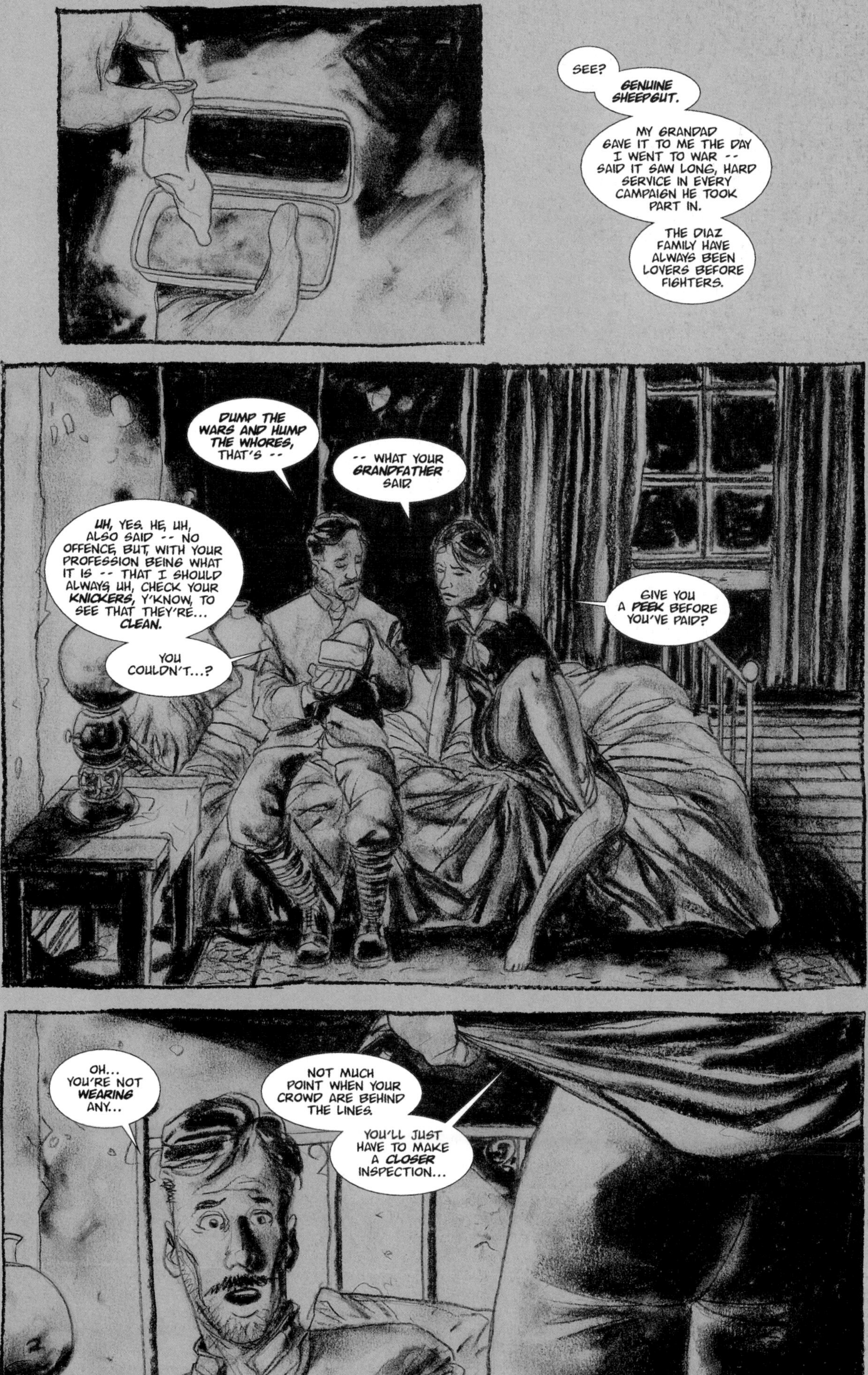
SEE?
GENUINE SHEEPGUT.
MY GRANDAD GAVE IT TO ME THE DAY I WENT TO WAR -- SAID IT SAW LONG, HARD SERVICE IN EVERY CAMPAIGN HE TOOK PART IN.
THE DIAZ FAMILY HAVE ALWAYS BEEN LOVERS BEFORE FIGHTERS.
DUMP THE WARS AND HUMP THE WHORES, THAT'S --
-- WHAT YOUR GRANDFATHER SAID.
UH, YES. HE, UH, ALSO SAID -- NO OFFENCE, BUT, WITH YOUR PROFESSION BEING WHAT IT IS -- THAT I SHOULD ALWAYS UH, CHECK YOUR KNICKERS, Y'KNOW, TO SEE THAT THEY'RE... CLEAN.
YOU COULDN'T...?
GIVE YOU A PEEK BEFORE YOU'VE PAID?
OH... YOU'RE NOT WEARING ANY...
NOT MUCH POINT WHEN YOUR CROWD ARE BEHIND THE LINES.
YOU'LL JUST HAVE TO MAKE A CLOSER INSPECTION...

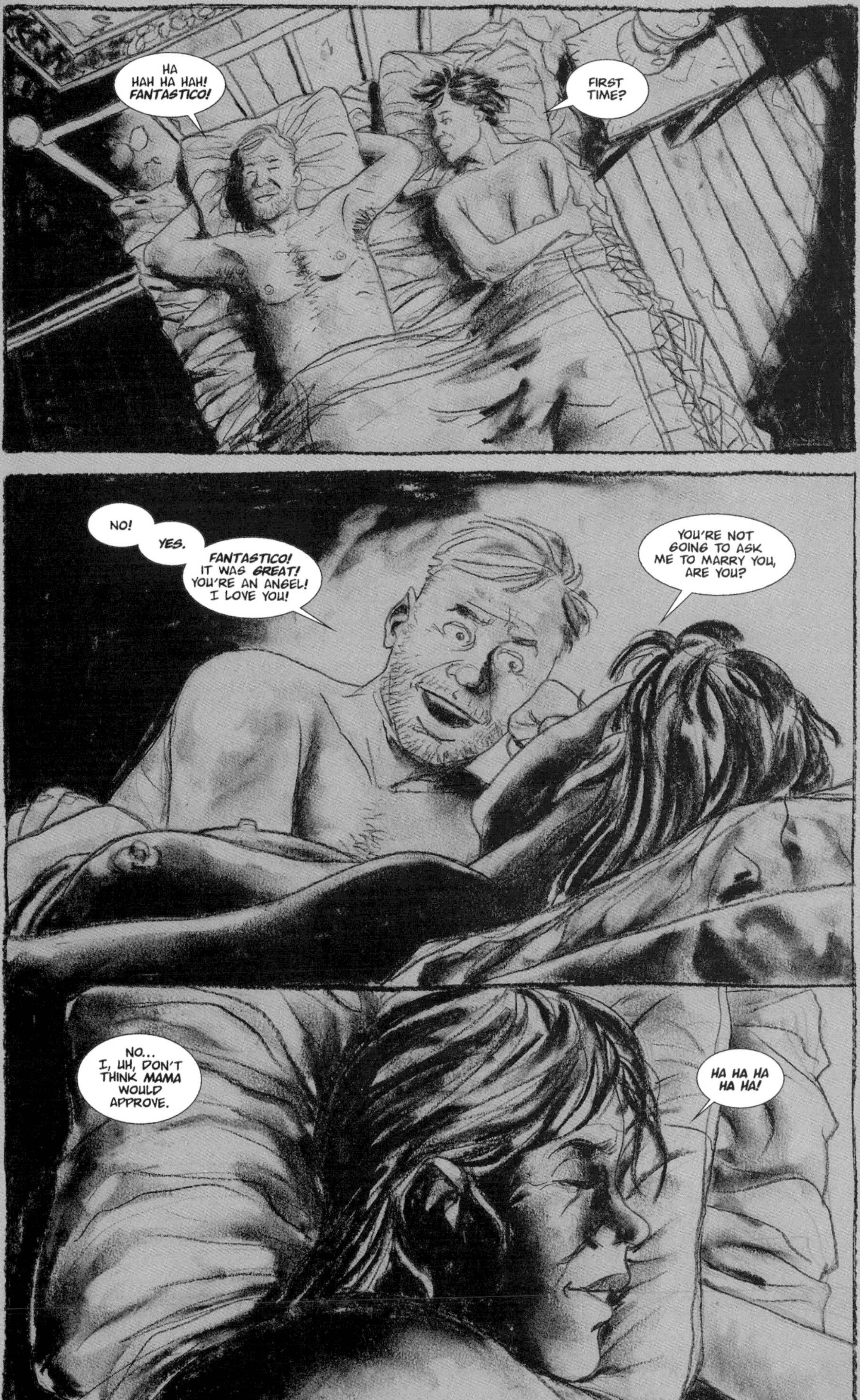
HA HAH HA HAH! FANTASTICO!
FIRST TIME?
NO!
YES.
FANTASTICO! IT WAS GREAT! YOU'RE AN ANGEL! I LOVE YOU!
YOU'RE NOT GOING TO ASK ME TO MARRY YOU, ARE YOU?
NO... I, UH, DON'T THINK MAMA WOULD APPROVE.
HA HA HA HA HA!

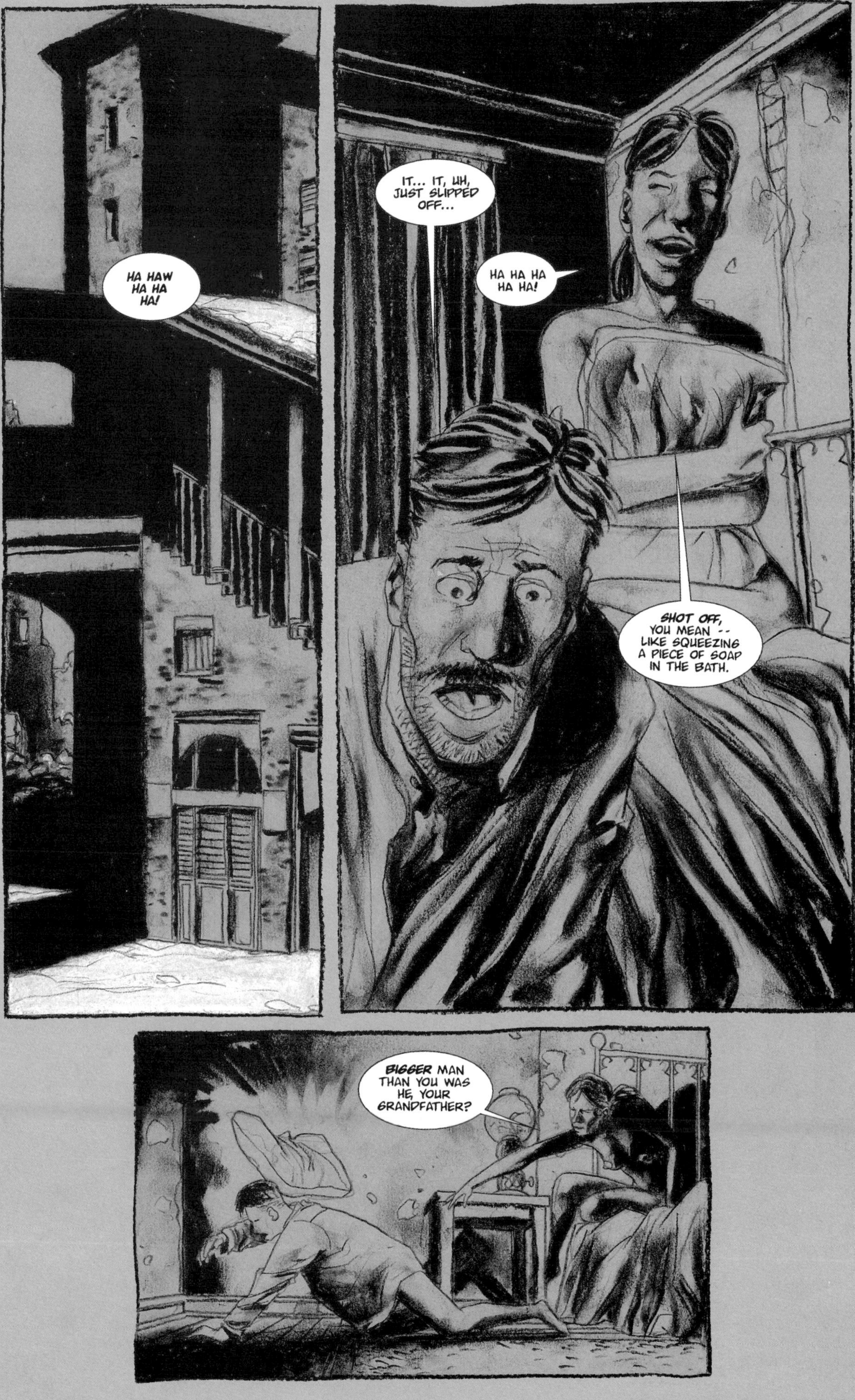
HA HAW
HA HA
HA!
IT... IT, UH,
JUST SLIPPED
OFF...
HA HA HA
HA HA!
SHOT OFF,
YOU MEAN --
LIKE SQUEEZING
A PIECE OF SOAP
IN THE BATH.
BIGGER MAN
THAN YOU WAS
HE, YOUR
GRANDFATHER?

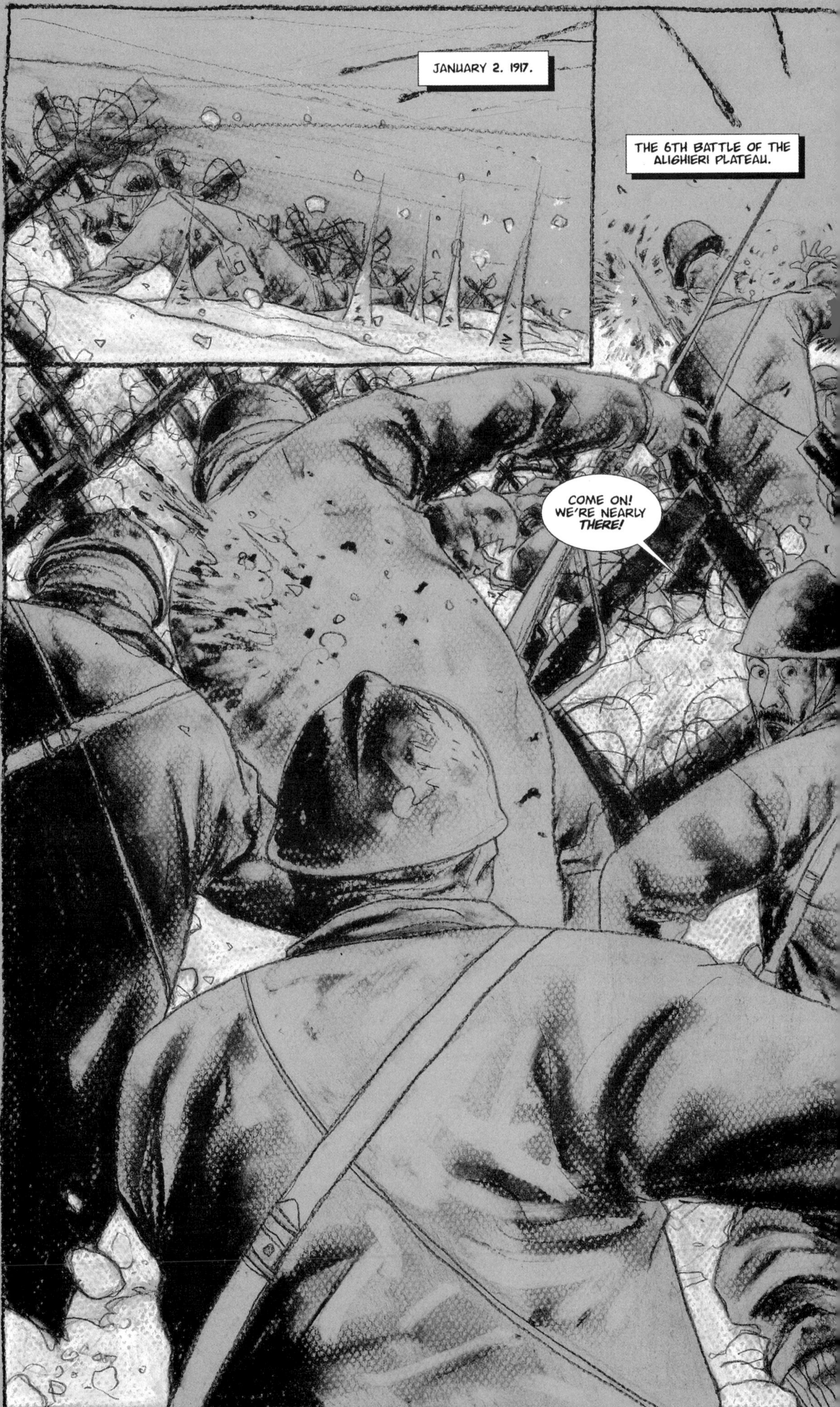
JANUARY 2. 1917.
THE 6TH BATTLE OF THE ALIGHIERI PLATEAU.
COME ON! WE'RE NEARLY THERE!

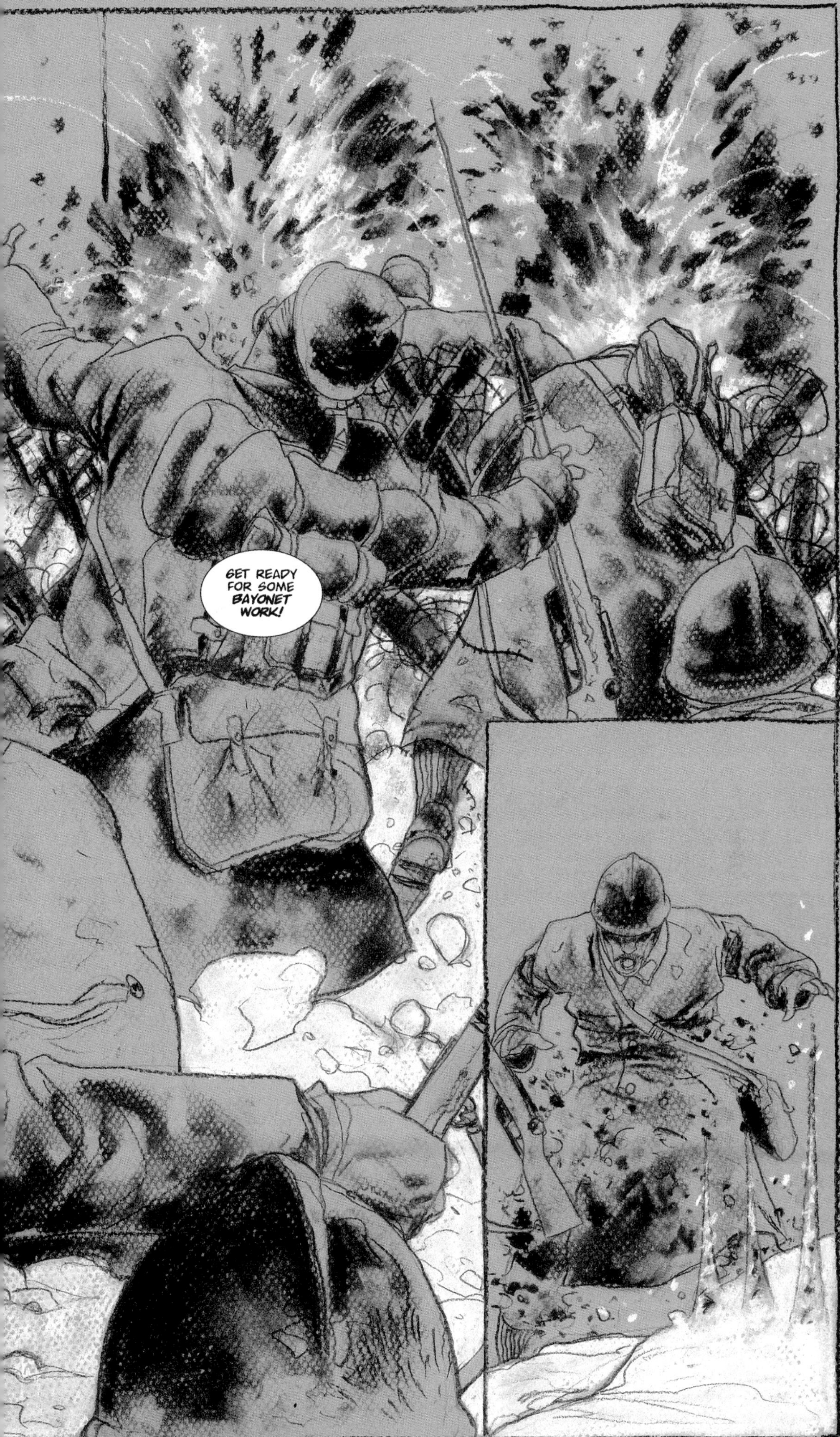
GET READY FOR SOME BAYONET WORK!

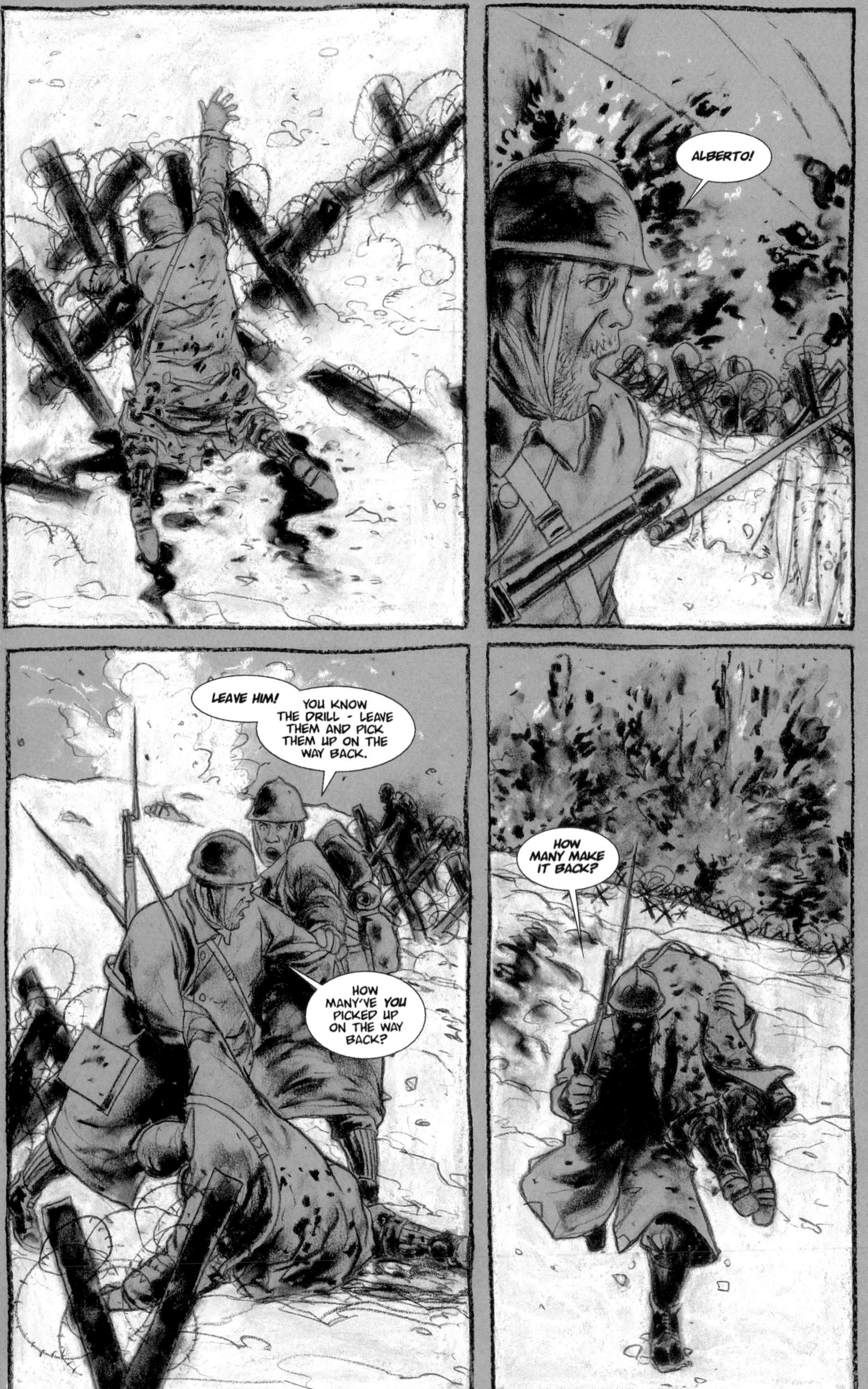
ALBERTO!
LEAVE HIM!
YOU KNOW THE DRILL - LEAVE THEM AND PICK THEM UP ON THE WAY BACK.
HOW MANY'VE YOU PICKED UP ON THE WAY BACK?
HOW MANY MAKE IT BACK?

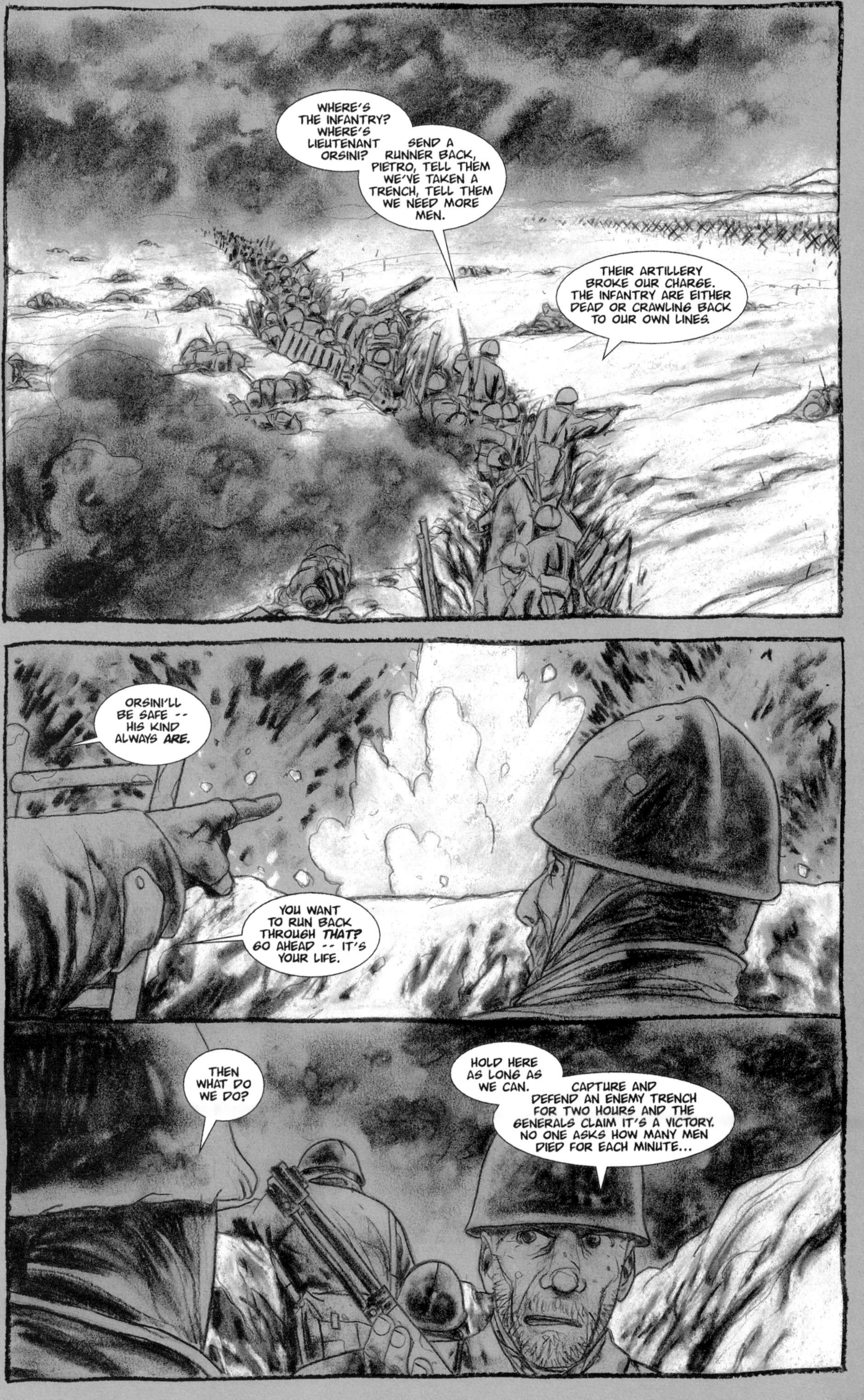
WHERE'S THE INFANTRY? WHERE'S LIEUTENANT ORSINI?
SEND A RUNNER BACK, PIETRO, TELL THEM WE'VE TAKEN A TRENCH, TELL THEM WE NEED MORE MEN.
THEIR ARTILLERY BROKE OUR CHARGE. THE INFANTRY ARE EITHER DEAD OR CRAWLING BACK TO OUR OWN LINES.
ORSINI'LL BE SAFE -- HIS KIND ALWAYS *ARE*.
YOU WANT TO RUN BACK THROUGH *THAT*? GO AHEAD -- IT'S YOUR LIFE.
THEN WHAT DO WE DO?
HOLD HERE AS LONG AS WE CAN.
CAPTURE AND DEFEND AN ENEMY TRENCH FOR TWO HOURS AND THE GENERALS CLAIM IT'S A VICTORY. NO ONE ASKS HOW MANY MEN DIED FOR EACH MINUTE...

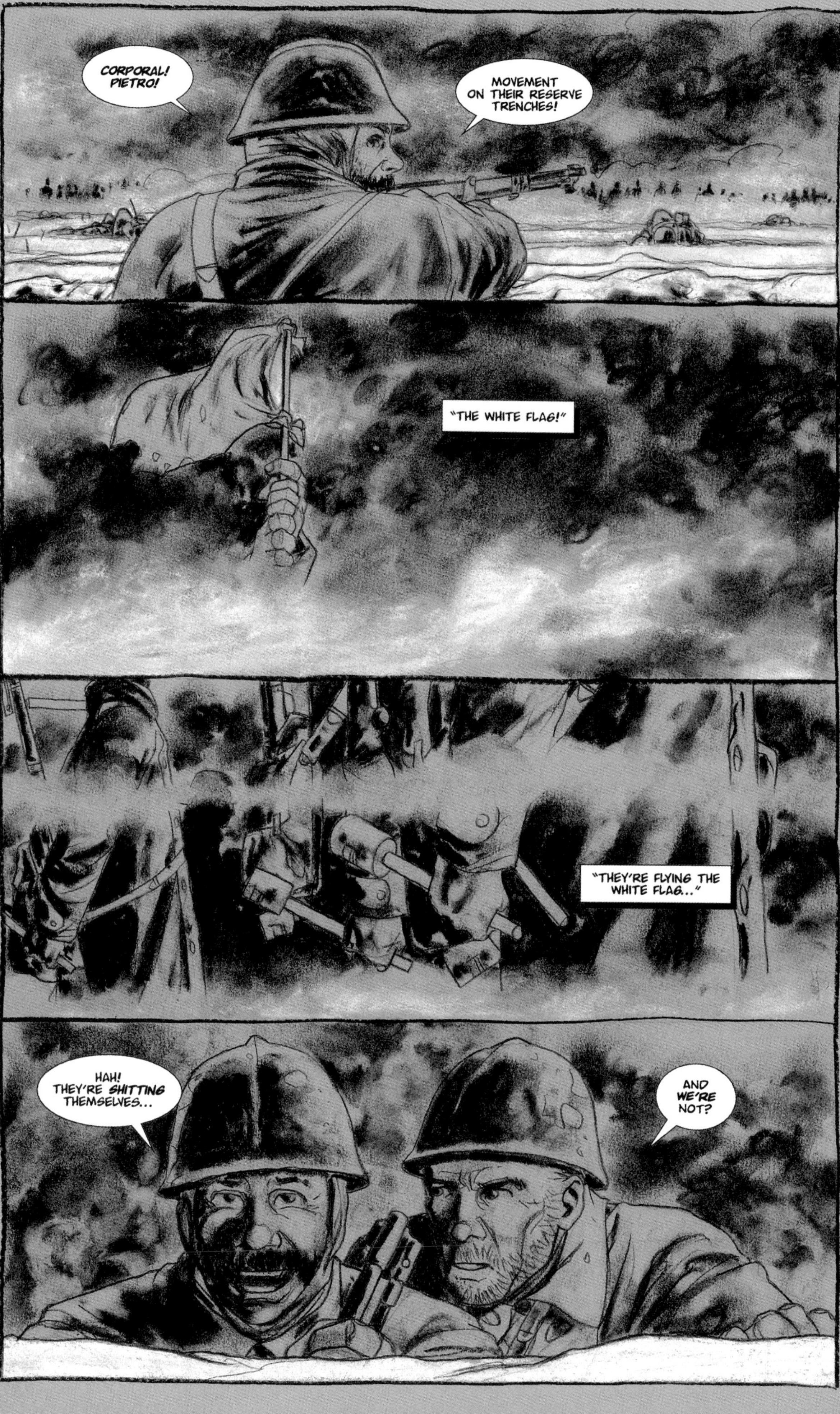
CORPORAL! PIETRO!
MOVEMENT ON THEIR RESERVE TRENCHES!
"THE WHITE FLAG!"
"THEY'RE FLYING THE WHITE FLAG..."
HAH! THEY'RE SHITTING THEMSELVES...
AND WE'RE NOT?

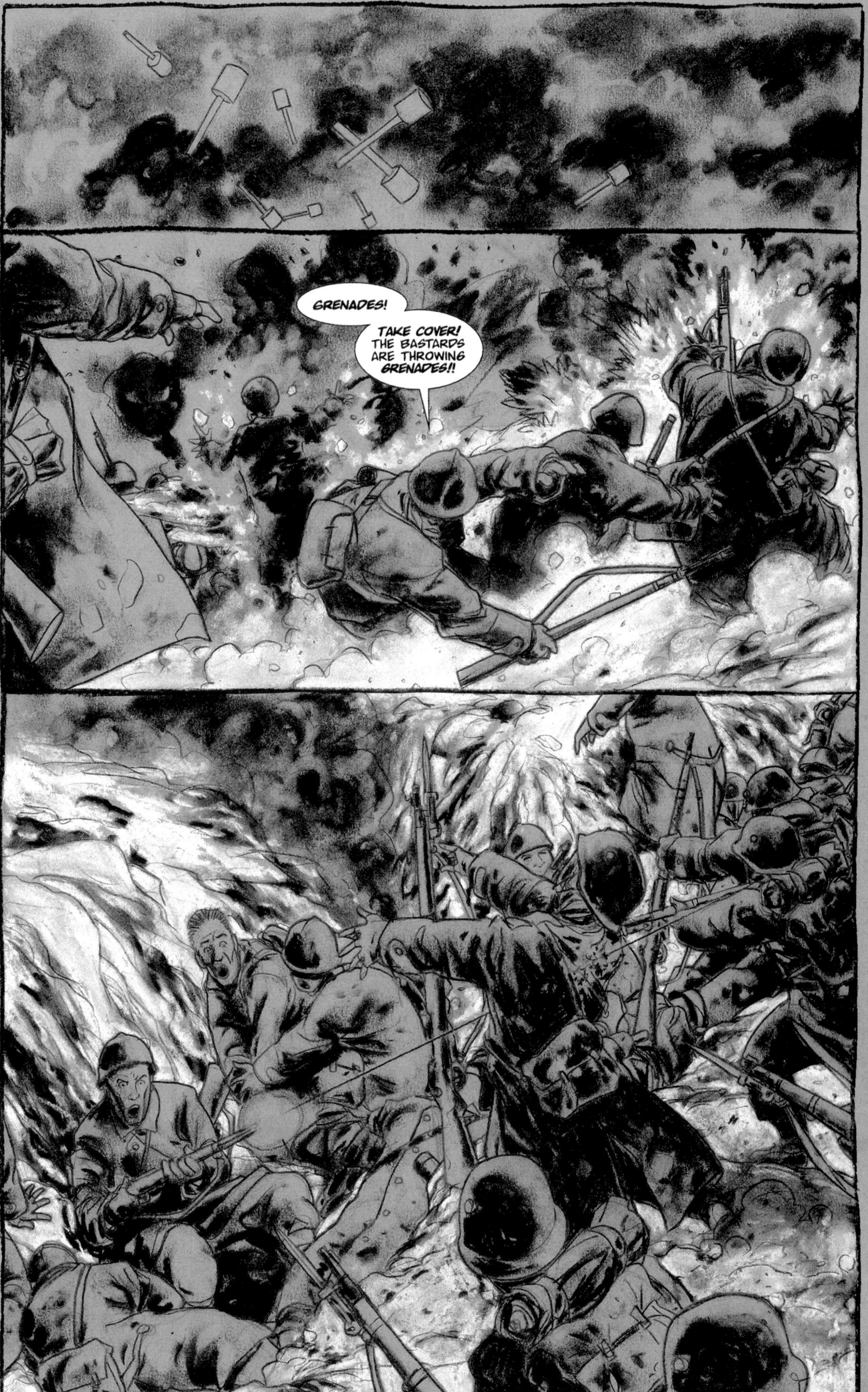
GRENADES!
TAKE COVER! THE BASTARDS ARE THROWING GRENADES!!

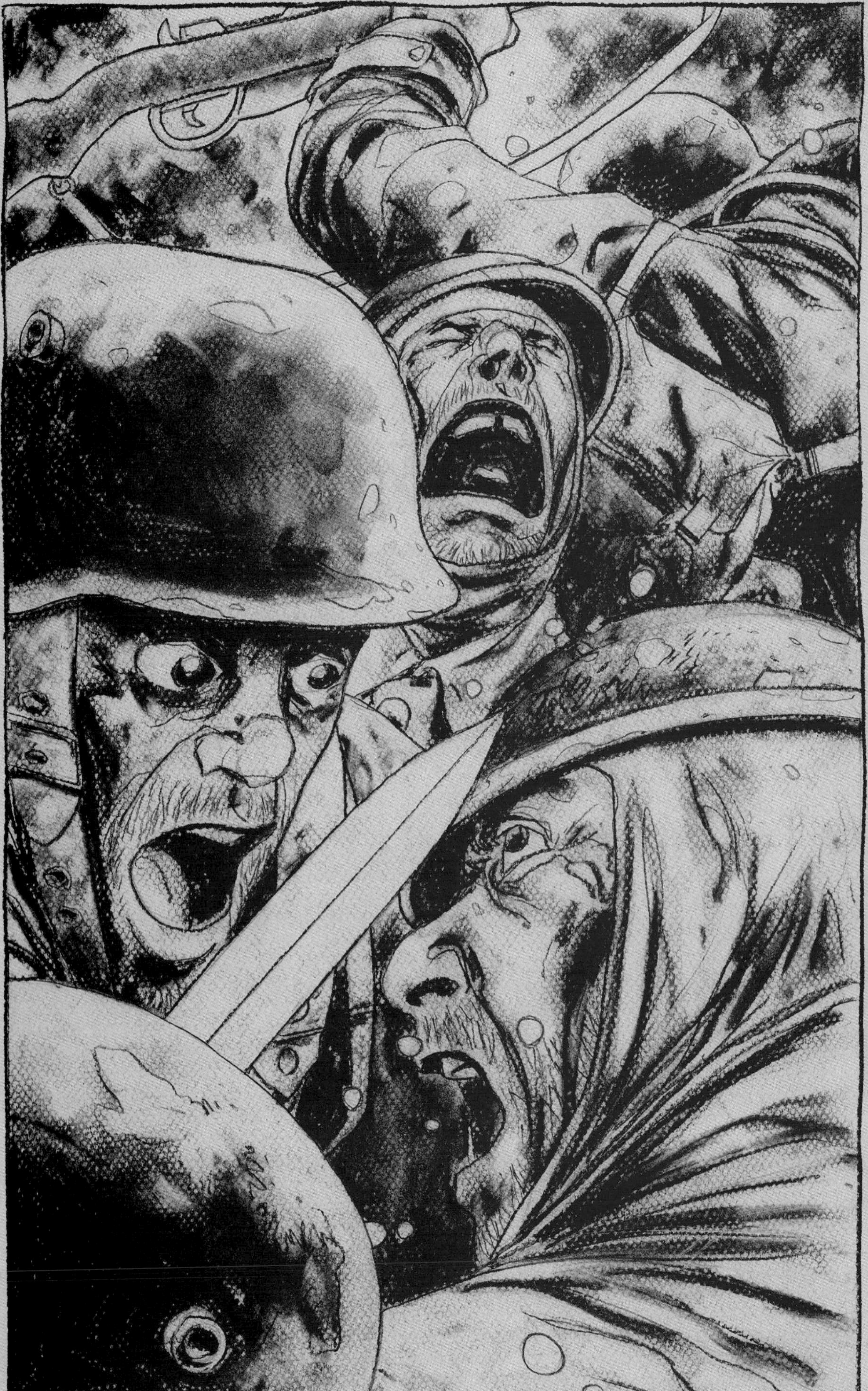

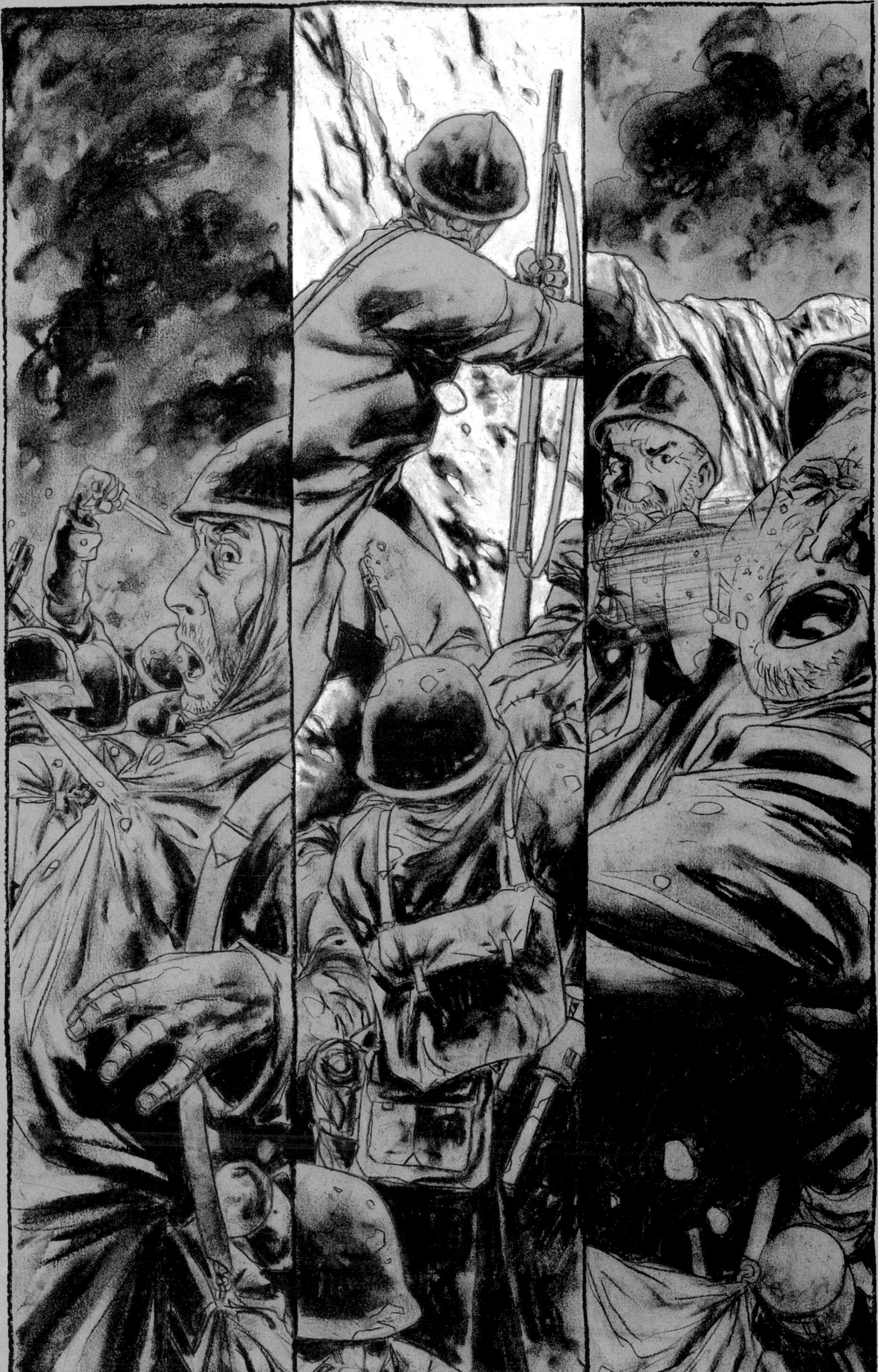

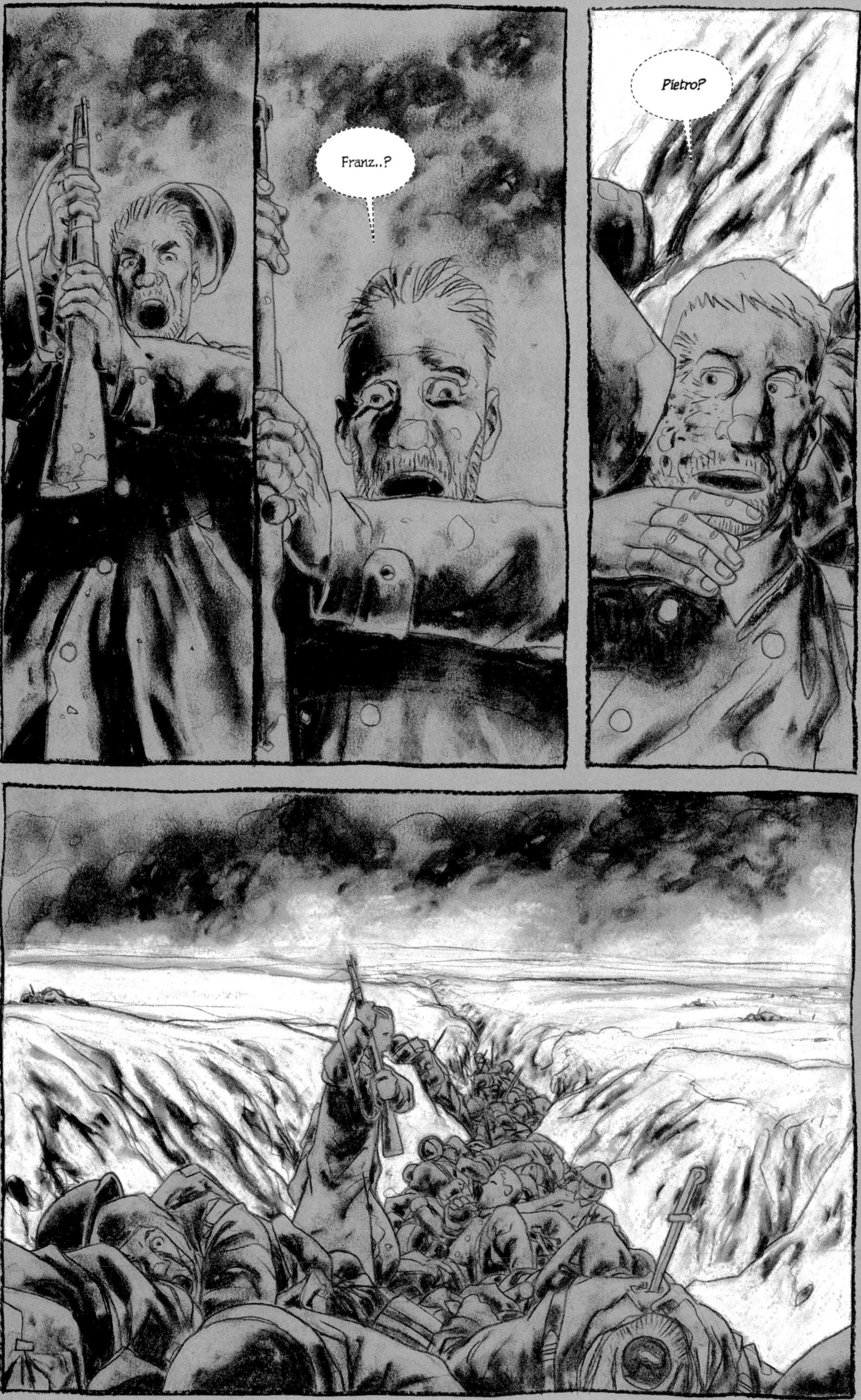
Franz..?
Pietro?

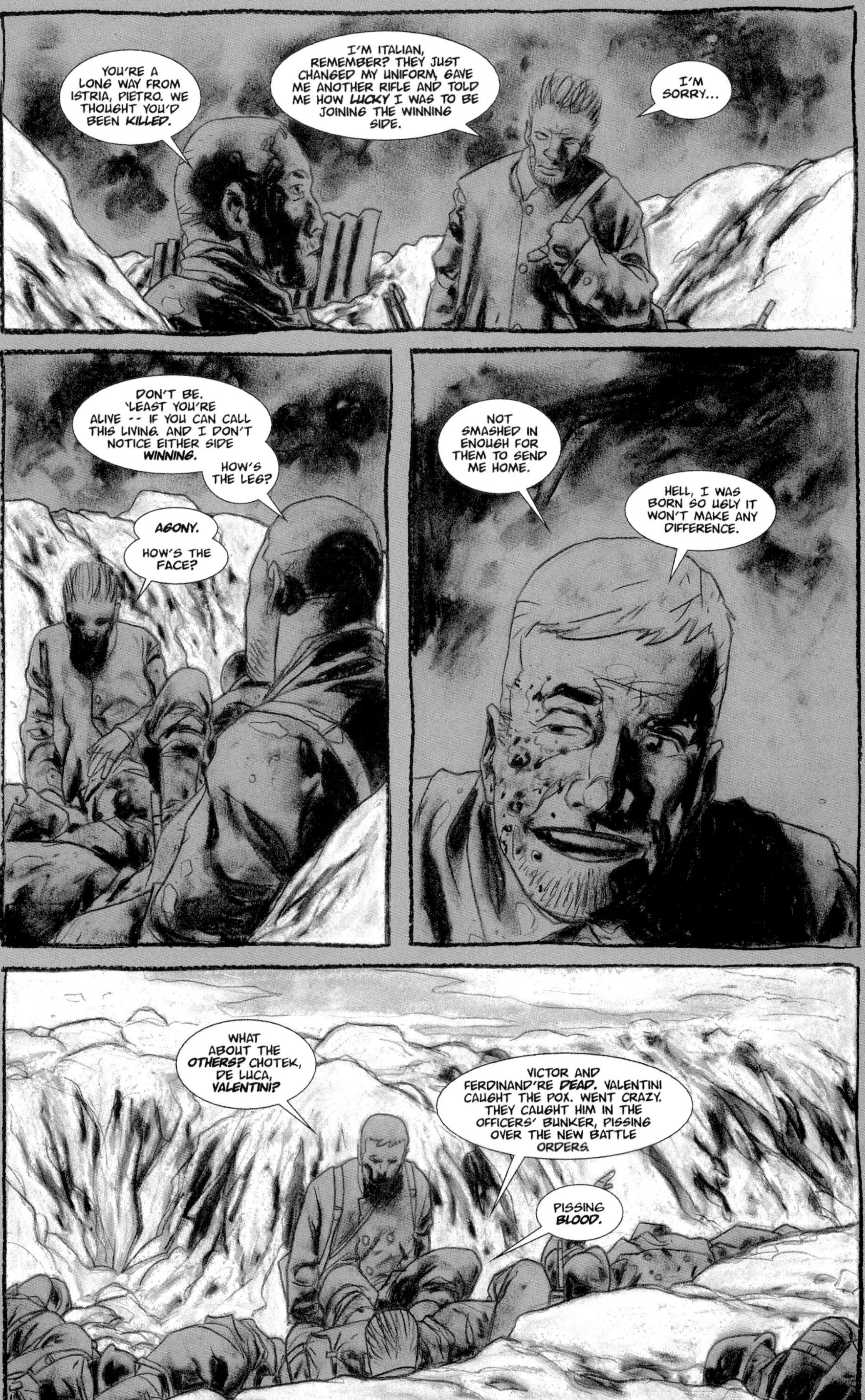
YOU'RE A LONG WAY FROM ISTRIA, PIETRO. WE THOUGHT YOU'D BEEN KILLED.
I'M ITALIAN, REMEMBER? THEY JUST CHANGED MY UNIFORM, GAVE ME ANOTHER RIFLE AND TOLD ME HOW LUCKY I WAS TO BE JOINING THE WINNING SIDE.
I'M SORRY...
DON'T BE. 'LEAST YOU'RE ALIVE -- IF YOU CAN CALL THIS LIVING. AND I DON'T NOTICE EITHER SIDE WINNING.
HOW'S THE LEG?
AGONY.
HOW'S THE FACE?
NOT SMASHED IN ENOUGH FOR THEM TO SEND ME HOME.
HELL, I WAS BORN SO UGLY IT WON'T MAKE ANY DIFFERENCE.
WHAT ABOUT THE OTHERS? CHOTEK, DE LUCA, VALENTINI?
VICTOR AND FERDINAND'RE DEAD. VALENTINI CAUGHT THE POX. WENT CRAZY. THEY CAUGHT HIM IN THE OFFICERS' BUNKER, PISSING OVER THE NEW BATTLE ORDERS.
PISSING BLOOD.

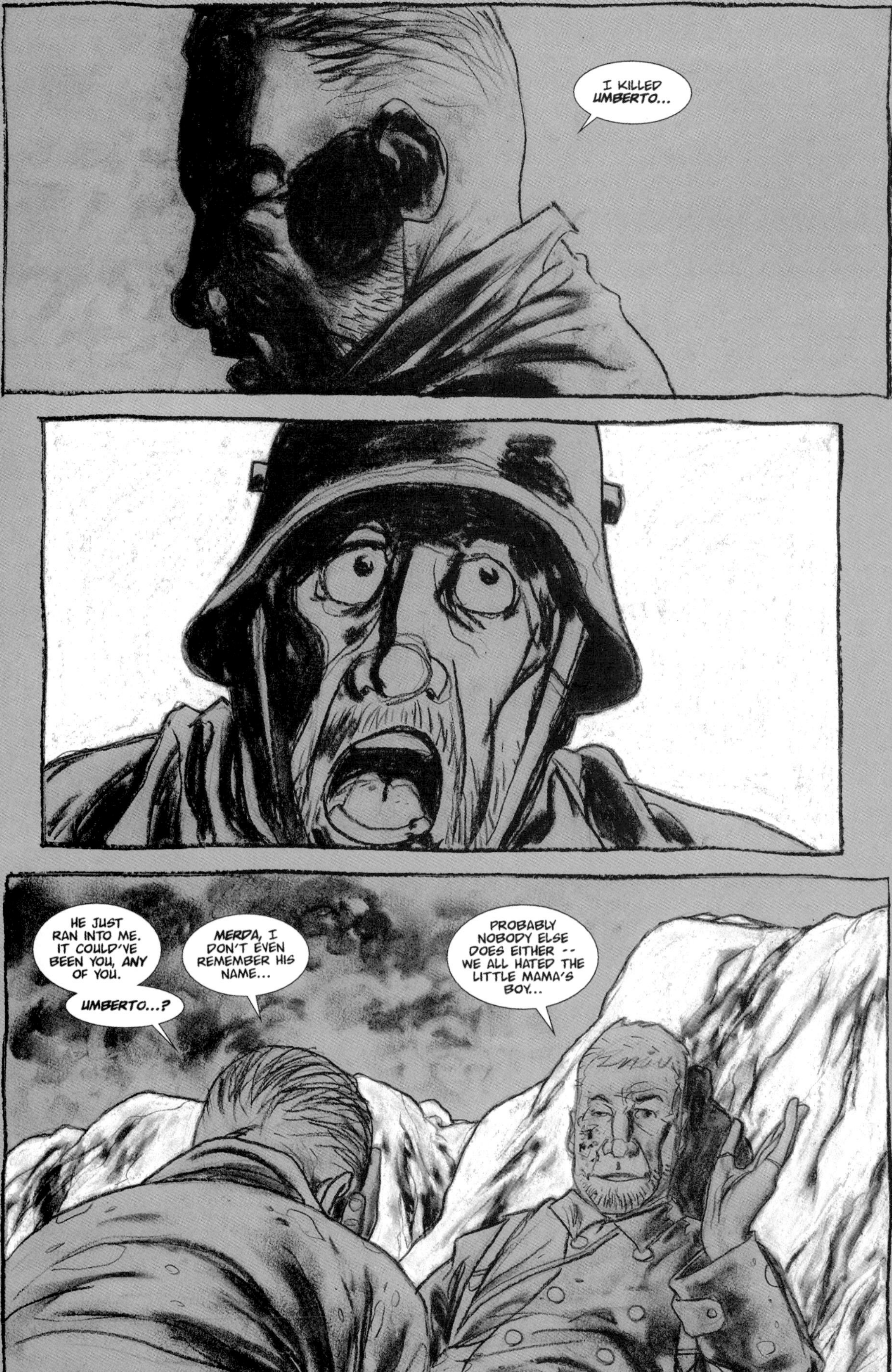
I KILLED UMBERTO...
HE JUST RAN INTO ME. IT COULD'VE BEEN YOU, ANY OF YOU.
UMBERTO...?
MERDA, I DON'T EVEN REMEMBER HIS NAME...
PROBABLY NOBODY ELSE DOES EITHER -- WE ALL HATED THE LITTLE MAMA'S BOY...

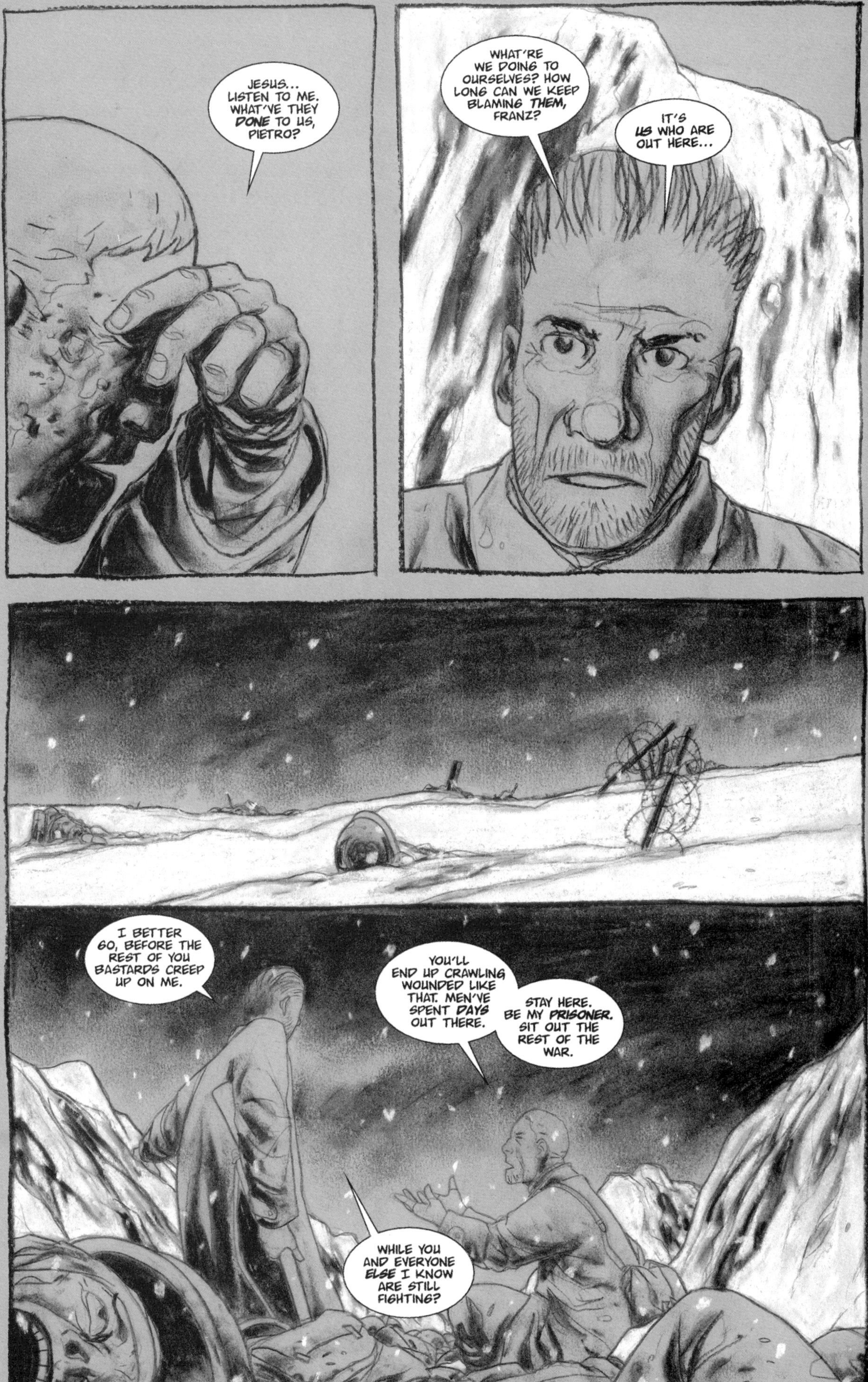
JESUS... LISTEN TO ME. WHAT'VE THEY DONE TO US, PIETRO?
WHAT'RE WE DOING TO OURSELVES? HOW LONG CAN WE KEEP BLAMING THEM, FRANZ?
IT'S US WHO ARE OUT HERE...
I BETTER GO, BEFORE THE REST OF YOU BASTARDS CREEP UP ON ME.
YOU'LL END UP CRAWLING WOUNDED LIKE THAT. MEN'VE SPENT DAYS OUT THERE.
STAY HERE. BE MY PRISONER. SIT OUT THE REST OF THE WAR.
WHILE YOU AND EVERYONE ELSE I KNOW ARE STILL FIGHTING?

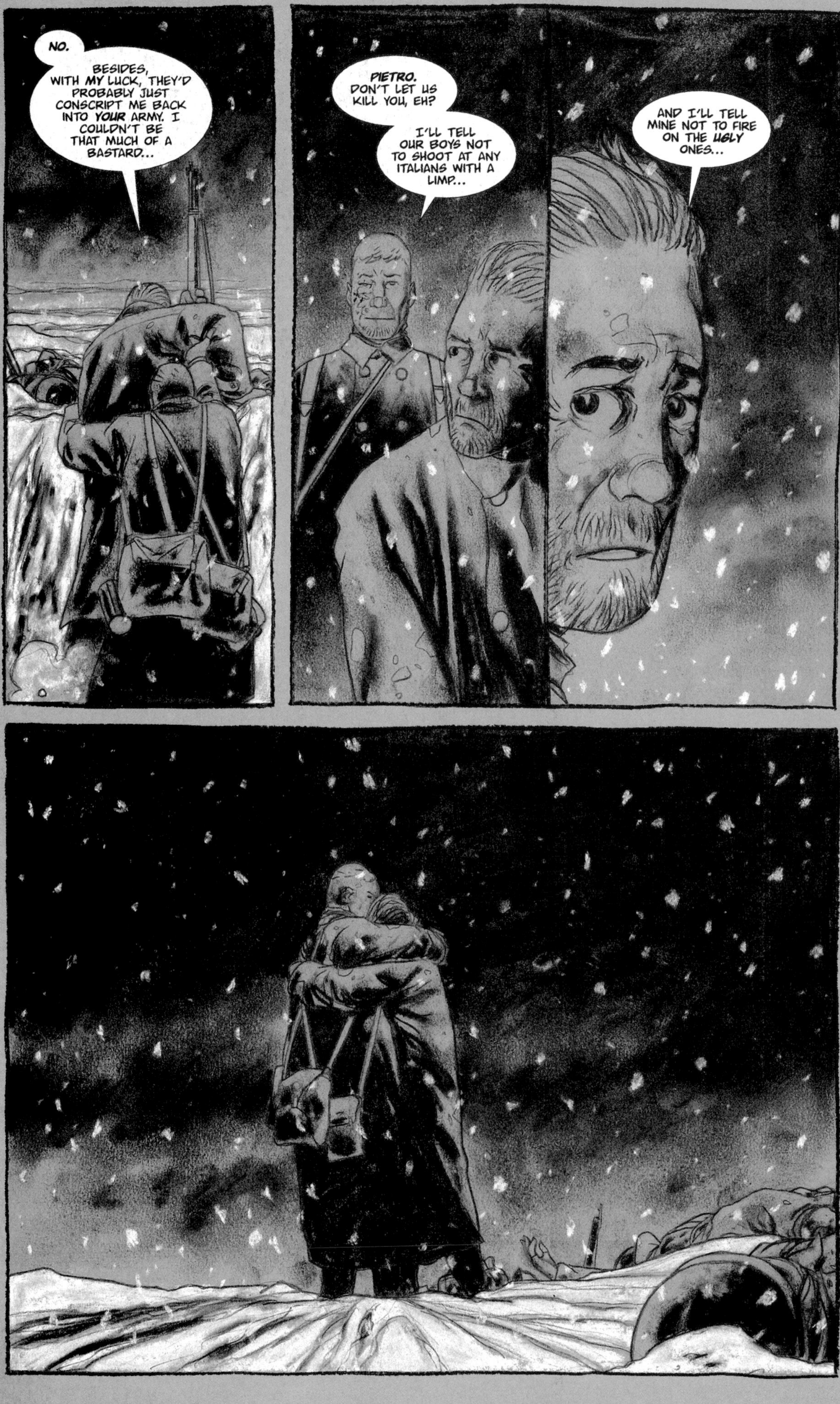NO.
BESIDES, WITH MY LUCK, THEY'D PROBABLY JUST CONSCRIPT ME BACK INTO YOUR ARMY. I COULDN'T BE THAT MUCH OF A BASTARD...
PIETRO. DON'T LET US KILL YOU, EH?
I'LL TELL OUR BOYS NOT TO SHOOT AT ANY ITALIANS WITH A LIMP...
AND I'LL TELL MINE NOT TO FIRE ON THE UGLY ONES...

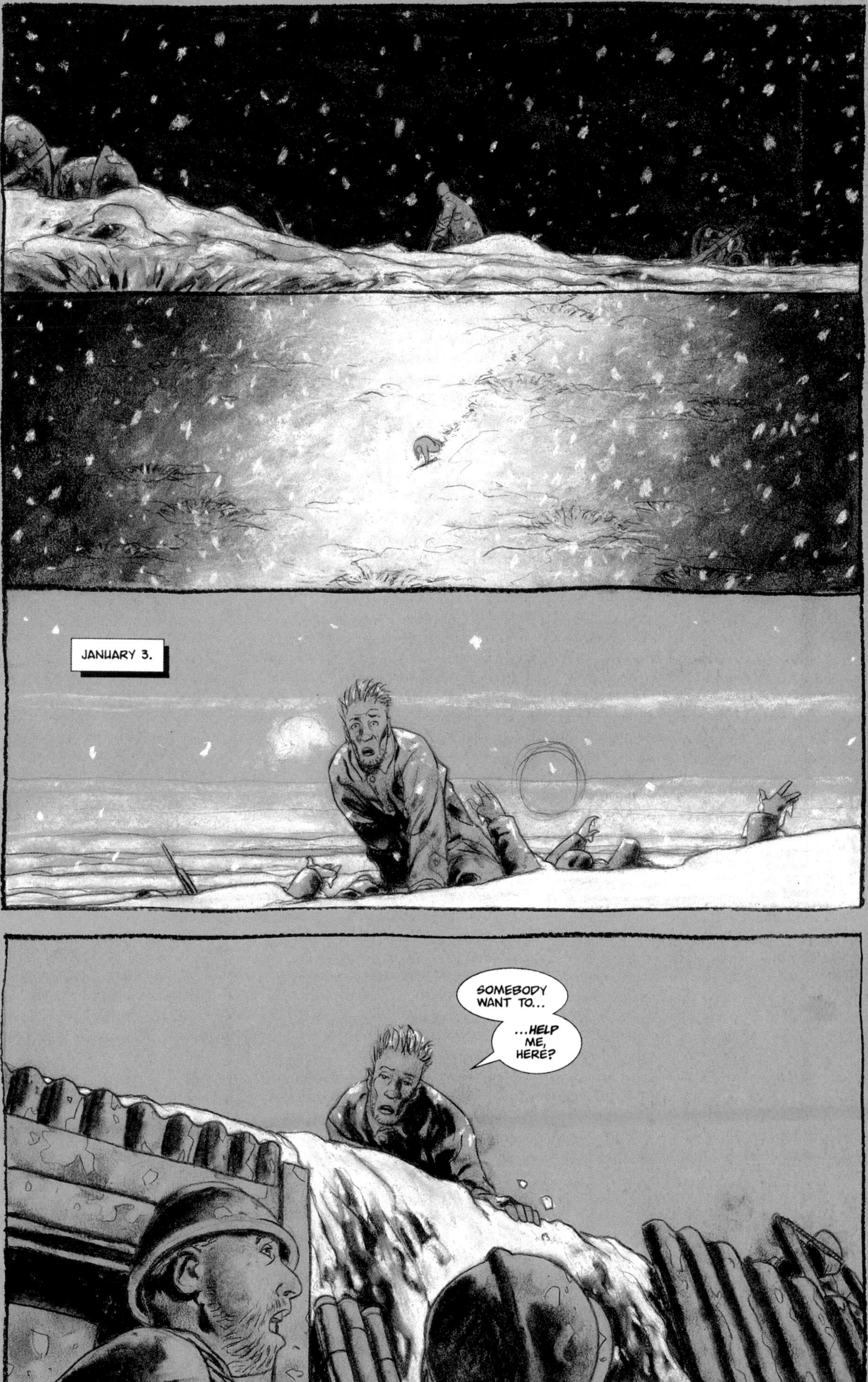
JANUARY 3.
SOMEBODY WANT TO...
...HELP ME, HERE?

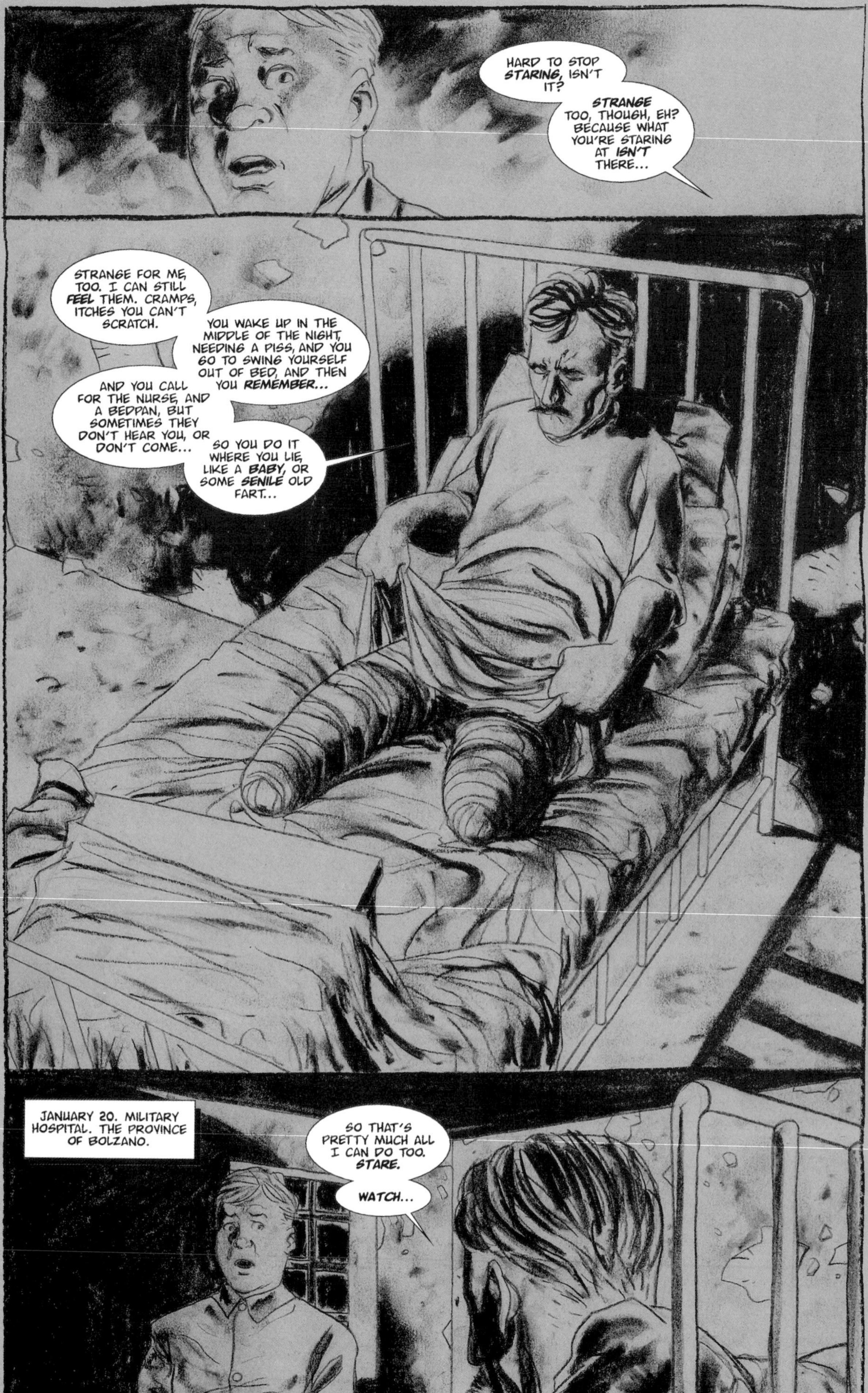
HARD TO STOP STARING, ISN'T IT?
STRANGE TOO, THOUGH, EH? BECAUSE WHAT YOU'RE STARING AT ISN'T THERE...
STRANGE FOR ME, TOO. I CAN STILL FEEL THEM. CRAMPS, ITCHES YOU CAN'T SCRATCH.
YOU WAKE UP IN THE MIDDLE OF THE NIGHT, NEEDING A PISS, AND YOU GO TO SWING YOURSELF OUT OF BED, AND THEN YOU REMEMBER...
AND YOU CALL FOR THE NURSE, AND A BEDPAN, BUT SOMETIMES THEY DON'T HEAR YOU, OR DON'T COME...
SO YOU DO IT WHERE YOU LIE, LIKE A BABY, OR SOME SENILE OLD FART...
JANUARY 20. MILITARY HOSPITAL. THE PROVINCE OF BOLZANO.
SO THAT'S PRETTY MUCH ALL I CAN DO TOO. STARE.
WATCH...

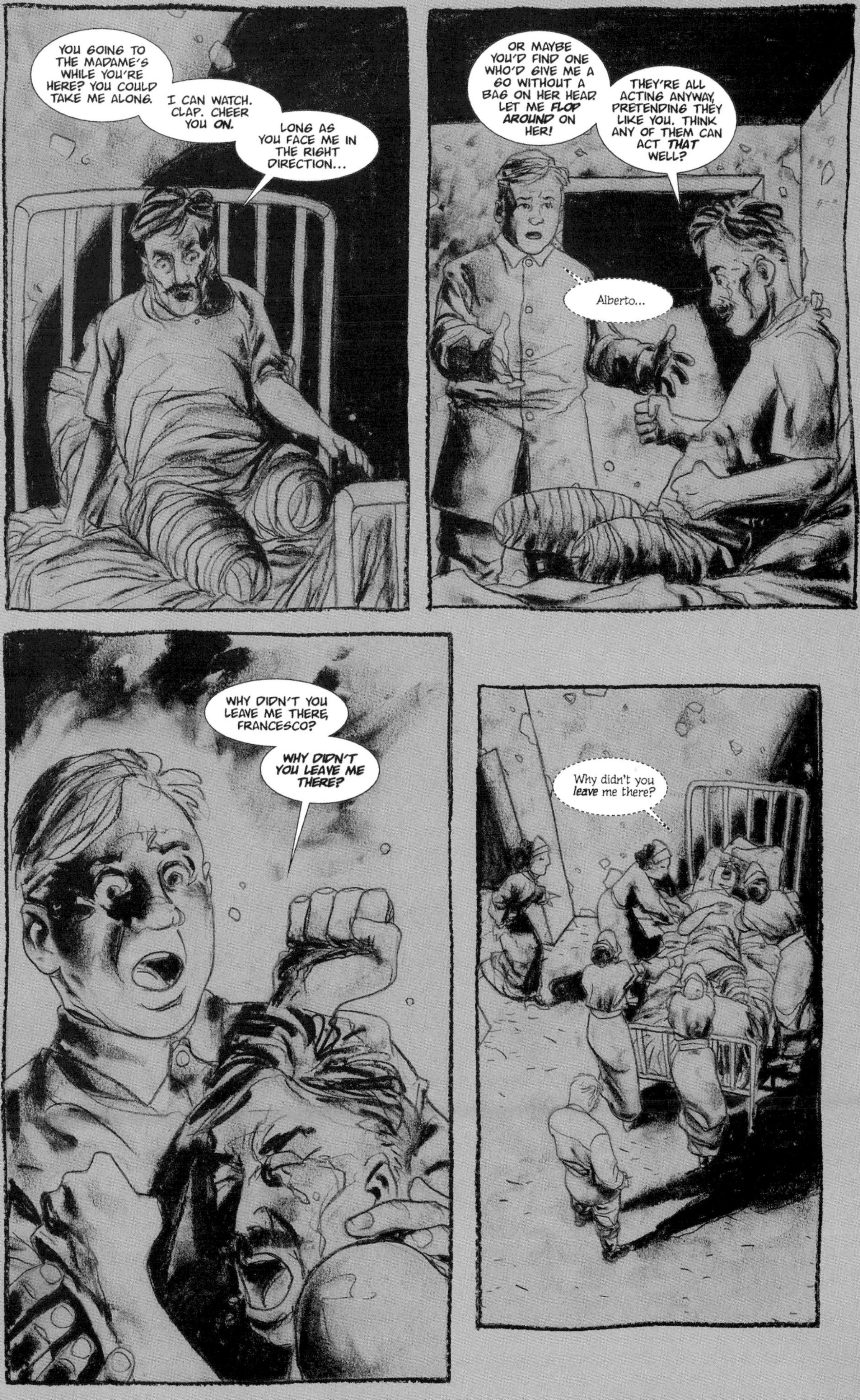
YOU GOING TO THE MADAME'S WHILE YOU'RE HERE? YOU COULD TAKE ME ALONG.
I CAN WATCH. CLAP. CHEER YOU **ON.**
LONG AS YOU FACE ME IN THE RIGHT DIRECTION...
OR MAYBE YOU'D FIND ONE WHO'D GIVE ME A GO WITHOUT A BAG ON HER HEAD. LET ME ***FLOP AROUND*** ON HER!
THEY'RE ALL ACTING ANYWAY, PRETENDING THEY LIKE YOU. THINK ANY OF THEM CAN ACT ***THAT*** WELL?
Alberto...
WHY DIDN'T YOU LEAVE ME THERE, FRANCESCO?
WHY DIDN'T YOU LEAVE ME THERE?
Why didn't you *leave* me there?

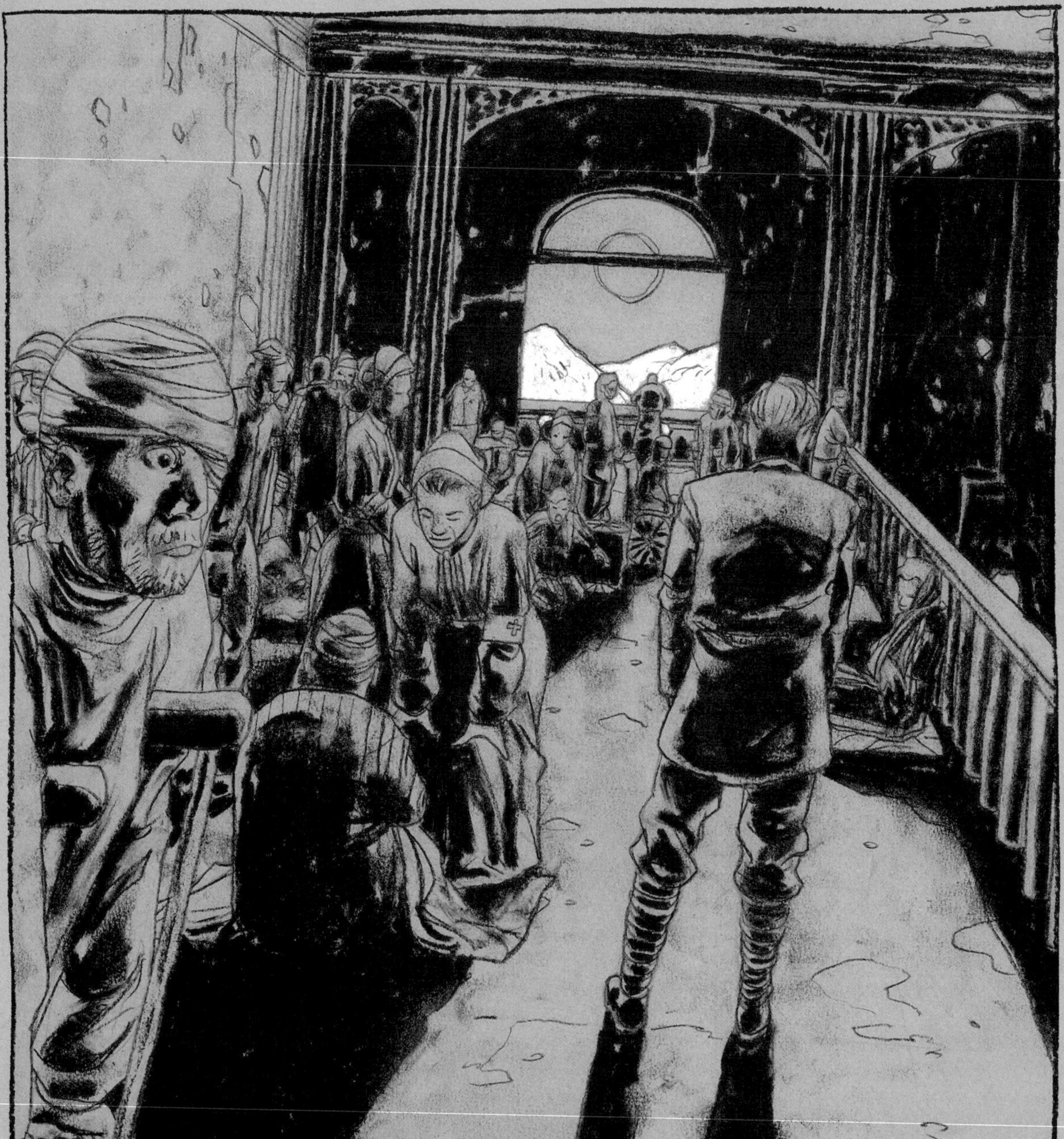
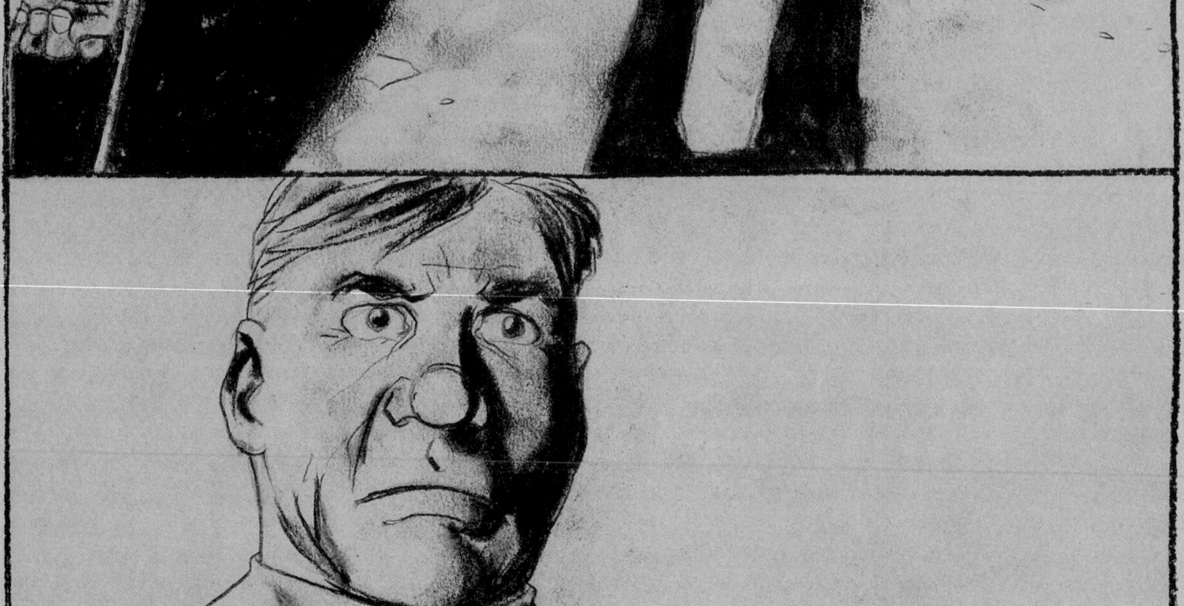

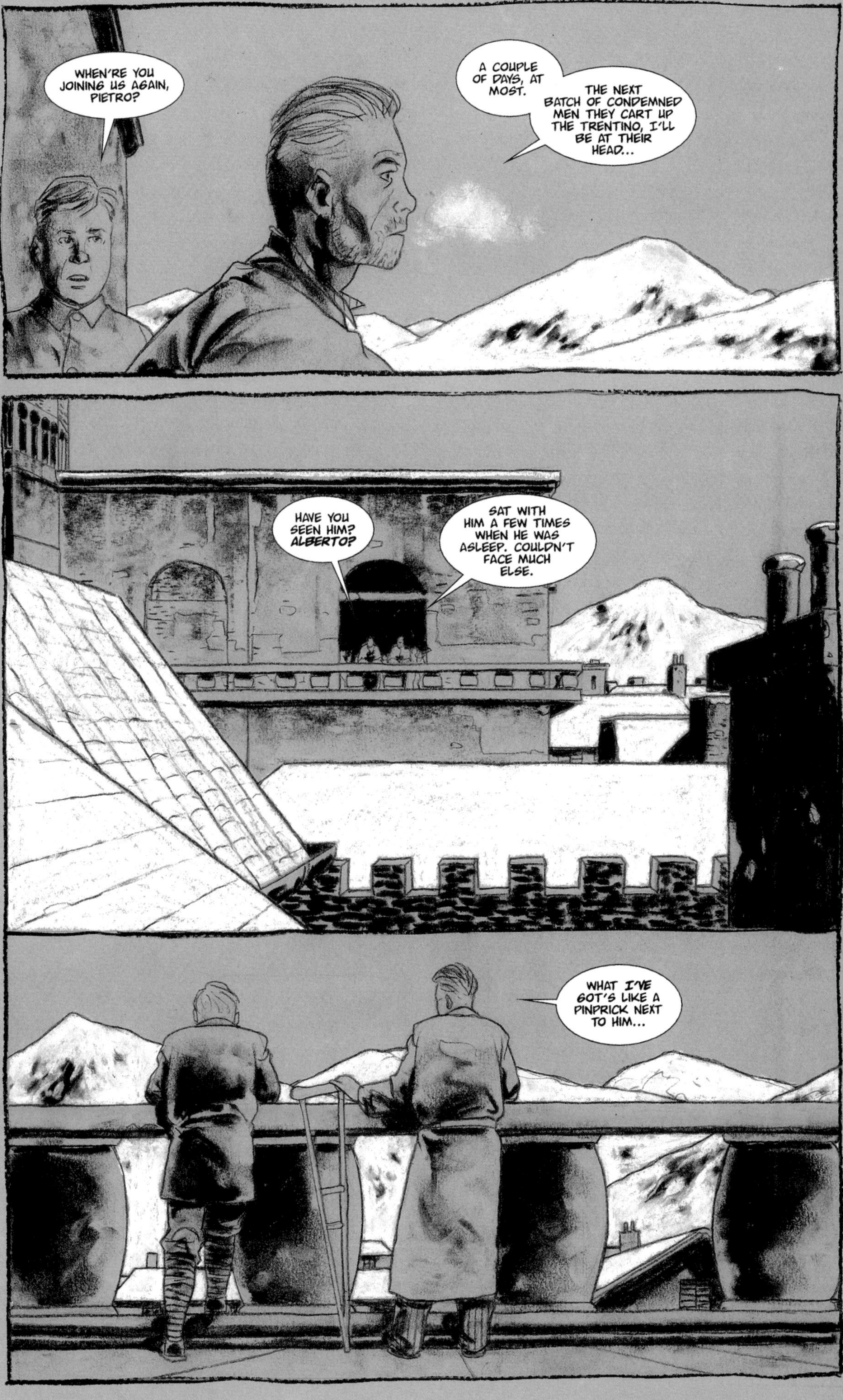
WHEN'RE YOU JOINING US AGAIN, PIETRO?
A COUPLE OF DAYS, AT MOST.
THE NEXT BATCH OF CONDEMNED MEN THEY CART UP THE TRENTINO, I'LL BE AT THEIR HEAD...
HAVE YOU SEEN HIM? ALBERTO?
SAT WITH HIM A FEW TIMES WHEN HE WAS ASLEEP. COULDN'T FACE MUCH ELSE.
WHAT I'VE GOT'S LIKE A PINPRICK NEXT TO HIM...

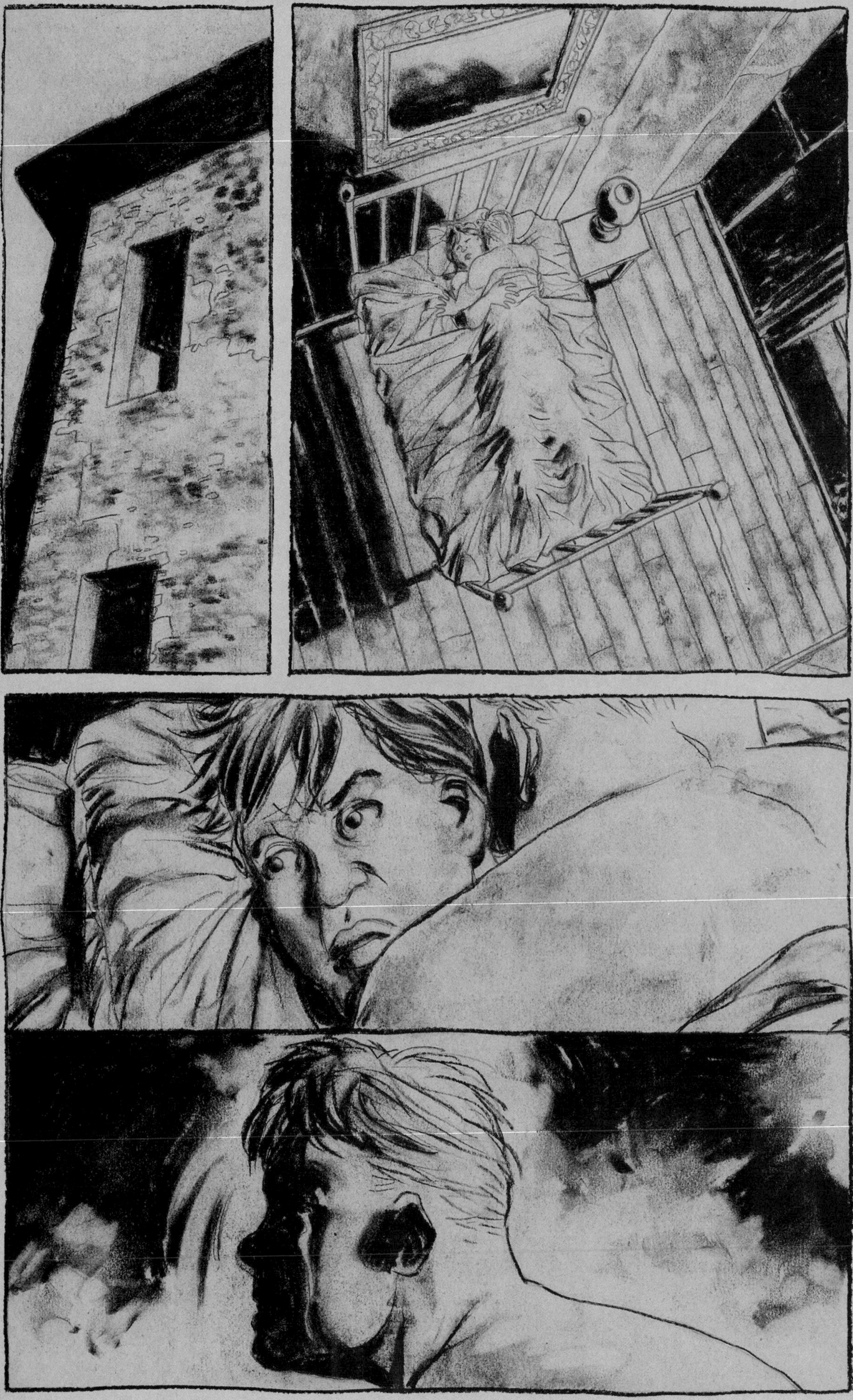

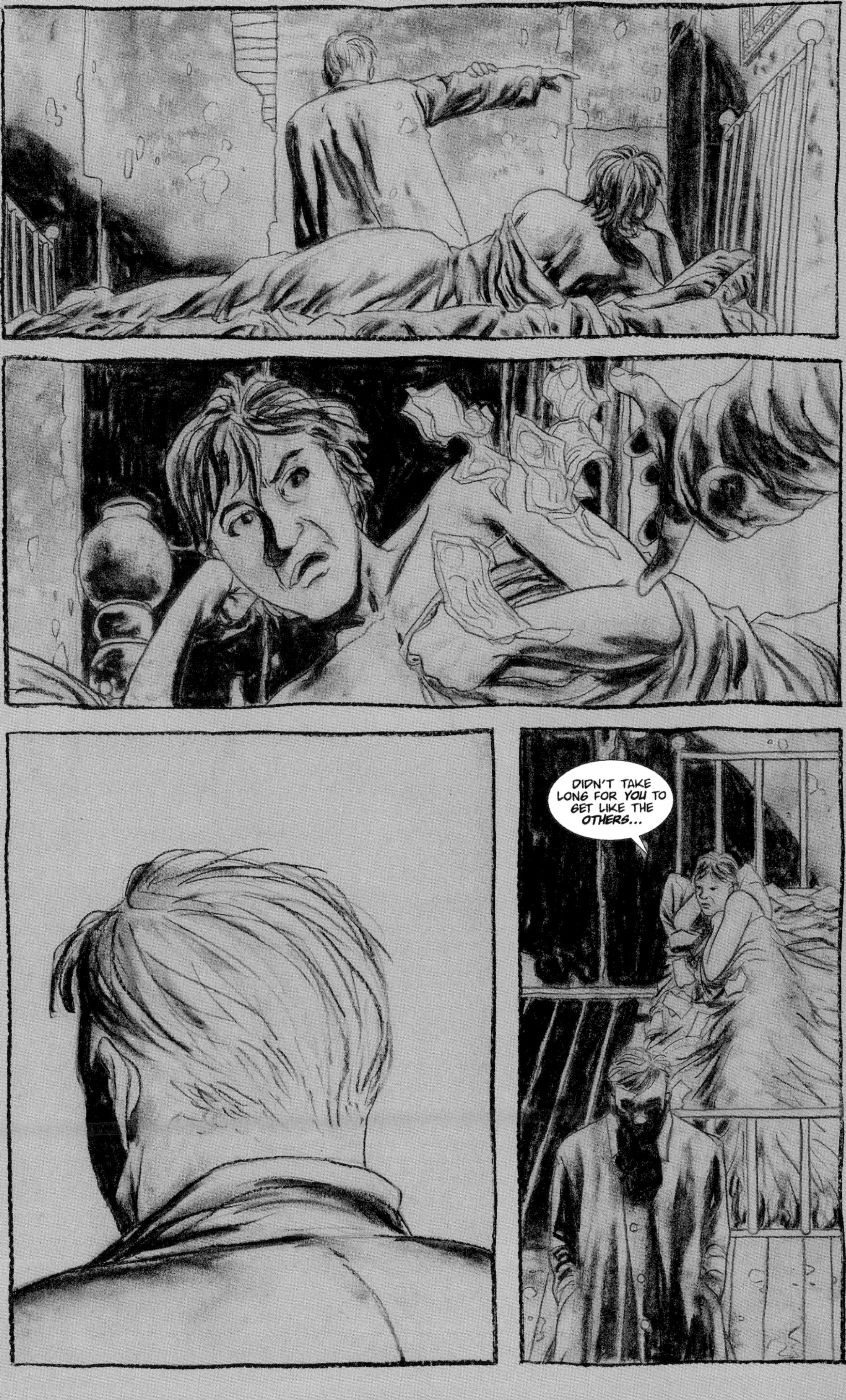
DIDN'T TAKE LONG FOR YOU TO GET LIKE THE OTHERS...

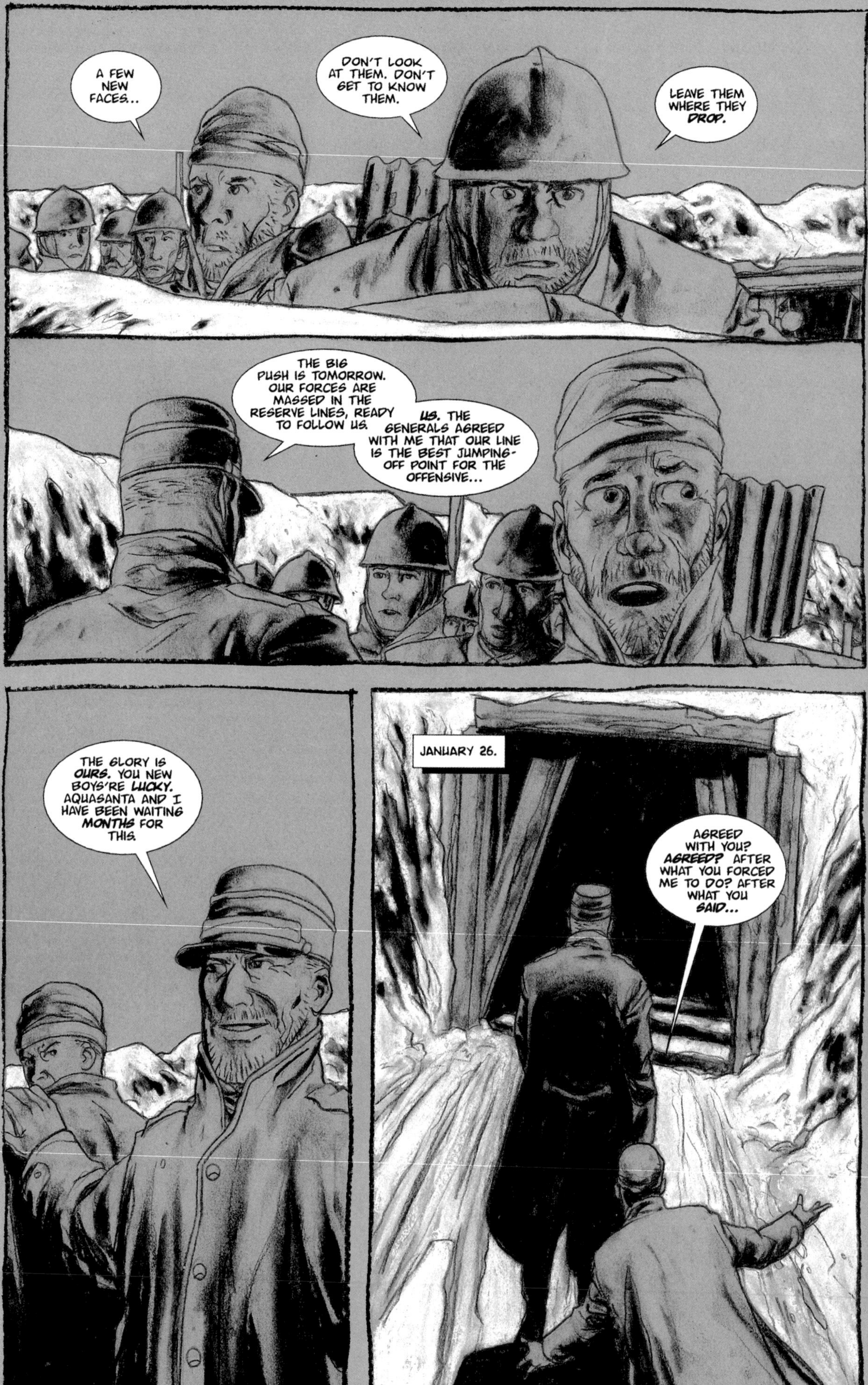
A FEW NEW FACES...
DON'T LOOK AT THEM. DON'T GET TO KNOW THEM.
LEAVE THEM WHERE THEY DROP.
THE BIG PUSH IS TOMORROW. OUR FORCES ARE MASSED IN THE RESERVE LINES, READY TO FOLLOW US.
US. THE GENERALS AGREED WITH ME THAT OUR LINE IS THE BEST JUMPING-OFF POINT FOR THE OFFENSIVE...
THE GLORY IS OURS. YOU NEW BOYS'RE LUCKY. AQUASANTA AND I HAVE BEEN WAITING MONTHS FOR THIS.
JANUARY 26.
AGREED WITH YOU? AGREED? AFTER WHAT YOU FORCED ME TO DO? AFTER WHAT YOU SAID...

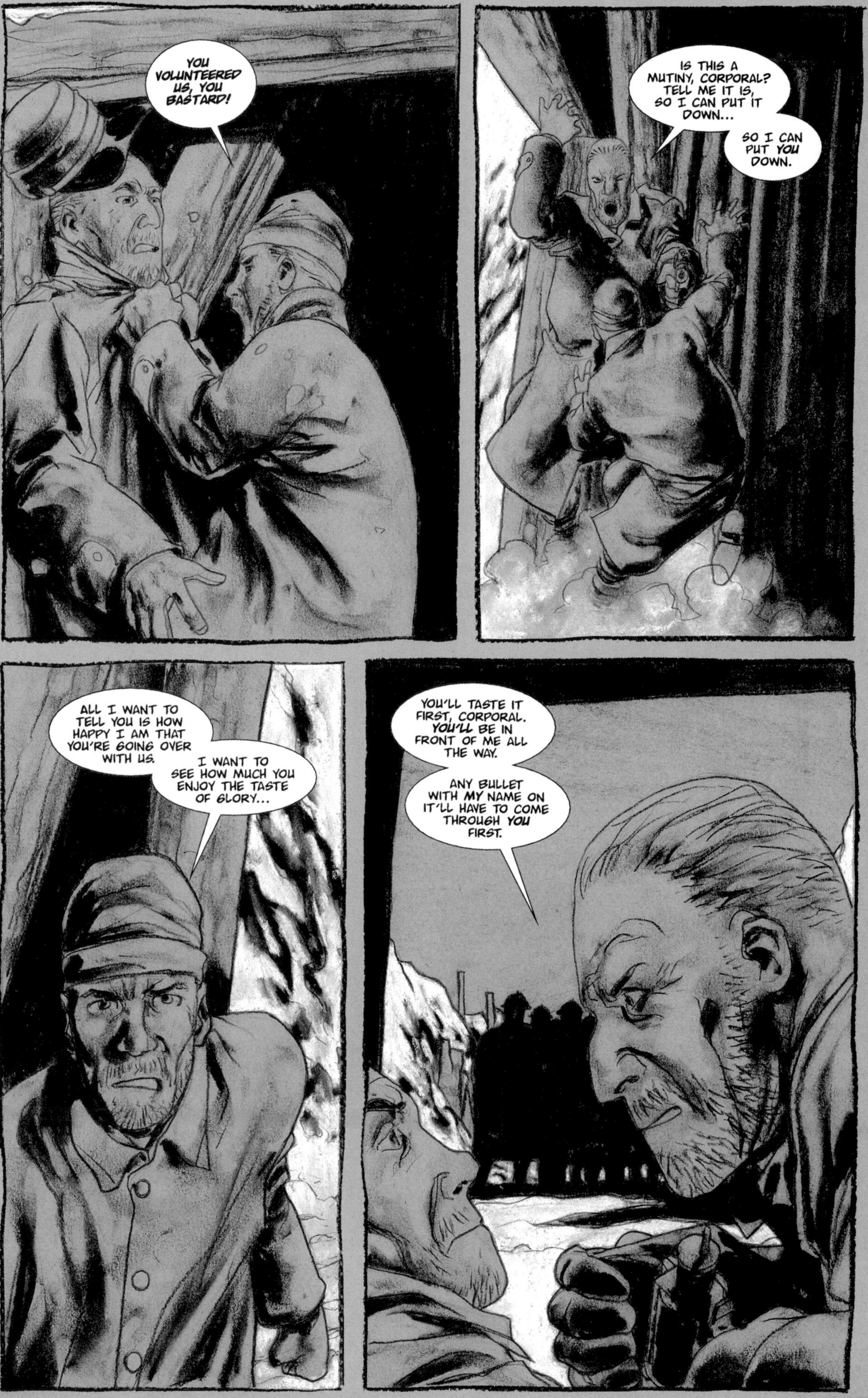
YOU VOLUNTEERED US, YOU BASTARD!
IS THIS A MUTINY, CORPORAL? TELL ME IT IS, SO I CAN PUT IT DOWN...
SO I CAN PUT YOU DOWN.
ALL I WANT TO TELL YOU IS HOW HAPPY I AM THAT YOU'RE GOING OVER WITH US.
I WANT TO SEE HOW MUCH YOU ENJOY THE TASTE OF GLORY...
YOU'LL TASTE IT FIRST, CORPORAL. YOU'LL BE IN FRONT OF ME ALL THE WAY.
ANY BULLET WITH MY NAME ON IT'LL HAVE TO COME THROUGH YOU FIRST.

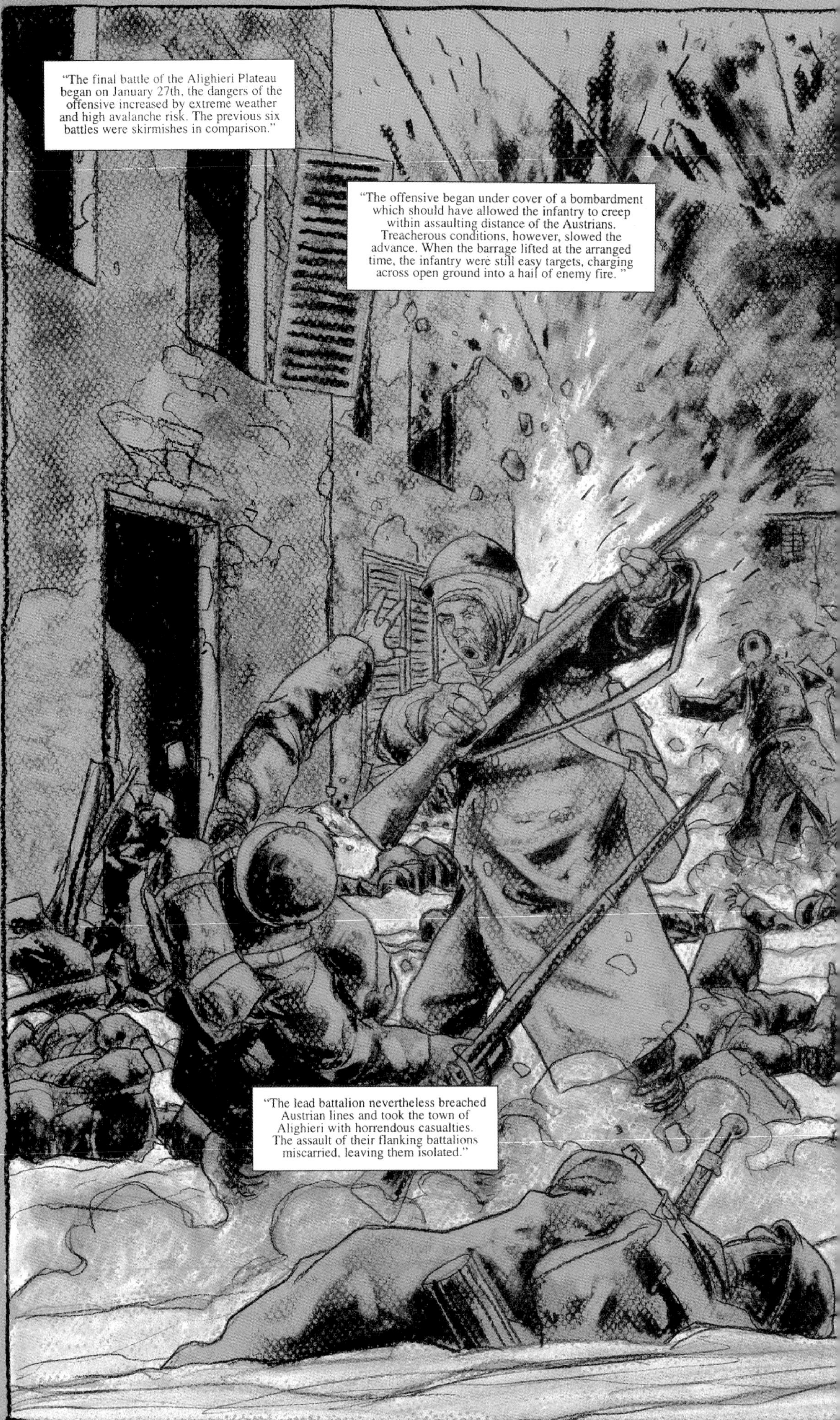
"The final battle of the Alighieri Plateau began on January 27th, the dangers of the offensive increased by extreme weather and high avalanche risk. The previous six battles were skirmishes in comparison."
"The offensive began under cover of a bombardment which should have allowed the infantry to creep within assaulting distance of the Austrians. Treacherous conditions, however, slowed the advance. When the barrage lifted at the arranged time, the infantry were still easy targets, charging across open ground into a hail of enemy fire."
"The lead battalion nevertheless breached Austrian lines and took the town of Alighieri with horrendous casualties. The assault of their flanking battalions miscarried, leaving them isolated."

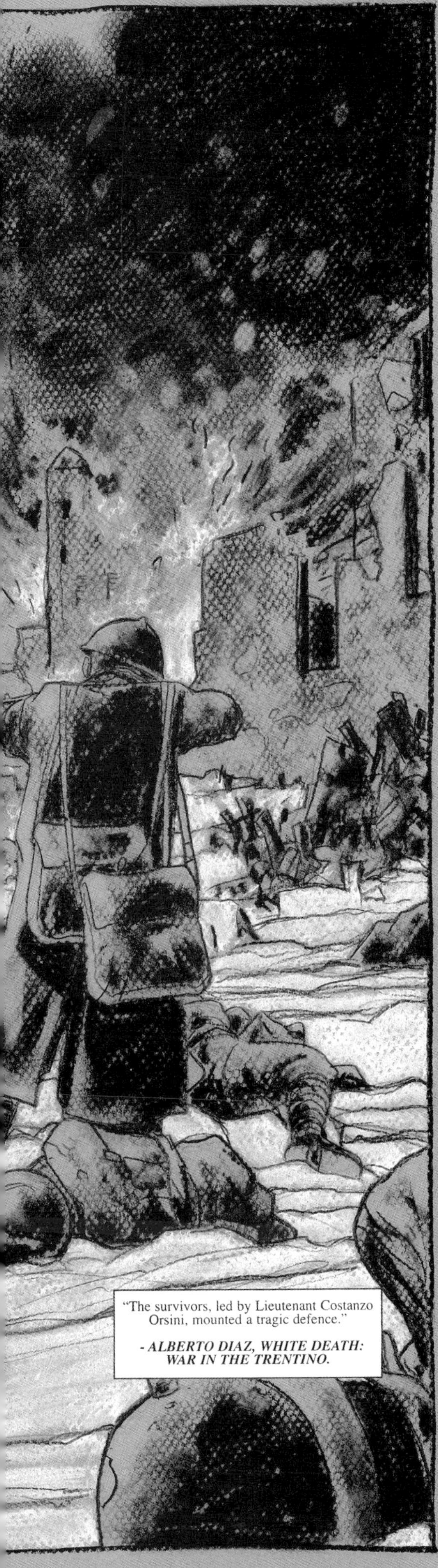
"The survivors, led by Lieutenant Costanzo Orsini, mounted a tragic defence."
- ALBERTO DIAZ, WHITE DEATH: WAR IN THE TRENTINO.

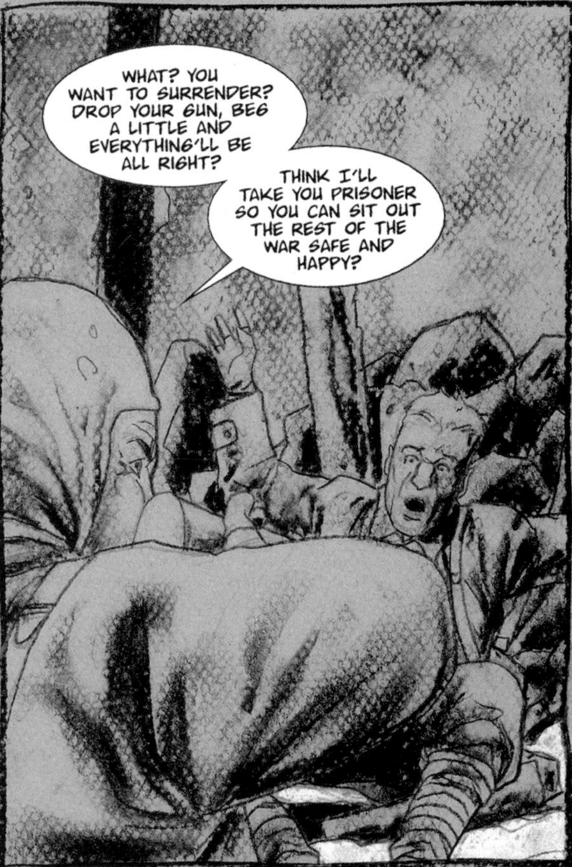
WHAT? YOU WANT TO SURRENDER? DROP YOUR GUN, BEG A LITTLE AND EVERYTHING'LL BE ALL RIGHT?
THINK I'LL TAKE YOU PRISONER SO YOU CAN SIT OUT THE REST OF THE WAR SAFE AND HAPPY?

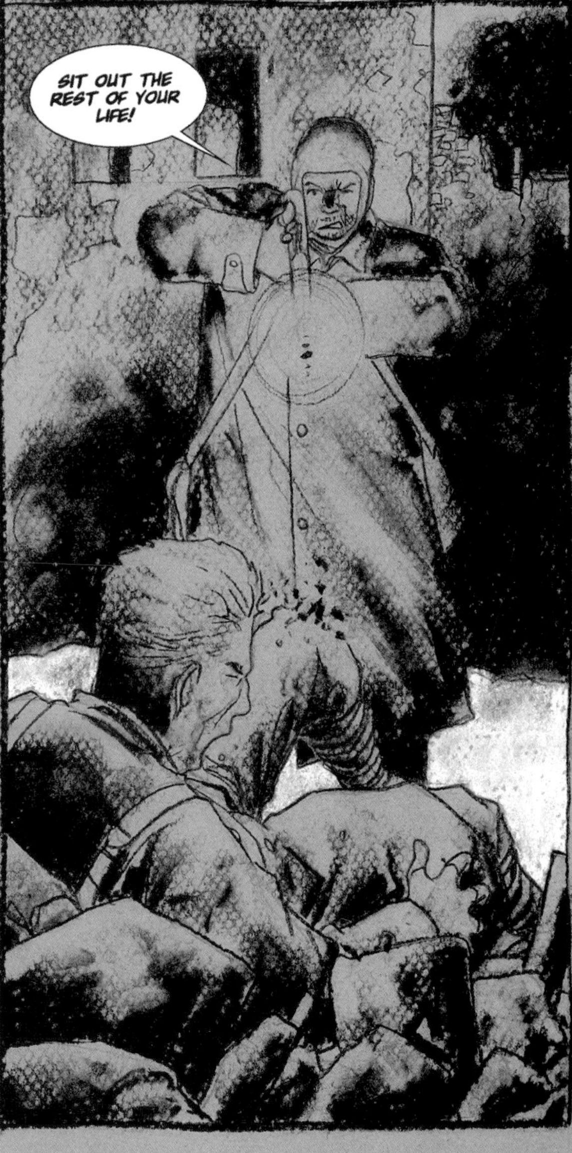
SIT OUT THE REST OF YOUR LIFE!

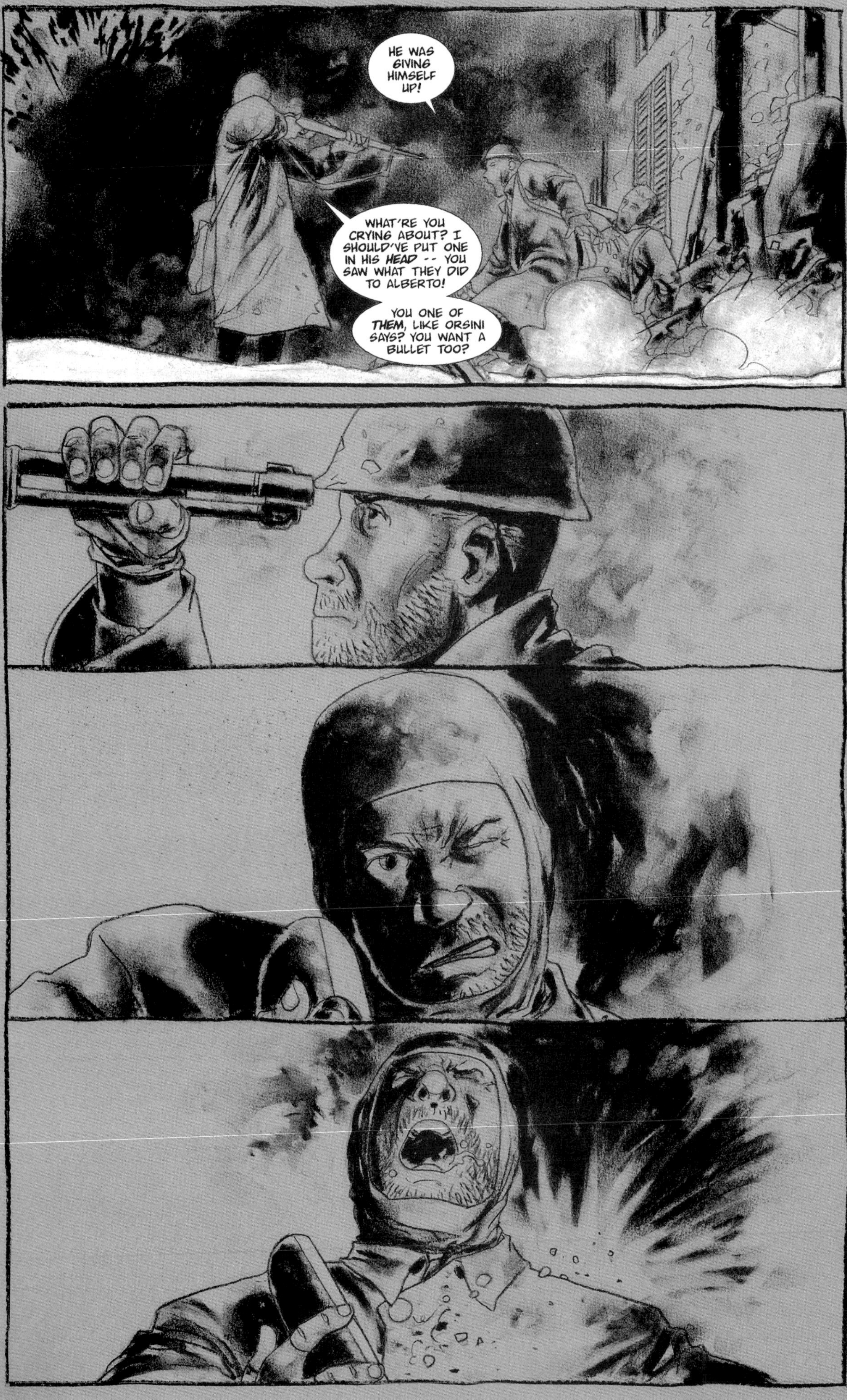
HE WAS GIVING HIMSELF UP!
WHAT'RE YOU CRYING ABOUT? I SHOULD'VE PUT ONE IN HIS HEAD -- YOU SAW WHAT THEY DID TO ALBERTO!
YOU ONE OF THEM, LIKE ORSINI SAYS? YOU WANT A BULLET TOO?

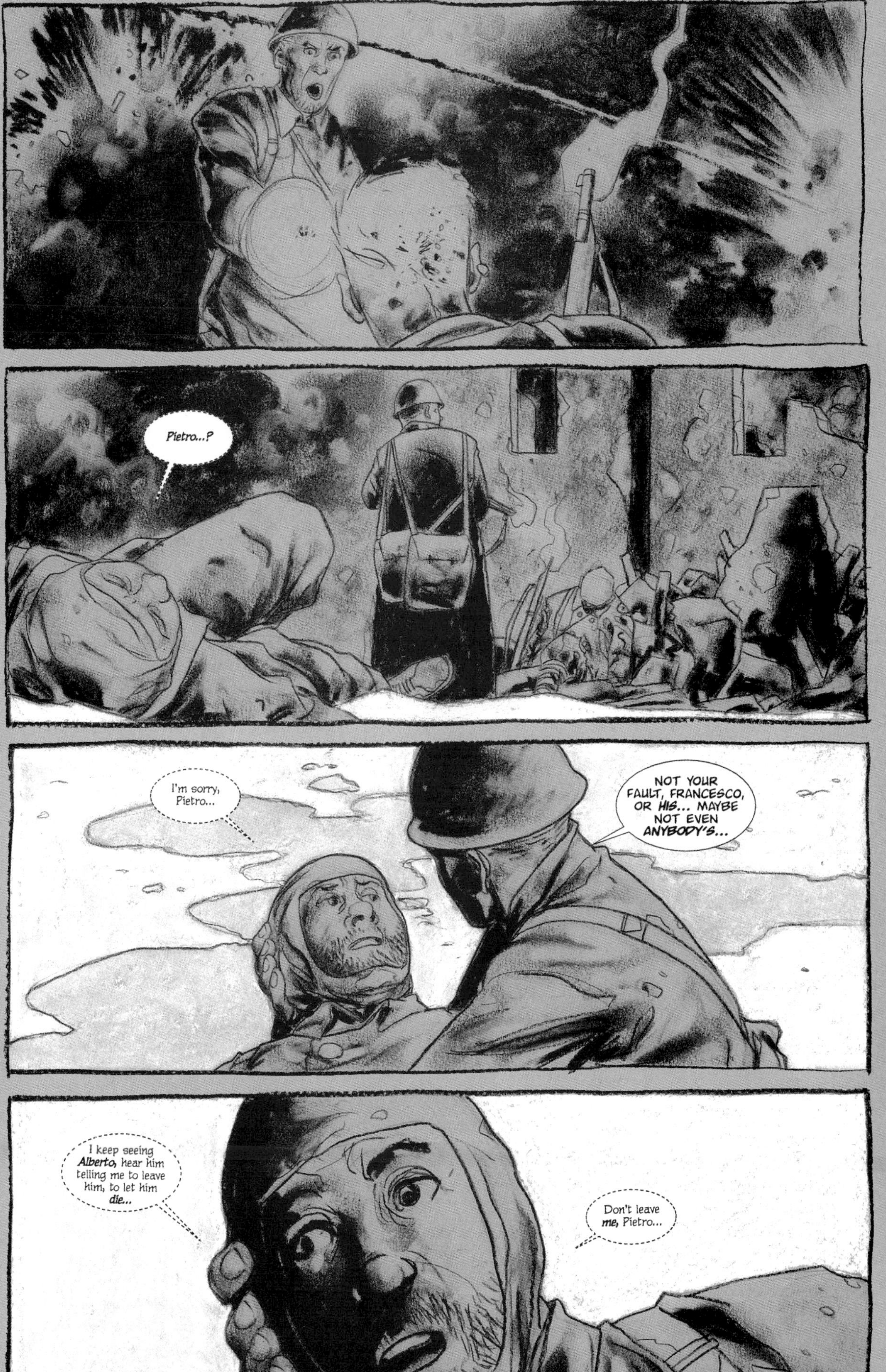
Pietro...?
I'm sorry, Pietro...
NOT YOUR FAULT, FRANCESCO, OR HIS... MAYBE NOT EVEN ANYBODY'S...
I keep seeing Alberto, hear him telling me to leave him, to let him die...
Don't leave me, Pietro...

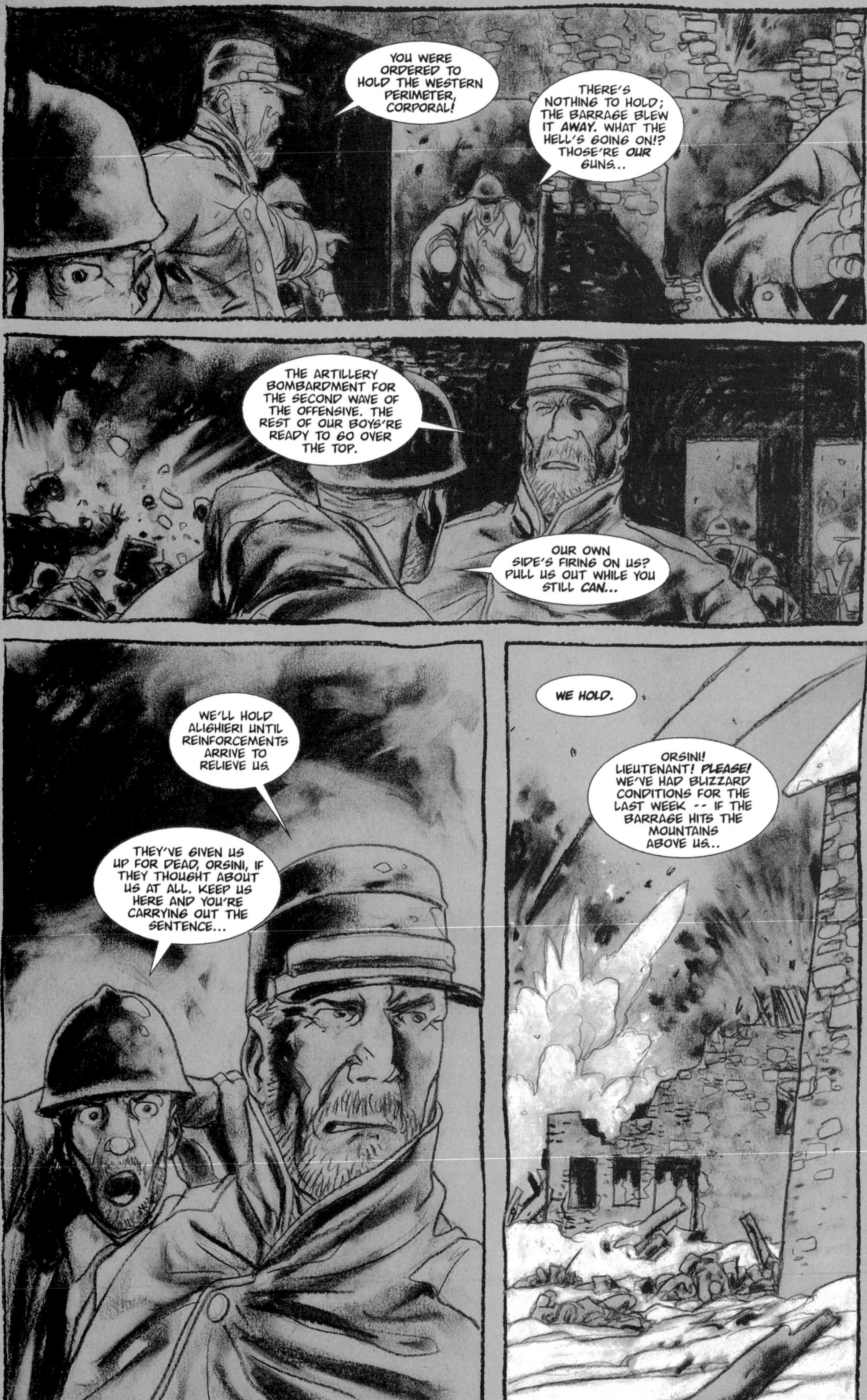
YOU WERE ORDERED TO HOLD THE WESTERN PERIMETER, CORPORAL!
THERE'S NOTHING TO HOLD; THE BARRAGE BLEW IT AWAY. WHAT THE HELL'S GOING ON!? THOSE'RE OUR GUNS...
THE ARTILLERY BOMBARDMENT FOR THE SECOND WAVE OF THE OFFENSIVE. THE REST OF OUR BOYS'RE READY TO GO OVER THE TOP.
OUR OWN SIDE'S FIRING ON US? PULL US OUT WHILE YOU STILL CAN...
WE'LL HOLD ALIGHIERI UNTIL REINFORCEMENTS ARRIVE TO RELIEVE US.
THEY'VE GIVEN US UP FOR DEAD, ORSINI, IF THEY THOUGHT ABOUT US AT ALL. KEEP US HERE AND YOU'RE CARRYING OUT THE SENTENCE...
WE HOLD.
ORSINI! LIEUTENANT! PLEASE! WE'VE HAD BLIZZARD CONDITIONS FOR THE LAST WEEK -- IF THE BARRAGE HITS THE MOUNTAINS ABOVE US...

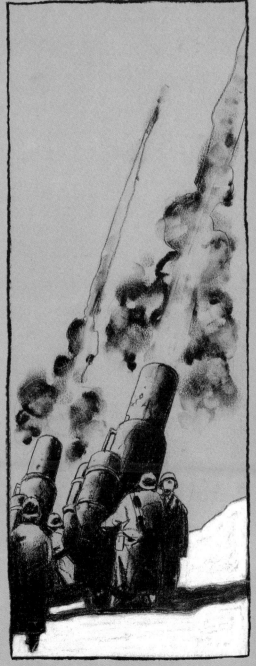

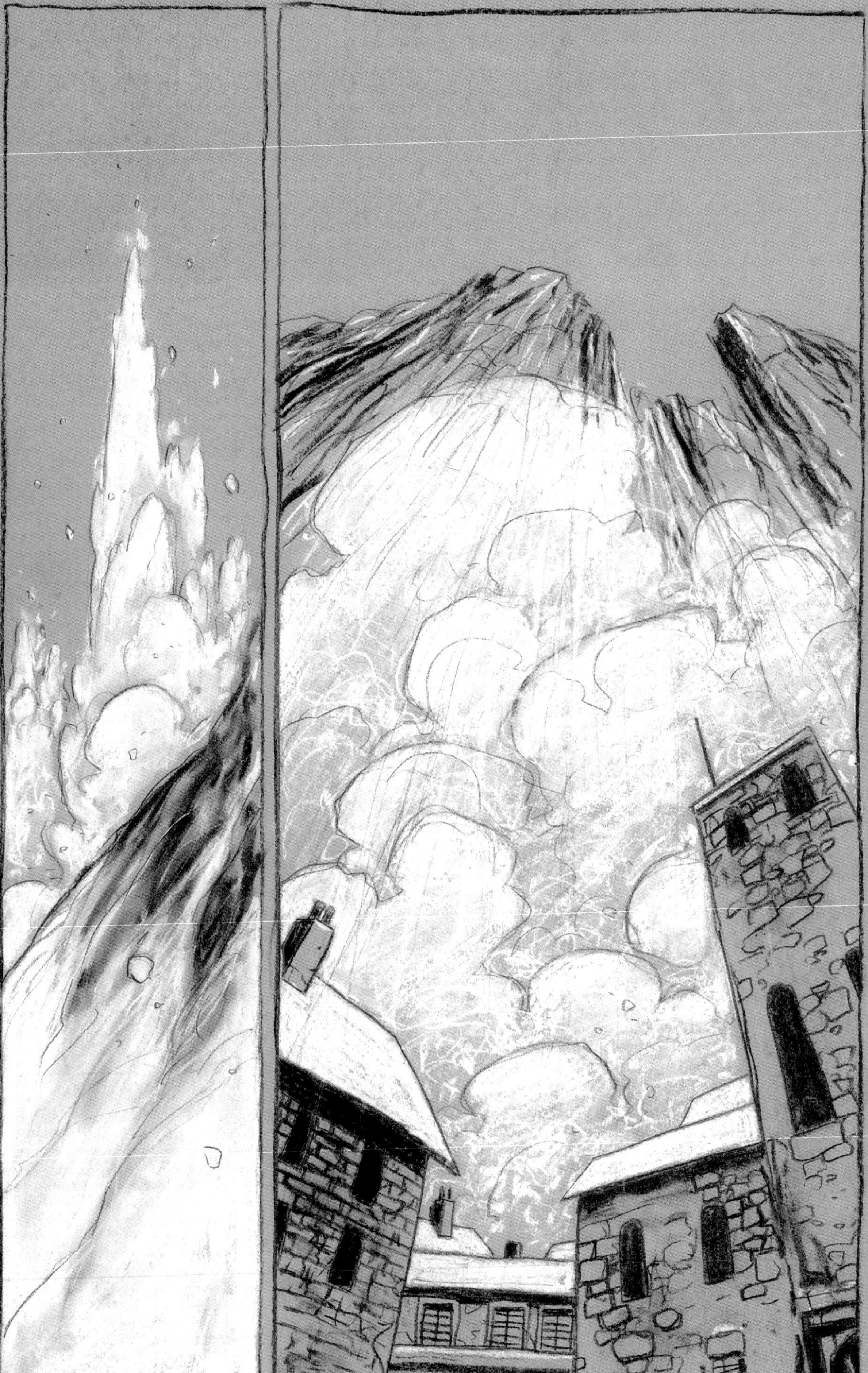

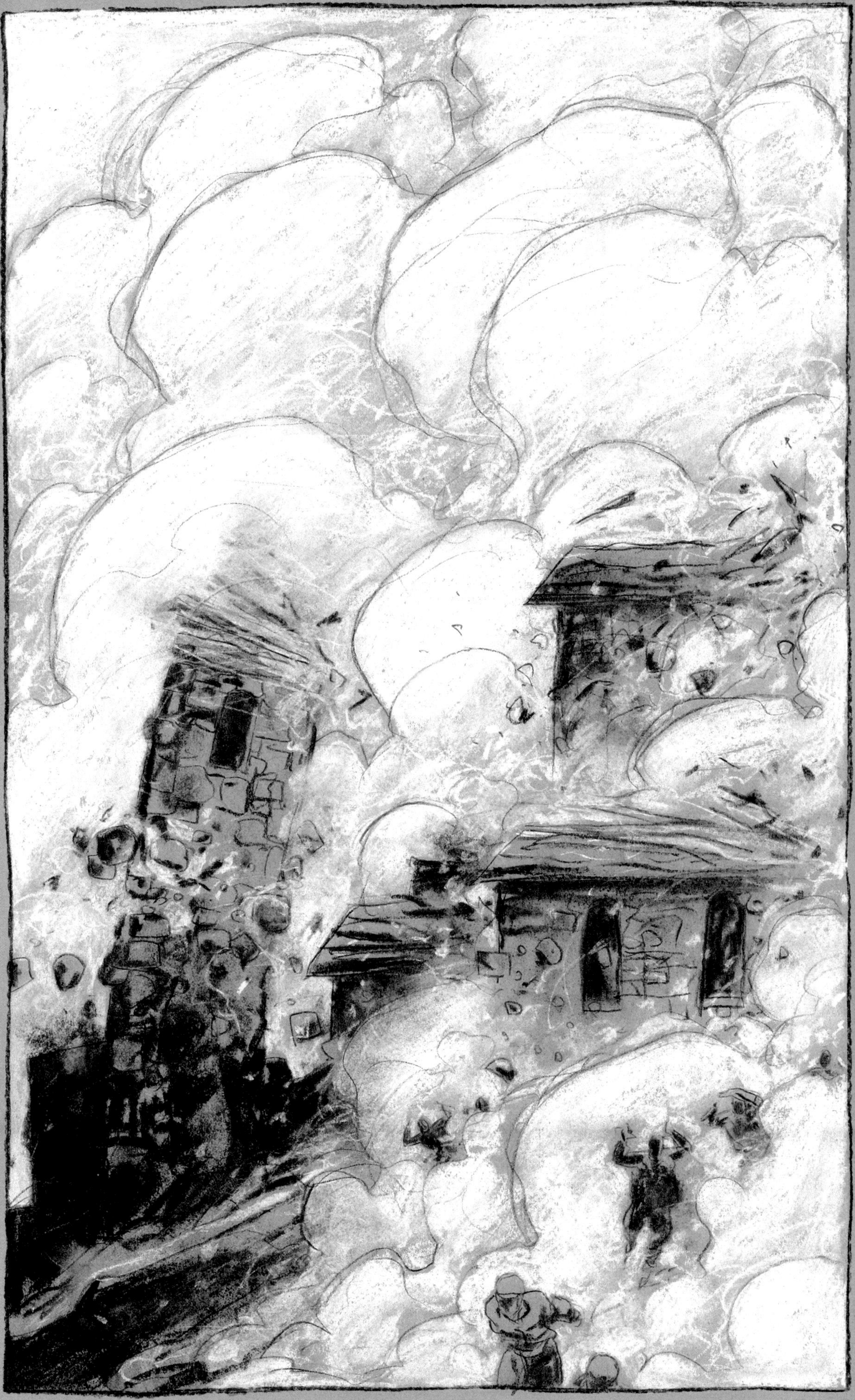

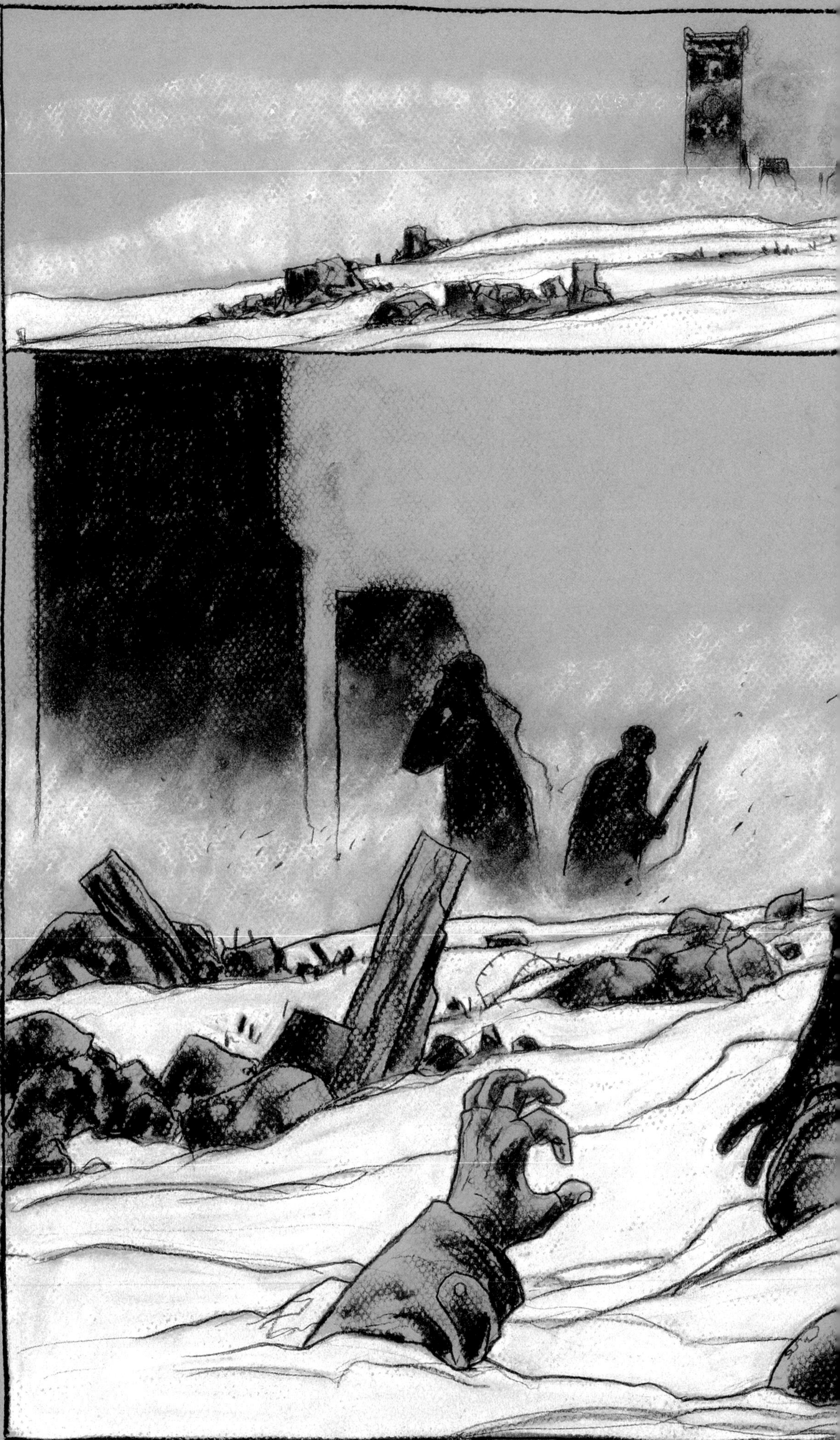

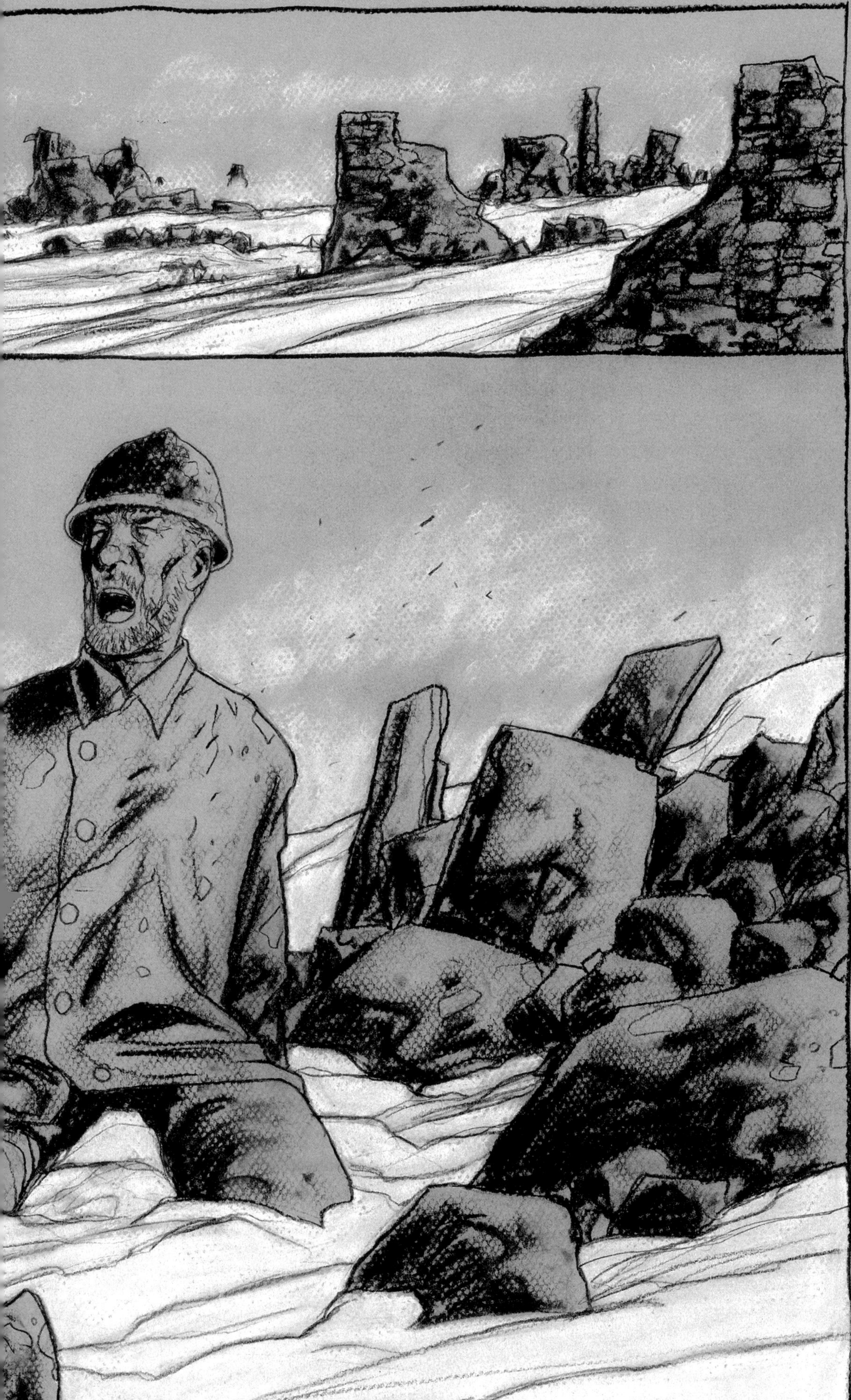

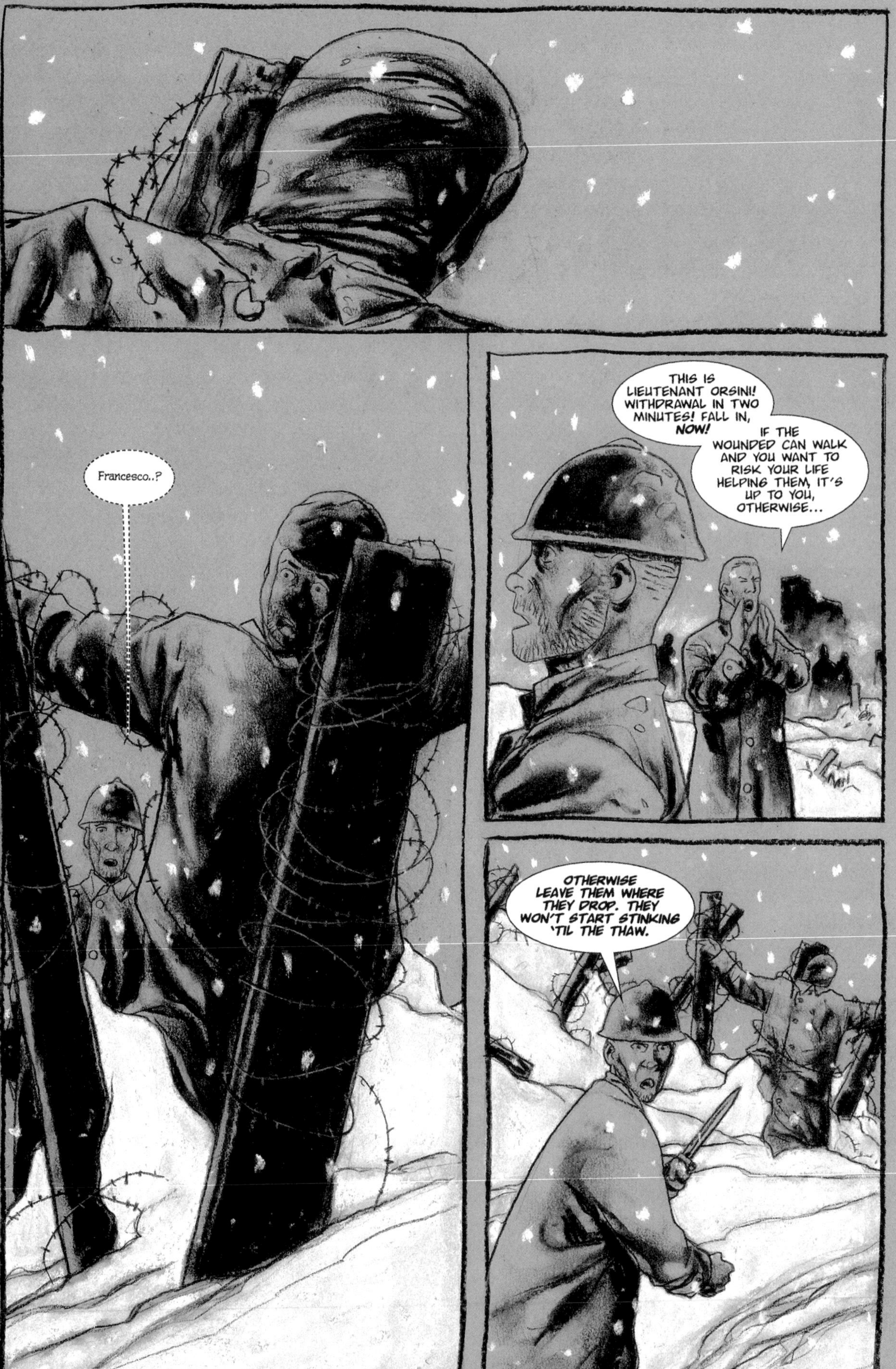
Francesco..?
THIS IS LIEUTENANT ORSINI! WITHDRAWAL IN TWO MINUTES! FALL IN, NOW!
IF THE WOUNDED CAN WALK AND YOU WANT TO RISK YOUR LIFE HELPING THEM, IT'S UP TO YOU, OTHERWISE...
OTHERWISE LEAVE THEM WHERE THEY DROP. THEY WON'T START STINKING 'TIL THE THAW.

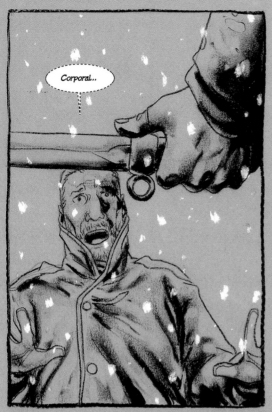

Corporal...

WELCOME TO ORSINI'S FRONT.

KILL OR BE KILLED.

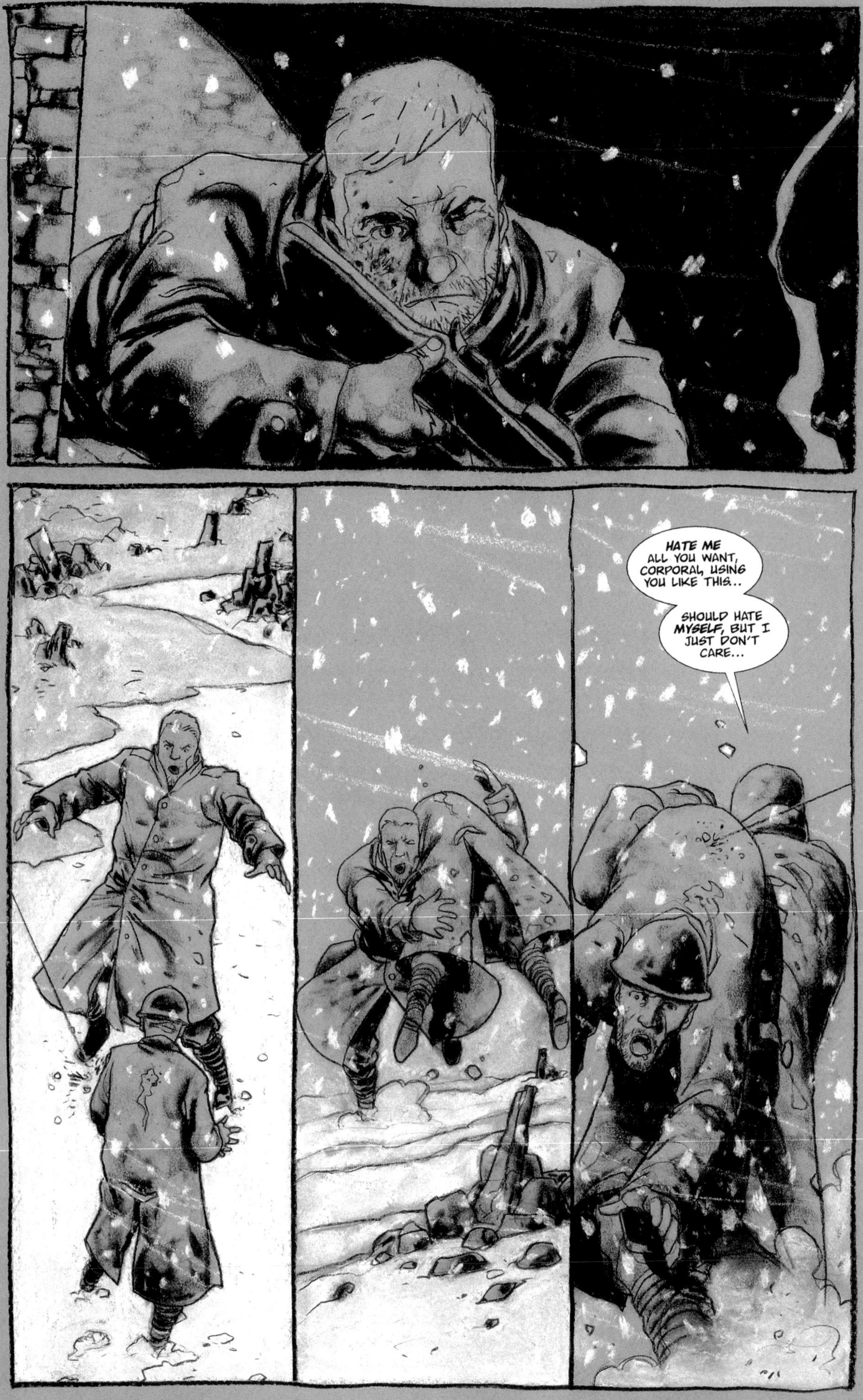
HATE ME ALL YOU WANT, CORPORAL, USING YOU LIKE THIS...
SHOULD HATE MYSELF, BUT I JUST DON'T CARE...

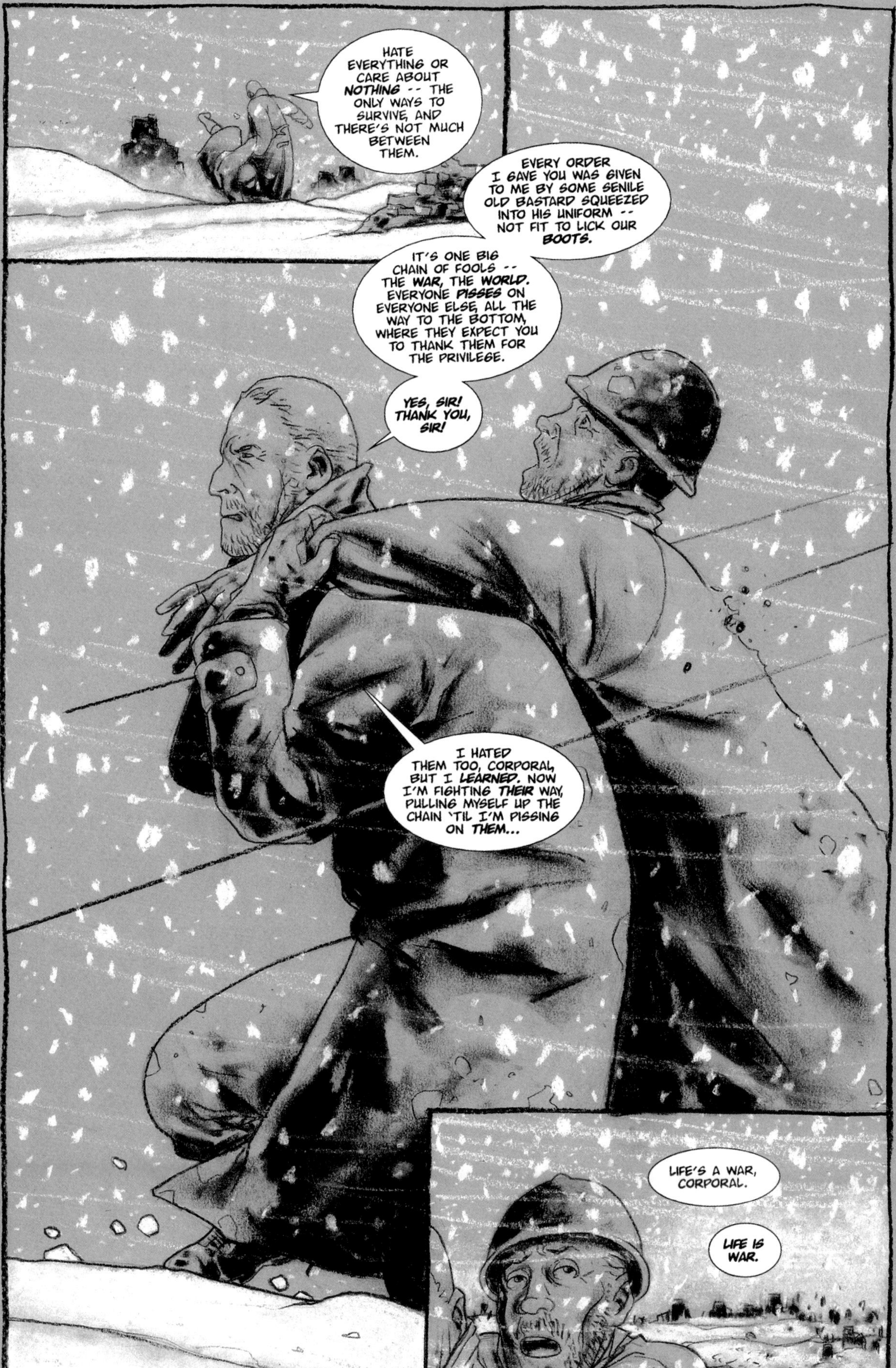
HATE EVERYTHING OR CARE ABOUT NOTHING -- THE ONLY WAYS TO SURVIVE, AND THERE'S NOT MUCH BETWEEN THEM.
EVERY ORDER I GAVE YOU WAS GIVEN TO ME BY SOME SENILE OLD BASTARD SQUEEZED INTO HIS UNIFORM -- NOT FIT TO LICK OUR BOOTS.
IT'S ONE BIG CHAIN OF FOOLS -- THE WAR, THE WORLD. EVERYONE PISSES ON EVERYONE ELSE, ALL THE WAY TO THE BOTTOM, WHERE THEY EXPECT YOU TO THANK THEM FOR THE PRIVILEGE.
YES, SIR! THANK YOU, SIR!
I HATED THEM TOO, CORPORAL, BUT I LEARNED. NOW I'M FIGHTING THEIR WAY, PULLING MYSELF UP THE CHAIN 'TIL I'M PISSING ON THEM...
LIFE'S A WAR, CORPORAL.
LIFE IS WAR.

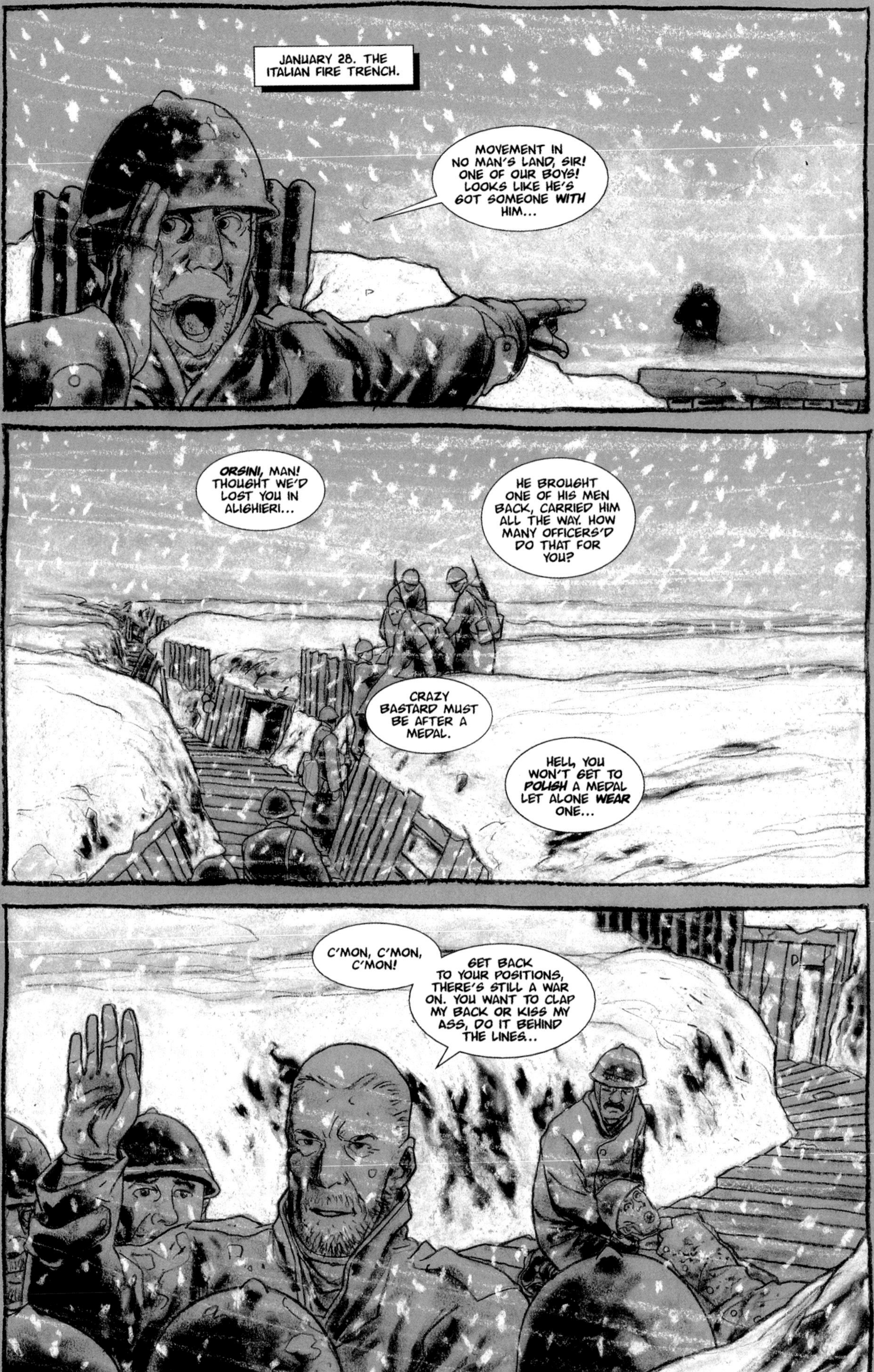
JANUARY 28. THE ITALIAN FIRE TRENCH.
MOVEMENT IN NO MAN'S LAND, SIR! ONE OF OUR BOYS! LOOKS LIKE HE'S GOT SOMEONE WITH HIM...
ORSINI, MAN! THOUGHT WE'D LOST YOU IN ALIGHIERI...
HE BROUGHT ONE OF HIS MEN BACK, CARRIED HIM ALL THE WAY. HOW MANY OFFICERS'D DO THAT FOR YOU?
CRAZY BASTARD MUST BE AFTER A MEDAL.
HELL, YOU WON'T GET TO POLISH A MEDAL LET ALONE WEAR ONE...
C'MON, C'MON, C'MON!
GET BACK TO YOUR POSITIONS, THERE'S STILL A WAR ON. YOU WANT TO CLAP MY BACK OR KISS MY ASS, DO IT BEHIND THE LINES..

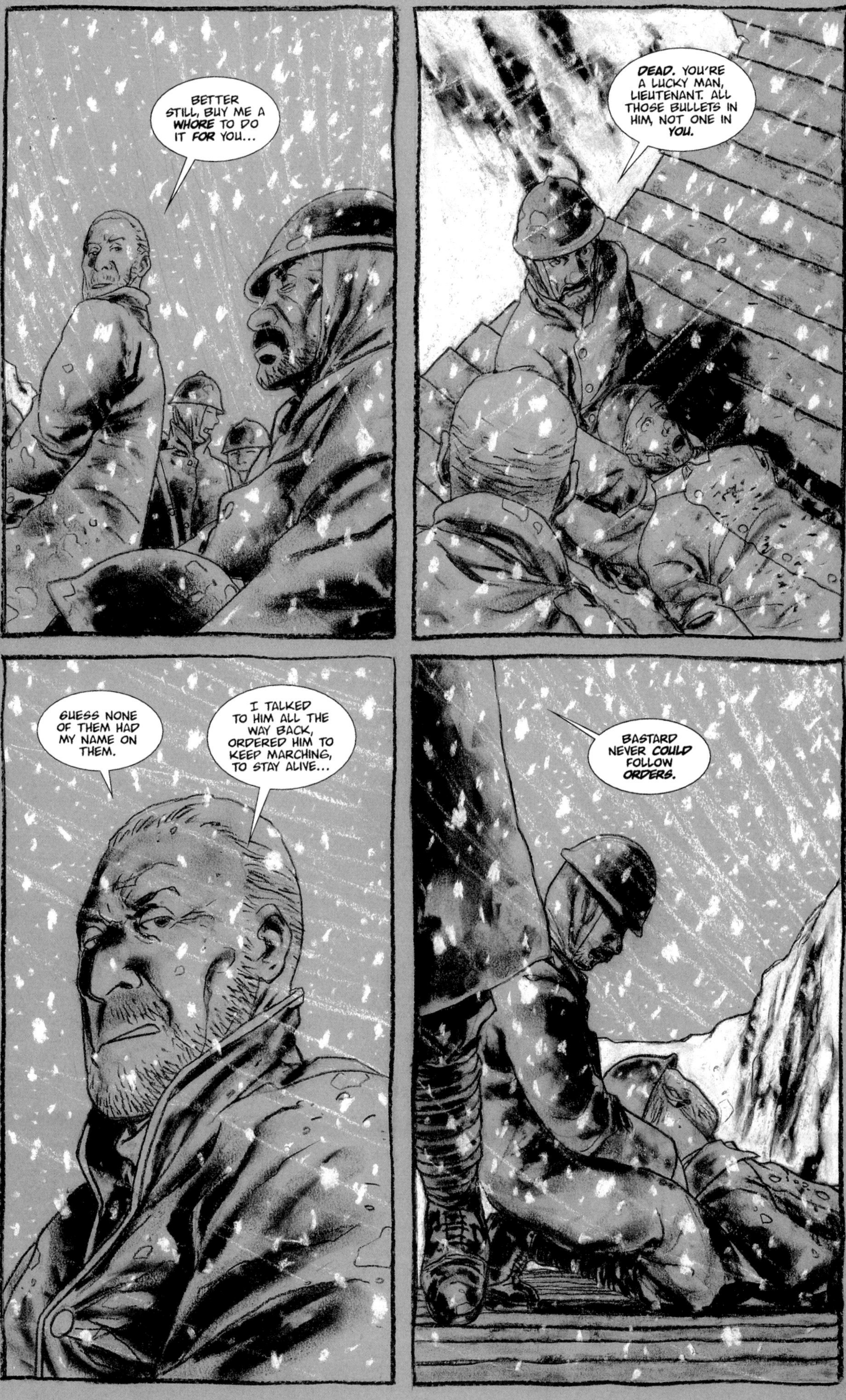
BETTER STILL, BUY ME A WHORE TO DO IT FOR YOU...
DEAD. YOU'RE A LUCKY MAN, LIEUTENANT. ALL THOSE BULLETS IN HIM, NOT ONE IN YOU.
GUESS NONE OF THEM HAD MY NAME ON THEM.
I TALKED TO HIM ALL THE WAY BACK, ORDERED HIM TO KEEP MARCHING, TO STAY ALIVE...
BASTARD NEVER COULD FOLLOW ORDERS.

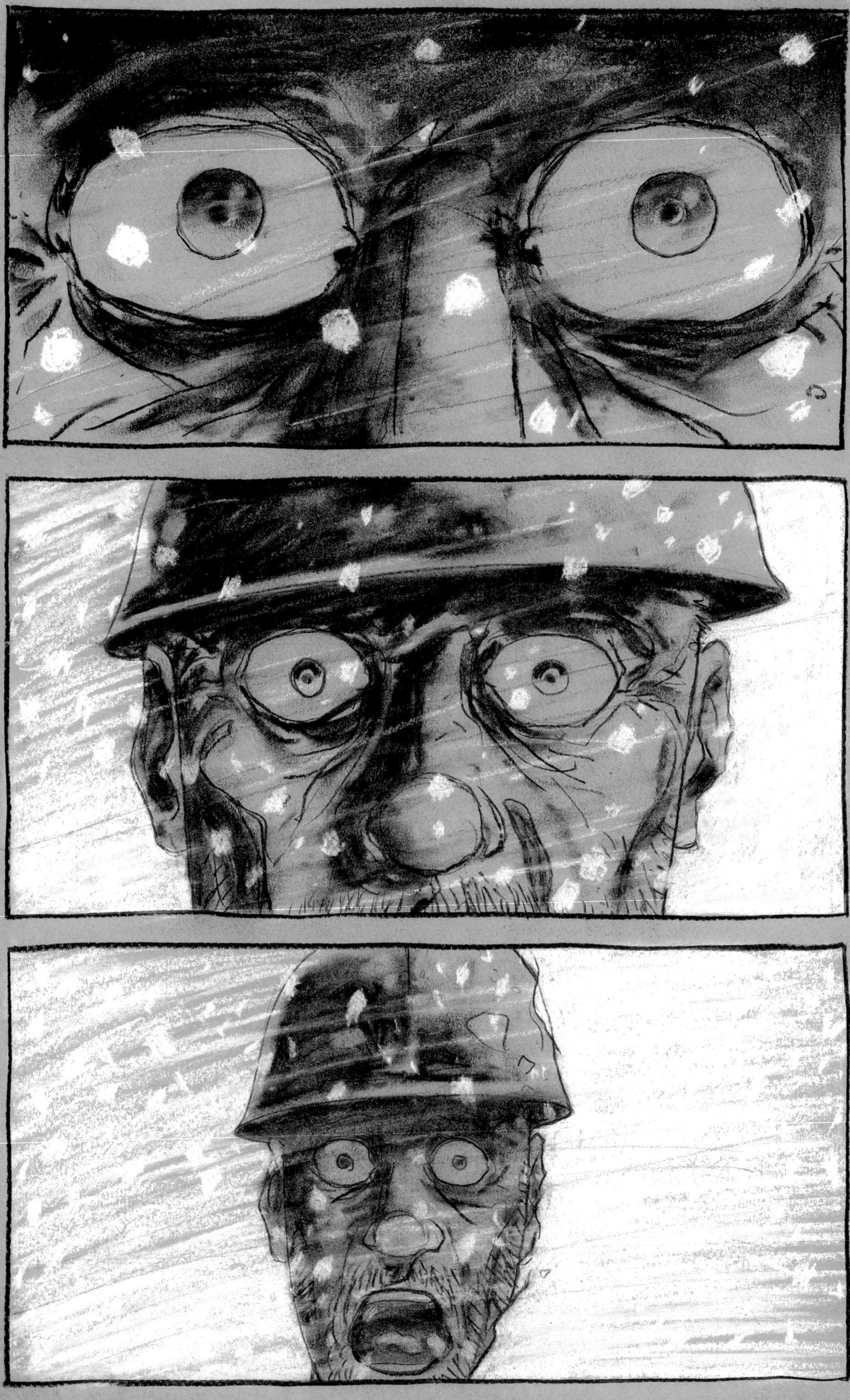

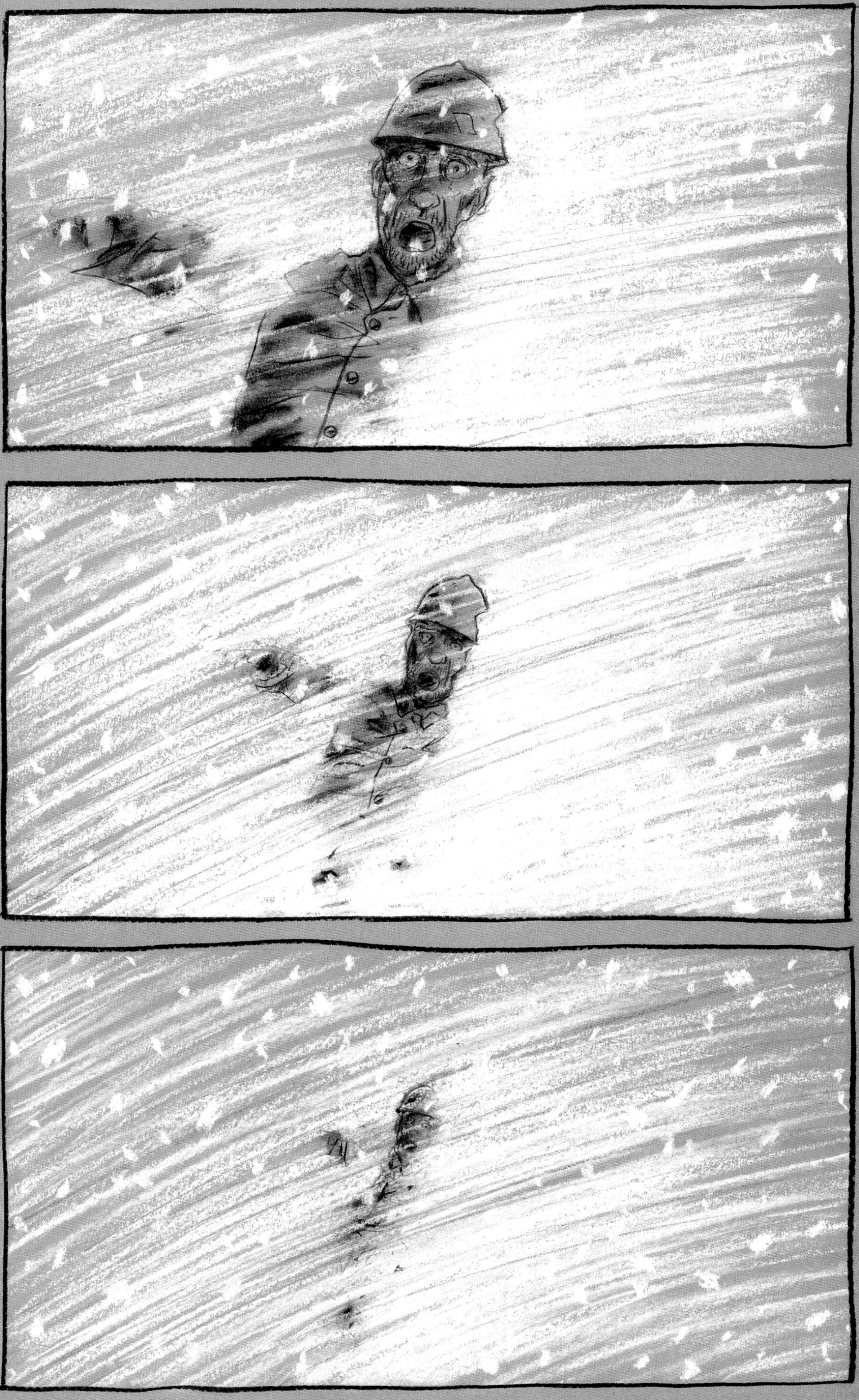

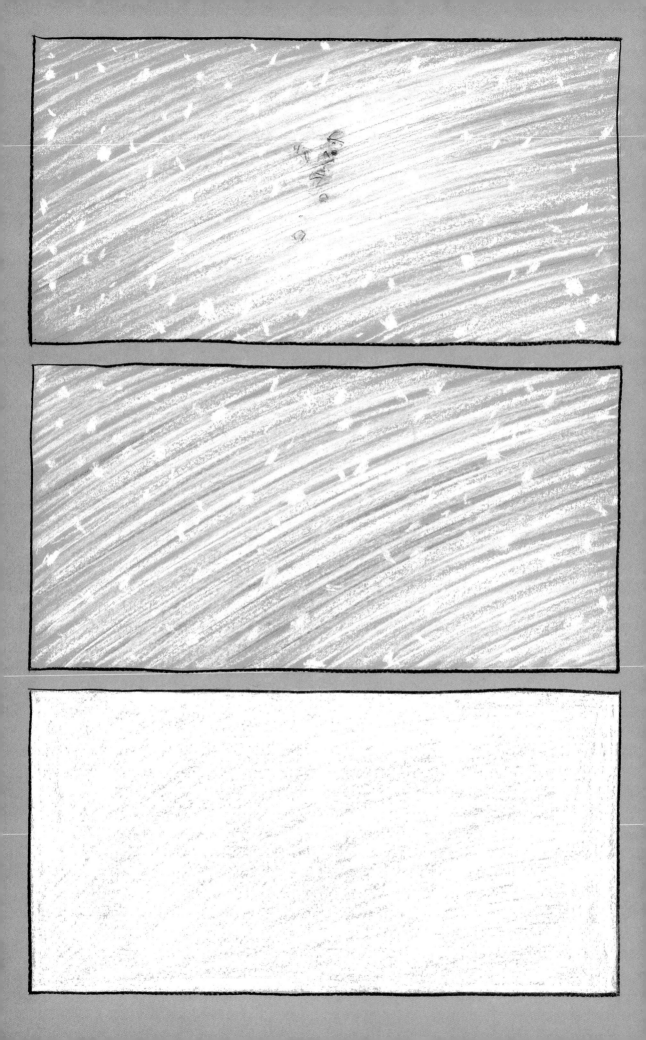

The following short story was produced as a promotional piece for the French comics magazine *Bo Dois*. It takes the form of a prologue to the main story, occurring shortly before Pietro Aquasanta and his comrades arrive at the Front.

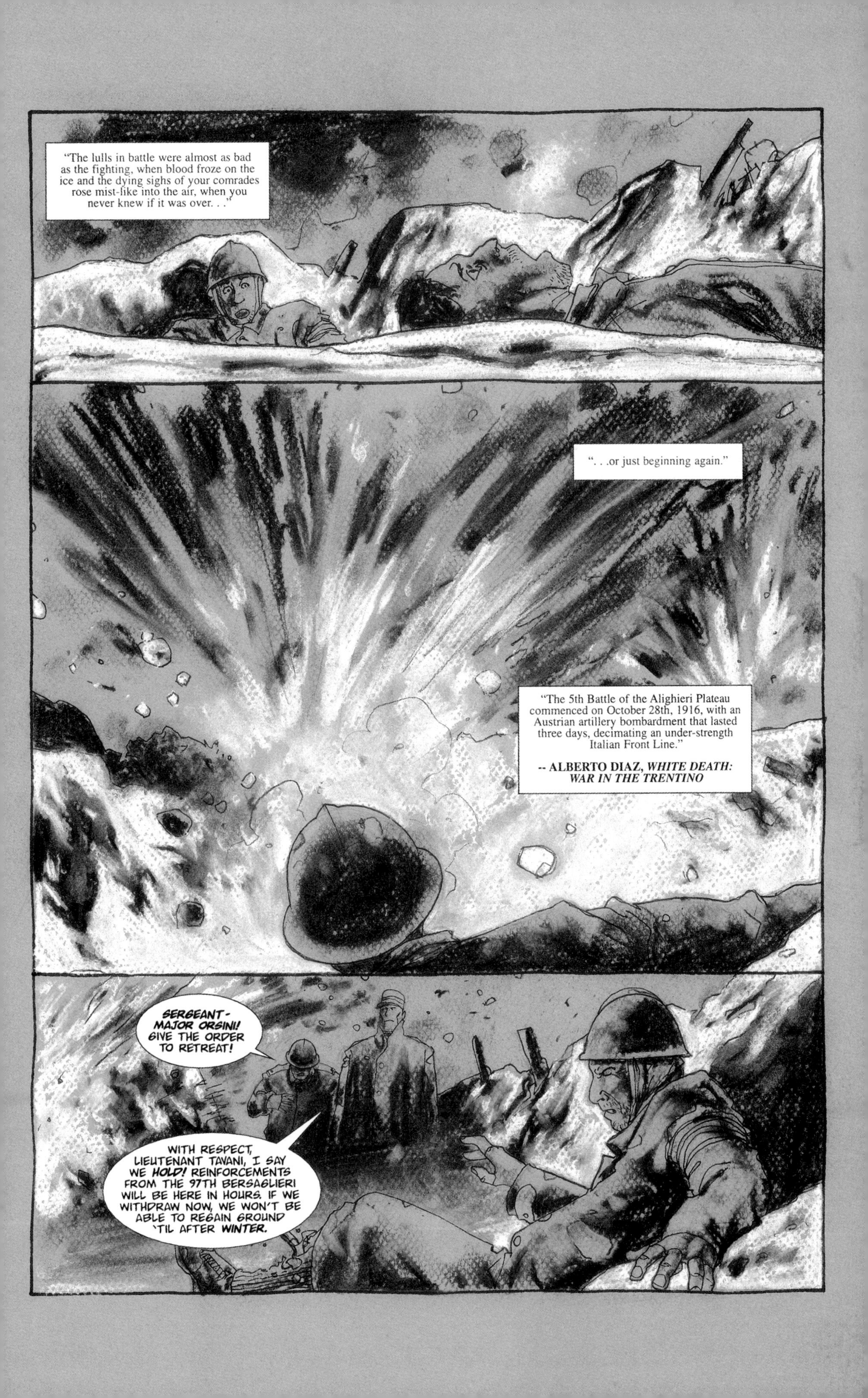
"The lulls in battle were almost as bad as the fighting, when blood froze on the ice and the dying sighs of your comrades rose mist-like into the air, when you never knew if it was over. . ."
". . .or just beginning again."
"The 5th Battle of the Alighieri Plateau commenced on October 28th, 1916, with an Austrian artillery bombardment that lasted three days, decimating an under-strength Italian Front Line."
-- ALBERTO DIAZ, WHITE DEATH: WAR IN THE TRENTINO
SERGEANT-MAJOR ORSINI! GIVE THE ORDER TO RETREAT!
WITH RESPECT, LIEUTENANT TAVANI, I SAY WE HOLD! REINFORCEMENTS FROM THE 97TH BERSAGLIERI WILL BE HERE IN HOURS. IF WE WITHDRAW NOW, WE WON'T BE ABLE TO REGAIN GROUND 'TIL AFTER WINTER.

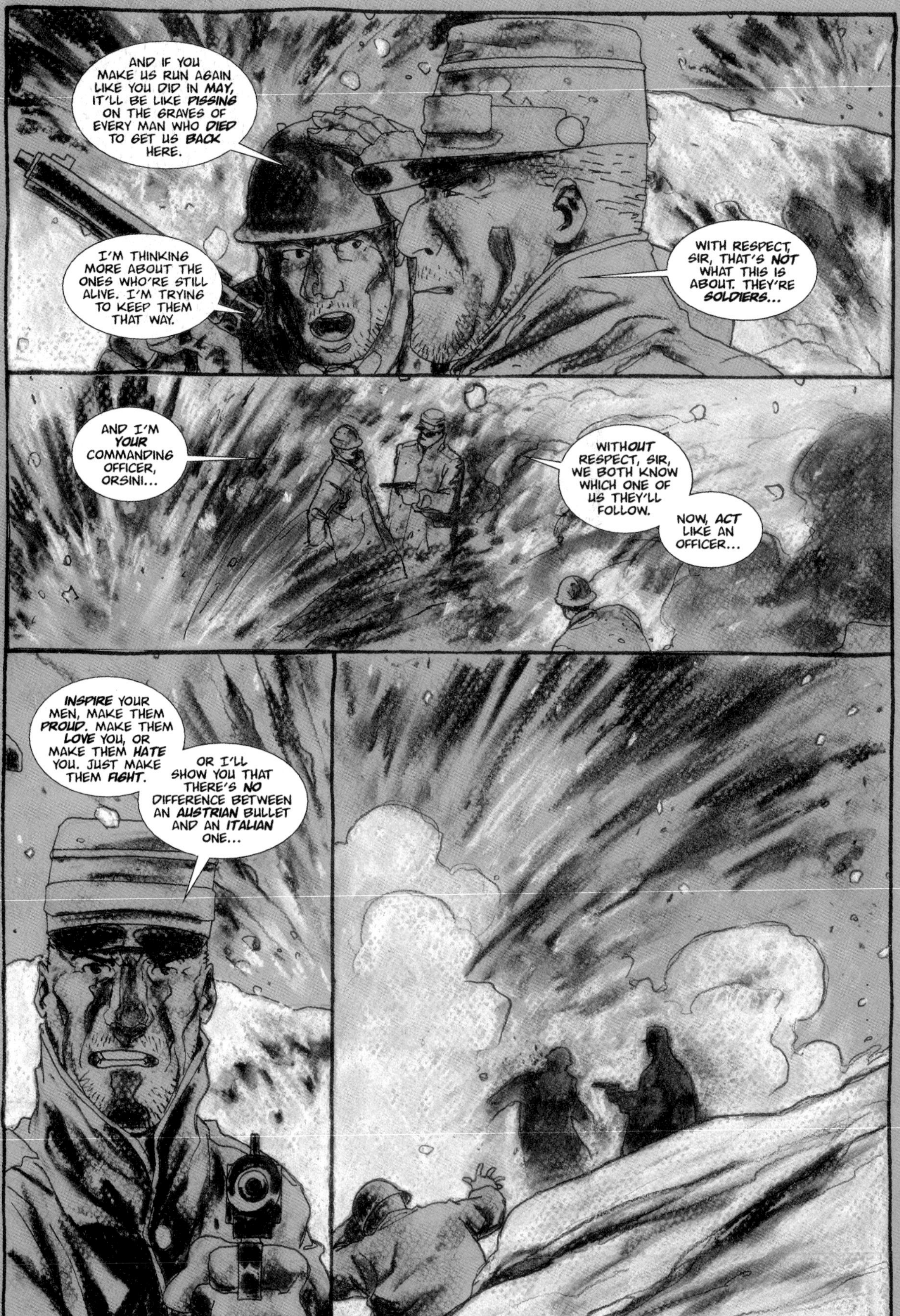
AND IF YOU MAKE US RUN AGAIN LIKE YOU DID IN MAY, IT'LL BE LIKE PISSING ON THE GRAVES OF EVERY MAN WHO DIED TO GET US BACK HERE.
I'M THINKING MORE ABOUT THE ONES WHO'RE STILL ALIVE. I'M TRYING TO KEEP THEM THAT WAY.
WITH RESPECT, SIR, THAT'S NOT WHAT THIS IS ABOUT. THEY'RE SOLDIERS...
AND I'M YOUR COMMANDING OFFICER, ORSINI...
WITHOUT RESPECT, SIR, WE BOTH KNOW WHICH ONE OF US THEY'LL FOLLOW.
NOW, ACT LIKE AN OFFICER...
INSPIRE YOUR MEN, MAKE THEM PROUD. MAKE THEM LOVE YOU, OR MAKE THEM HATE YOU. JUST MAKE THEM FIGHT.
OR I'LL SHOW YOU THAT THERE'S NO DIFFERENCE BETWEEN AN AUSTRIAN BULLET AND AN ITALIAN ONE...

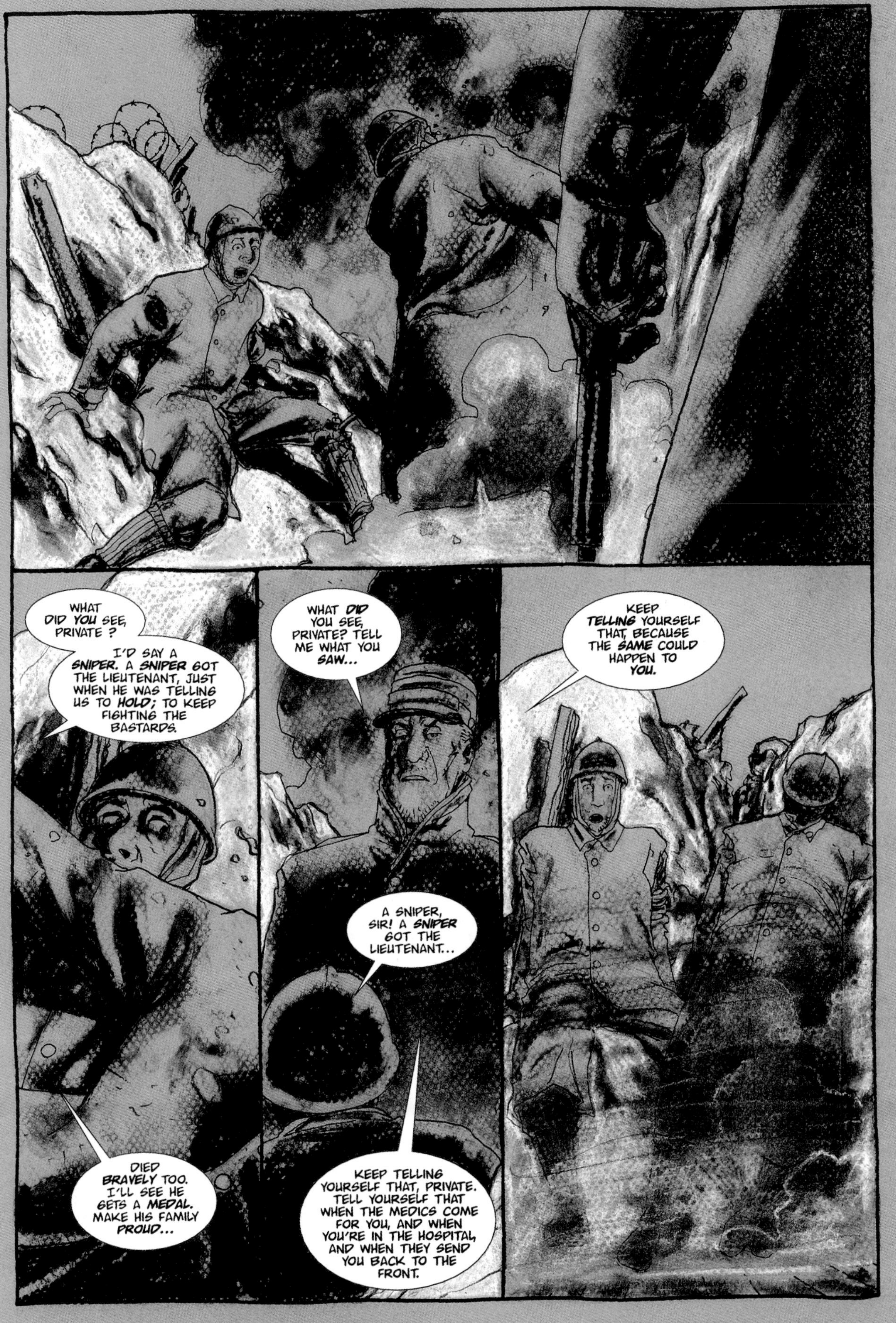
WHAT DID YOU SEE, PRIVATE ?
I'D SAY A SNIPER. A SNIPER GOT THE LIEUTENANT, JUST WHEN HE WAS TELLING US TO HOLD; TO KEEP FIGHTING THE BASTARDS.
DIED BRAVELY TOO. I'LL SEE HE GETS A MEDAL. MAKE HIS FAMILY PROUD...
WHAT DID YOU SEE, PRIVATE? TELL ME WHAT YOU SAW...
A SNIPER, SIR! A SNIPER GOT THE LIEUTENANT...
KEEP TELLING YOURSELF THAT, PRIVATE. TELL YOURSELF THAT WHEN THE MEDICS COME FOR YOU, AND WHEN YOU'RE IN THE HOSPITAL, AND WHEN THEY SEND YOU BACK TO THE FRONT.
KEEP TELLING YOURSELF THAT, BECAUSE THE SAME COULD HAPPEN TO YOU.

FROM ORIGINAL SCRIPT TO FINISHED ART #1

1. Slightly Low Angle, Close, Cadorna, clean, freshly shaven, stares at us with a horror and anguish that no one of his relative youth should have to experience.

> **DIAZ**
> (Off Panel)
> HARD TO STOP STARING, ISN'T IT?

> **DIAZ**
> (Off Panel)
> STRANGE TOO, THOUGH, EH? BECAUSE
> WHAT YOU'RE STARING AT ISN'T THERE.

2. Big Pic: Diaz stares at us from a hospital bed, hauling the covers away to reveal the tragic consequences of his wounds. His legs are missing - one from the knee down, the other from mid-thigh - the stumps swathed in bandages. Half-sitting, propped up by pillows, he immodestly pulls his hospital gown up to give his friend a 'better' view.

> **DIAZ**
> STRANGE FOR ME, TOO. I CAN STILL
> FEEL THEM. CRAMPS, ITCHES YOU CAN'T
> SCRATCH.

> **DIAZ**
> YOU WAKE UP IN THE MIDDLE OF THE
> NIGHT, NEEDING A PISS, AND YOU GO
> TO SWING YOURSELF OUT OF BED, AND
> THEN YOU REMEMBER...

> **DIAZ**
> AND YOU CALL FOR THE NURSE, AND A
> BEDPAN, BUT SOMETIMES THEY DON'T
> HEAR YOU, OR DON'T COME.

> **DIAZ**
> SO YOU DO IT WHERE YOU LIE, LIKE A
> BABY, OR SOME SENILE OLD FART.

3. Interior Location Shot, a small bare hospital room, Diaz on the bed, shrugging now, Cadorna hovering at the foot of the bed, frozen, helpless.

> BOX
> **JANUARY 20. MILITARY HOSPITAL. THE**
> **PROVINCE OF BOLZANO.**

> **DIAZ**
> SO THAT'S PRETTY MUCH ALL I CAN DO
> TOO.

> **DIAZ**
> STARE. WATCH.

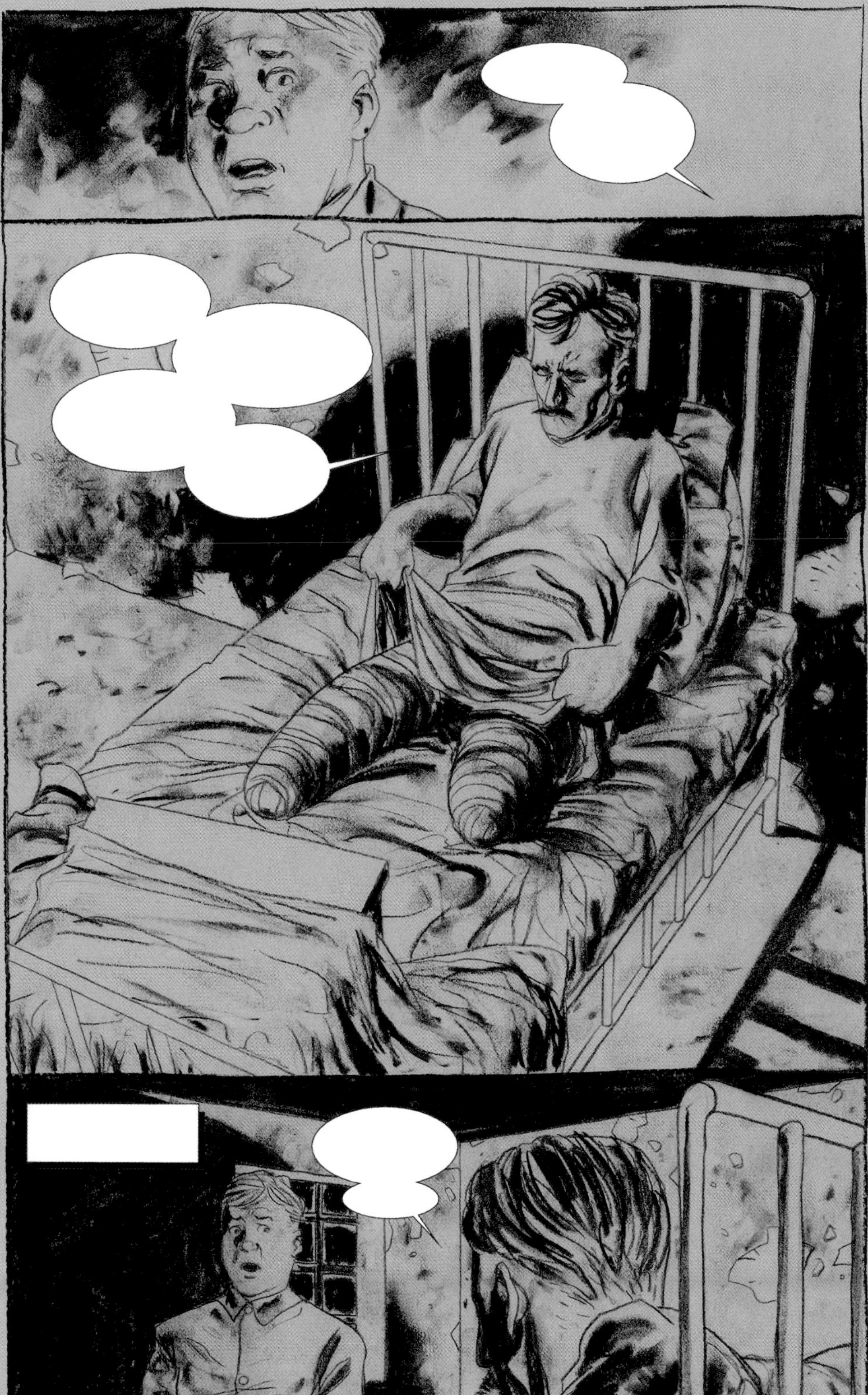

FROM ORIGINAL SCRIPT TO FINISHED ART #2

1. Tight Medium Shot, Diaz, getting progressively closer to losing control, slapping the palm of one hand against a bandaged thigh in a clapping motion

> DIAZ
> YOU GOING TO THE MADAME'S WHILE YOU'RE HERE? YOU COULD TAKE ME ALONG.

> DIAZ
> I CAN WATCH. CLAP. CHEER YOU ON.

> DIAZ
> LONG AS YOU FACE ME IN THE RIGHT DIRECTION...

2. Diaz, tears of impotent rage streaming down his face, begins rocking his lips in a violent, bitter approximation of fucking, his arms and shoulders moving as well.

Cadorna finally finds the courage to move towards his friend, arms outstretched to hug him, comfort him.

> DIAZ
> OR MAYBE YOU'D FIND ONE WHO'D GIVE ME A GO WITHOUT A BAG ON HER HEAD. LET ME FLOP AROUND ON HER!

> DIAZ
> THEY'RE ALL ACTING ANYWAY, PRETENDING THEY LIKE YOU. THINK ANY OF THEM CAN ACT THAT WELL!?

> CADORNA
> ALBERTO...

3. Tight medium Shot, Diaz hammers at Cadorna with his fists as his friend tries to embrace him.

> DIAZ
> WHY DIDN'T YOU LEAVE ME THERE, FRANCESCO!?

> DIAZ
> WHY DIDN'T YOU LEAVE ME THERE!?

4. High Angle Shot, the door to the room open now, nurses surrounding Diaz, sedating him, Cadorna, standing apart from them at the foot of the bed, or slowly backing away with helpless, guilty horror.

> DIAZ
> WHY DIDN'T YOU LET ME DIE?

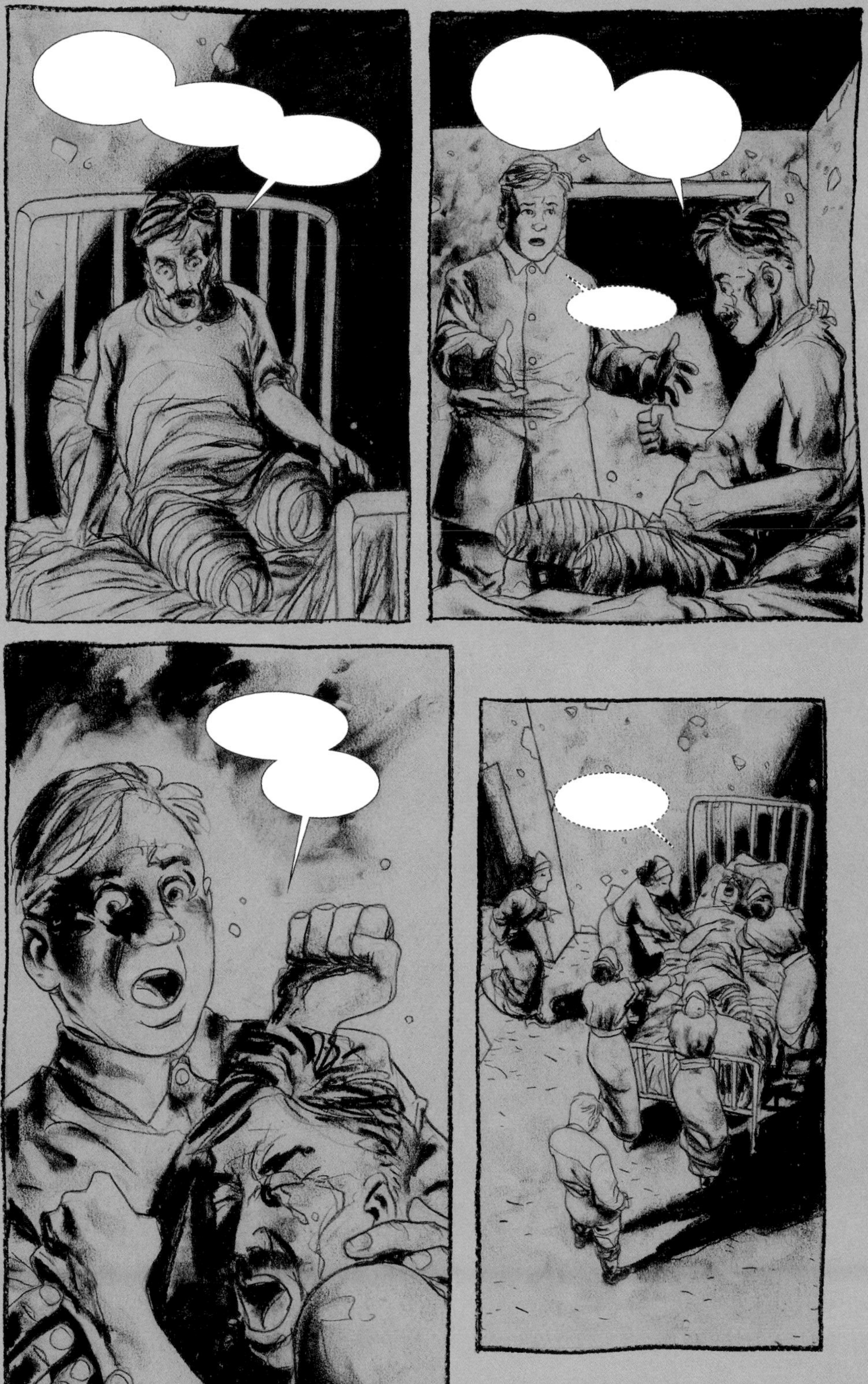

<u>FROM ORIGINAL SCRIPT TO FINISHED ART #3</u>

A Splash Page Panel 1, Charlie, with Panel 2 Inset?

1. Splash Panel: Wounded soldiers 'recuperate' on the large balcony of an upper floor of the hospital, a surprisingly warm winter afternoon sun shining down on them.

It's a harrowing image: Shattered bodies trapped in wheelchairs; half-men lurching scarecrow-like on crutches; missing limbs; disfigured faces; shell-shocked expressions.

Nurses move amongst them, administering medicines and empathy, as much veterans of the war as the invalids, a bond of conflict and shared suffering between them.

The mountains of the Trentino provide a harsh backdrop, implacable, inescapable...

2. Close, Cadorna observes the above scene with quiet anguish, his illusions of heroism and patriotic duty shattered as he confronts the true horror of war for possibly the first time.

Sometimes, the survivors suffer most...

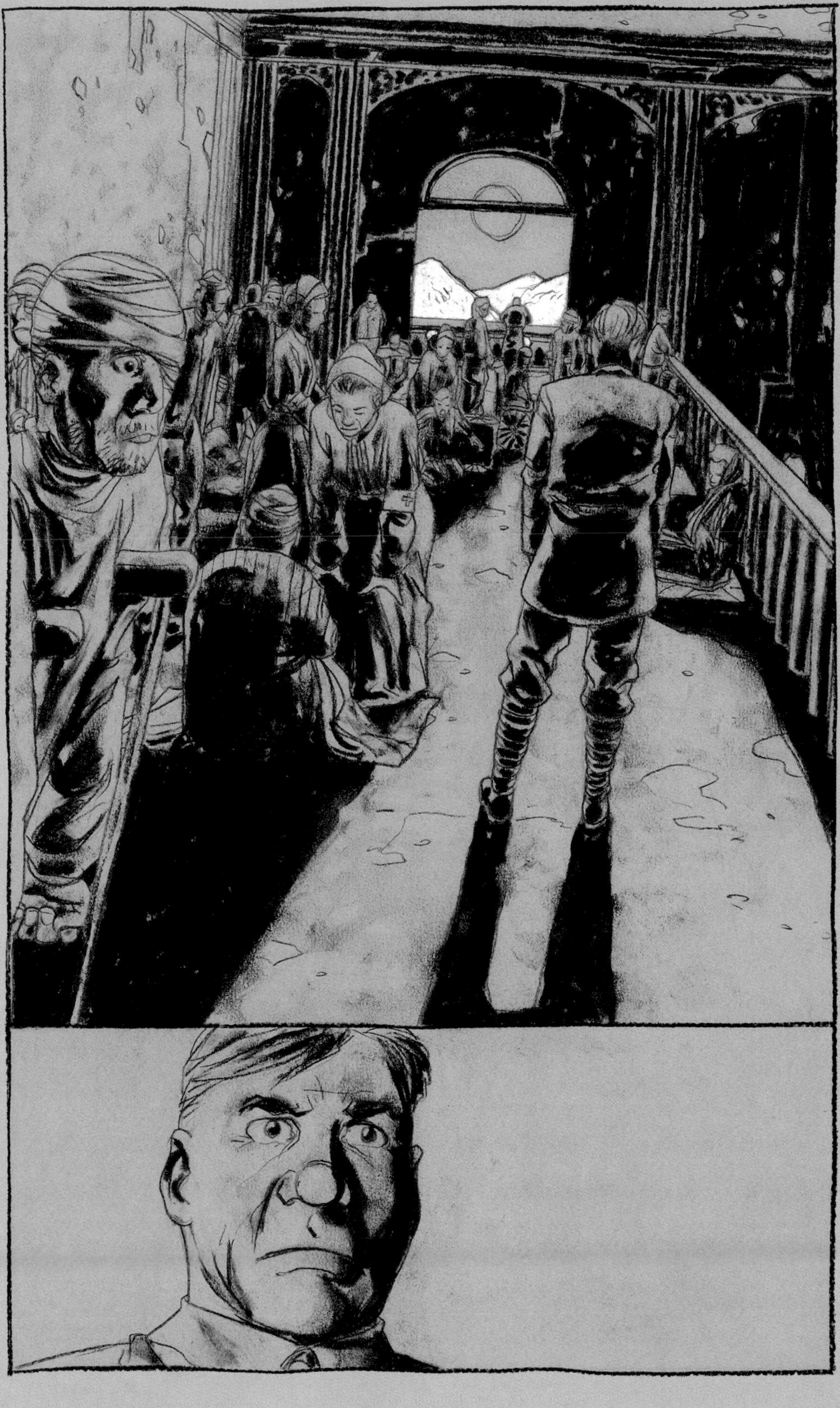

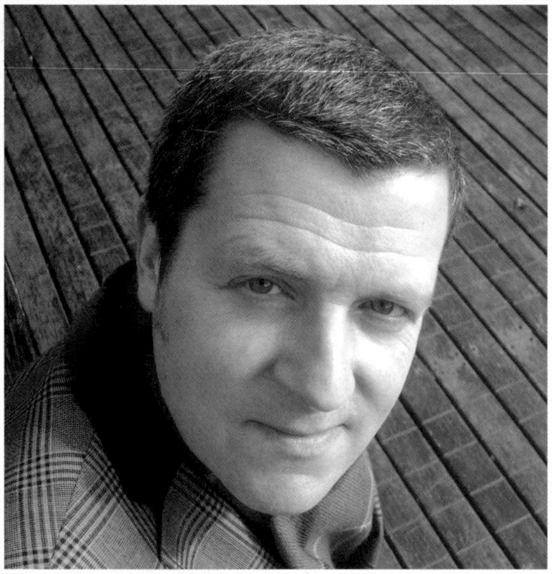

Photo © Deborah Tate

Robbie Morrison is the writer of the graphic novels *WHITE DEATH*, co-created with *THE WALKING DEAD* artist Charlie Adlard, and *DROWNTOWN* (art by Jim Murray), an epic adventure set in a flooded, futuristic London, published in the UK by Jonathan Cape.

Born in Helensburgh, Scotland, he is best known to date for the Eagle award-winning *NIKOLAI DANTE* saga; serialised in iconic UK comic *2000AD* from 1997-2012 and collected as 11 graphic novels.

In a 20-year career, he has created many popular series/characters, including *BLACKHEART* (art Frank Quitely), *SHAKARA* and *THE BENDATTI VENDETTA*. He is a regular writer of *JUDGE DREDD*, and has scripted *BATMAN* and *SPIDER-MAN*. He has worked with Dave Gibbons on the *WATCHMEN* artist's digital comic *TREATMENT*, and is the writer of the new *DR. WHO* series from Titan Comics and the BBC.

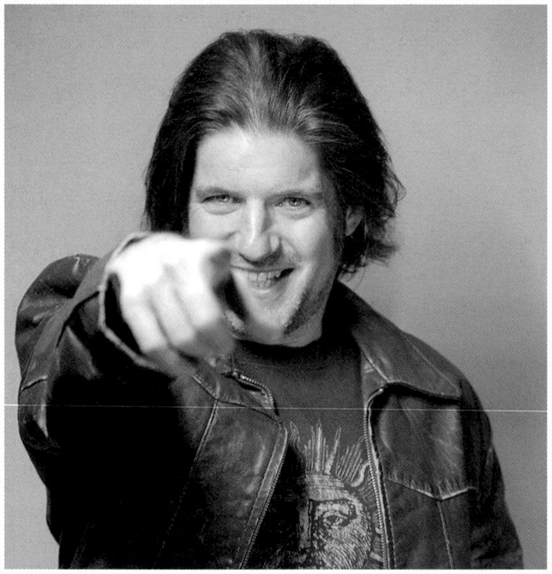

Photo © Olivier Roller

Charlie has been a "veteran" of the comic industry for over 20 years. He's spent the majority of his time since 2004 working on *THE WALKING DEAD* for which he has received many industry awards. In his time as a cartoonist he has worked on many other projects as far reaching as *MARS ATTACKS*, the *X-FILES*, *JUDGE DREDD*, *SAVAGE*, *BATMAN*, *X-MEN*, *SUPERMAN*, etc., and creator-owned projects closer to his heart like *ASTRONAUTS IN TROUBLE*, *CODEFLESH*, *ROCK BOTTOM*, and *WHITE DEATH*.

He was born on the 4th August 1966 in the town of Shrewsbury, England and, having moved away to study film and video at art college, eventually moved back and still resides there today.

Before moving back to Shrewsbury, he spent a brief stint in London, finding out that the BA he'd earned at art college was pretty useless in getting a job in the film industry, and after failing to set the world alight playing the drums in a rock band, eventually settled on the "third" option, which was comics. An option he finally realised should have been number one right from the beginning.

After spending two years back in Shrewsbury, working on a portfolio, he eventually found his first work at the *JUDGE DREDD MEGAZINE* in 1992 and hasn't looked back since.

Charlie is married with two children and one cat. Life is good...